WORKERS' POLITICS
THE ETHICS OF SOCIALISM

William Ash

Introduction to the Indian Edition
Randhir Singh

Acknowledgements

For ideas in connection with the theoretical application of Marxism to questions of morality I am deeply indebted to the late Professor George Thomson. I am as deeply indebted to the late Reg Birch for my appreciation of the practical application of Marxism to the conditions of the working class in Britain. An account of Reg Birch's contribution can be found in *Reg Birch: engineer, trade unionist, communist*, by Will Podmore, ISBN 0-947967-33-8,(2004).

WORKERS' POLITICS : THE ETHICS OF SOCIALISM
William Ash

First Published in India, 2010

ISBN 978-93-5002-036-4 (Hb)

Published in Great Britain by Bread Books, Coventry
Indian edition published with the permission from the Author

Published by
AAKAR BOOKS
28 E Pocket IV, Mayur Vihar Phase I, Delhi-110 091
Phone : 011-2279 5505 Telefax : 011-2279 5641
aakarbooks@gmail.com; www.aakarbooks.com

Printed at
Arpit Printographers, Shahdara, Delhi-110 032
arpitprinto@yahoo.com

CONTENTS

PREFACE

2007

Workers' Politics is a reprint of *Marxist Morality*, written and published in India in 1998. Since then there have occurred historical events which further demonstrate the moral necessity of a socialist understanding of society as the basis for united action to end the exploitation of working people by capitalist corporatists and begin the establishment of a free, peaceful and truly democratic world.

The Cold War, which *Marxist Morality* recognised as the fight of the capitalist United States to wipe communism off the face of the earth, had begun before the end of World War II with the criminal nuclear bombing of Hiroshima and Nagasaki in an already defeated Japan – just to show the Soviet Union the overwhelming power of the country it dared oppose with its socialist principles and practices. The United States proceeded to act aggressively against the progressive movements in any part of the western world over which it exercised any military or economic dominance – supplying arms and financial aid to anarchic forces like the Contras in Nicaragua, applying sanctions against any country that harboured them or with its own military strength carrying out vicious attacks against such parties.

The United States was also active in the rest of the world – taking advantage of the Soviet Union's absence from the United Nations Security Council to get approval for a war against Korea, supporting the reactionary government of Indonesia in its round-up and massacre of thousands of communists, involving itself in war against those Vietnamese supporting the socialist leader Ho Chi Minh. Only in the last case the United States was soundly defeated – the most powerful nation on earth brought to its knees and driven out of the country by the progressive Vietnamese people! In Cuba, too, under the leadership of Fidel Castro and Che Guevara progressive Cubans were able to stand off threats from the mighty United States only ninety miles away!

The collapse of the Soviet Union could be called the end of the Cold War. Not the end of socialism, it is pointed out in the *Marxist Morality* chapter 'Marxism Socialism in Practice'. "What expired in 1991 was certainly not the dictatorship of the proletariat which was Marx's name for democratic socialism when there were still class enemies within the country and external enemies without. If what was born in Lenin's October Revolution had remained democratic socialism, it could not have been disposed of without major resistance on the part of the Soviet Union's united people. The best description of what had collapsed into anarchy is state socialism which had been allowed to decline into bureaucratic stagnation."

One of the events of the new Twentyfirst Century was the collapse into capitalist anarchy of those countries in Eastern Europe which had adopted communism under Soviet influence. This, too, was used as proof that socialism could not last. All it proved was that socialism cannot be imposed on a country from above; it has to be won by the working people themselves uniting and liberating themselves from their exploiters.

The Twentyfirst Century was to see the closest ever alliance between the United States and Britain. The end of the Cold War had contributed to the establishment of global capitalism in which the huge corporations of the United States played a predominant role. A consequence of this was that groups of people in different parts of the world suffered in one way or another from America's economic and political dominance. The class struggle between working people and their capitalist exploiters which had been the subject of much of the conflict dealt with in *Marxist Morality* had now, with much less political significance, been largely replaced by religious and American dominance. Hence the September 11th attack on New York's twin towers. President George Bush's reaction to this shattering act was to declare war on terrorists. And who were the terrorists? Anyone who took any kind of action against America's 'benign' control of the world. Prime Minister Tony Blair declared Britain to be Bush's closest ally in this war against terrorism.

Bush was considering as a major target for this war Saddam Hussein's Iraq. Iraq might not represent a country likely to carry out an attack like the bombing of the twin towers, but it did have a huge amount of oil American corporations would like to get their hands on. While there had been no objection by the United Nations to actions like forcefully breaking up Yugoslavia or invading Afghanistan to end Taliban rule, there was no approval for war against Iraq. In spite of the failure of a resolution to that end and the opposition in Britain against war on Iraq Blair supported Bush slavishly and supplied troops and arms for the invasion. It might be said that the relation some two hundred years earlier between imperialist Britain and its main colony, the United States, had now been reversed with Britain becoming the imperialist America's main colony.

The Twentyfirst Century began with New Labour in power in Britain. In opposition Tony Blair had strongly opposed Mrs.Thatcher's anti-trade union laws and privatisation of the railways. In office Blair not only left the anti trade-union laws in place and the railways in the hands of privateers but proceeded under sly under the counter ways to begin privatising other public services like education and health.

What Blair was demonstrating was what *Marxist Morality* has made clear – that in a capitalist country with political control basically in the hands of the ruling class owners of the means of production there was no parliamentary road to socialism. Real democratic socialism would only be achieved by the working class uniting its much larger forces and taking political power away from the capitalist ruling class by assuming-control itself of the means of production and thus being in a position to ensure the formation of a government truly democratic and socialist.

Some would-be socialists believe that the Labour Party can be purged of New Labour and become once more the idealistic means of achieving socialism. But real socialists have to realise that just as Blair's political rule has become indistinguishable from Thatcher's so 'social democracy' under capitalist domination will always turn into some form of fascism.

The historical events since *Marxist Morality's* publication continue to demonstrate that the Marxist socialism defined in its pages is the only moral answer to the evils of global capitalism. *Workers' Politics* is dedicated to the international collaboration of the organised working class in the revolutionary disempowerment of corporate capitalists in order to begin the establishment of a free, peaceful and truly democratic world.

William Ash, October 2007.

INTRODUCTION TO THE INDIAN EDITION

A specific feature of the current situation in the world is the ideological and cultural sweep of capitalist ideas and values that, in its own way, defines the current phase of globalisation Capitalism's technological ingenuity has made it possible for its principles to find their way into social, institutonal and cultural spaces that even a few decades ago were beyond their reach. Commodity relations and moralities of the market are penetrating into every aspect of our lives, producing profit of course but also ravaging morals and culture everywhere. A process of culture penetration is on – including what is described as 'McDonaldisation', 'the American way of life', 'homogenisation or leveling down of cultures', or simply as 'consumerist culture' – whereby the bourgeoisie today 'makes the world in its own image' with an immunity almost unparalleled since Marx wrote these words 150 odd years ago. This culture penetration is not just an extension but integral part of globalisation as imperialist domination. Imperialism has never been merely an economic-military system of control and exploitation. Cultural domination, an effort to penetrate and dominate the cultural life of the popular classes in order to reorder the values, behaviour, institutions and identity of the oppressed peoples to conform with the interests of the imperial classes, was always an integral part of it. So it is now with globalisation as a new, latest form of imperialism. Besides, there are now direct material benefits to be had, as never before. Recognising American economic and cultural domination in the ongoing globalisation, James Petras has written:

> US cultural imperialism has two goals – one economic and the other political – to capture markets for its cltural commodities and to establish hegemony by shaping popular consciousness. The export of entertainment commodities is one of the most important sources of capital accumulation and global profits, displacing manufacturing exports. In the political sphere, cultural imperialism plays a major role in dissociating people from their cultural roots and traditions of solidarity, replacing them with media created 'needs', which change with every publicity campaign. The poltical effect is to alienate people

> from traditional class and community bonds, atomising and separating individuals from each other.

(It may be mentioned that religious fundamentalism – especially the Islamic – so rampant today, is, significant, party at least, for its opposition to 'consumerism of the west' or 'the American way of life', the imperialist cultural domination it is resourceless to understand or overcome. But it has acquired this significance primarily because the traditional Left alternatives, in particular the great revolutionary traditions of Marxism and communism seem to have become, for the time being at least, unavailable.)

To be pariticularly noticed is the ideological domination or hegemony that capitalism has come to acquire in the current phase of capitalist globalisation. With capitalism become all but universal, it has also become ideologically hegemonic as never before. It is today so powerful and pervasive as to have become invisible, and is all the more powerful for being invisible. You no longer mention or recognize it or even refer to it by its proper name. It is 'globalisation', 'liberalisation', 'structural adjustment', 'economic reform', 'new economic policy' (and with the new votaries from the Left in India joining in) 'industrialisation', 'development and progress', even 'civilisation', etc. – that is anythig but capitalism. A consensus on behalf of capitalism has emerged that makes it virtually immune against criticism or any discussion of alternatives (which, incidentally also makes nonsense of the much-vaunted pluralism of bourgeois democracy, gaining for it a spurious credibility only by a bizarre blowing up of minor differences among competitors in the politics of 'actually existing capitalism'). Given the failure of the revolutionary experiment in the Soviet Union and the collapsed Soviet regime's spurious identification with socialism, bourgeois ideologues have gone to town proclaiming the inevitability and virtues of capitalism. It is not only that the world is noisy with the refrain that 'there is no alternative', that the 'economic reforms' are 'irreversible' and that the world must adjust to the so-called rationality and efficiency requirements of 'the ecomomy', today every human practice, every socilal relationship, virtually everything under the sun including the natural environment is subject to the requirements of profit-maximisation. As Michael Löwy has noted:

> Indeed, never until the end of the 20th century has capital succeeded in exerting such a complete, absolute, undivided, and unlimited sway over the whole world. Never in the past has it had its current ability to impose its rules, its policies, its dogmas. and its interests upon all the nations of the globe. Never have international finance capital and multinational corporations been so out of control by states and peoples. Never before now has there existed such a dense network of international institutions– Intenational Monetary Fund, World Bank, World Trade Organisation – devoted to controlling, governing, and adiministering human life according to the strict rules of the capitalist free market and unrestricted pursuit of capitalist profitability. Finally, never in any preceding epoch have all spheres of human life – social relationships, culture, art, politics, sexuality, health, education, sports, recreation – been so completely dominated by capital, so deeply submerged in 'the icy water of egotistical calculation'.

Underpinning this ideological domination are new information and communication technologies which have added immensely to the power of those in command of the mass media, advertisement and entertainment, to control popular consciousness, to turn whole people, like individuals glued to their TV sets, into what the German poet Hans Magnus Enzensberger has called 'secondary illiterates', those who need neither memory nor any thinking or learning to sustain themselves. These are of little worth to them, the passive subjects in a world where the reigning ideology is consumerism with its exclusive concern for 'instant gratification' and 'contentment'. A market-driven 'mass culture' has come up which on the one hand aims at developing consumer instincts in the people to the utmost and thereby expanding markets for the greater glory of late-capitalist profit-making and, on the other hand, at ideological brainwashing of the people, diverting them from any advanced social ideals and implanting in their minds bland, illusory and often downright false and reactionary views of social and political realities.

A 'true idiot culture', Carl Bernstein has called It, where for 'the first time in history the weird and the stupid and the vulgar are becoming our cultural norm, even our cultural ideal'. Even as a 'stupid and vulgar' culture is mass purveyed via television screens, tabloid newspapers, glossy magazines and similar other means, the tendency is to pitch all message to the lowest level of mental capacity. Knowledge is reduced to slick, pre-digrested, easy to understand capsules, inducing people to want simple answers to difficult problems. People's consciousness is transferred on to philistine, narrow-minded lines, and interest in truth which demands hard, complex and subtle exercise of mind, simply recedes into the background. The overall consequence is a dilution and dispersal of people's questioning spirit, their angry or combustible sentiments, an emasculation of their critical consciousness. There is a general enervation of civil society, its members rendered incapable of 'Answering back' as C. Wright Mills once phrased it. According to Jean Baudrillard, the very possibilites of critical examination and reflection are destroyed. In other words, the inundations of consumerism and 'mass culture' leave the alienated individuals of contemporary late-capitalist society eminently vulnerable to capitalism's hegemonic control. Though oppressed and exploited, they are now more open to 'colonisation of the mind' – victims' internalisation of the cliche 'there is no alternative', their willing suspension of ideals and acceptance of a sub-autonomous existence in the interest of maintaining a secondary or even a tertiary position in the obtaining 'reality' – be it the capitalist society or for that matter the global capitalist system. For that is also what the 'third world mentality' is all about.

As hinted at above, the disappearance of the Soviet Union, a putative alternative social order has, in its own way, contributed to this ideological domination of capitalism. So have the deformations of its socialism. For example, throughout its history socialism and democracy were invariably seen to be positively interlinked. Today the link is tenuous, almost no more, in large part because of the Soviet experience. Marx's 'dictatorship of the proletariat' never happened in the Soviet Union. It was indeed 'the great absence' in the historical experiment of 'building socialism' in the Soviet Union. Soviet socialism's authoritarian deformation, has had the consequence of opening up a gulf between socialism and democracy. It indeed gifted away democracy to capitalism to be used as an ideological weapon to defend and promote its interest at home and abroad, even build or restore capitalism in its name. This is what allows a free-marketeering Obama to dismiss the socialist choice of a democratically planned economy, that is democracy in the sphere of economy, as 'an oppressive government-run economy' and is an important reson why –

as more than one bourgeois ideologue has noted with obvious relief – the current crisis of capitalism has not produced a corresponding advocacy of socialism. All this both expresses and confirms the prevailing ideological domination of capitalism.

Such then is the historical and ideological context of William Ash's *Workers' Politics – the ethics of socialism.* (The book, it may be noted, is a reprint of *Marxist Morality*, originally written and published in india in 1998).

As noted above, capitalism, is today so powerful and pervasive as to have become invisible, and it is all the more powerful for being invisible. You no longer see or recognise it, even refer to it by its proper name. But if you connot *see* or *think* capitalism, you obviously cannot argue or act against it. And if capitalism is not recognised, its negation, socialism, too disappears from your theory and practice.

The current historical and ideological context, therefore, also points to the relevance of William Ash's book. For *Workers' Politics – the ethics of socialism* is a book about capitalism and socialism, it is above all a Marxist intervention in behalf of socialism, raising issues which are forgotten or forbidden in these 'our dark times'.

I had read Ash's *Marxism and Moral Concepts* (published by Monthly Review Press in 1964) a long time back. But I came to know of his life and work only recently when I met him and Ranjana Ash during one of their annual visits to India, which, for reasons of age and health, William Ash, can, unfortunately, no longer undertake. Ash is a truly remarkable human being, indeed 'one of a rare breed'. Ash gave up his American citizenship and came to England to join in the war against fascism. Serving as a fighter pilot he was shot down over France and then created a record of sorts by his dozen odd attempts to break out of German POW camps – the story later told in the best selling *Under The Wire*, coauthored with a friend. Decorated as a war hero, and electing to settle down in London, he found employment as a journalist with the BBC to be later dismissed for his anti-imperialist politics. Author of *Marxism and Moral Concepts*, an authoritative book on *How To Write Radio Drama*, a pioneering work on the Albanian revolution, *Pickaxe and Rifle*, and a dozen odd works of political fiction set in conflict situations in different parts of the world, William Ash is above all an active revolutionary, a communist, who has remained one though the old and more recent vicissitudes of the movement. For me it is a privilege to count Bill and Ranjana among my friends.

William Ash opens his argument with Marx's famous moral injunction: 'The philosophers have only interpreted the world in different ways; the point is to change it' and goes on to state, with Marx, what in a way is the methodological principle governing his inquiry into the ethics of socialism: 'Where speculation ends – in real life – there real positive science begins: the representation of the practical activity, of the practical process of the development of man. Empty talk about consciousness ceases, and real knowledge has to take its place. When reality is depicted, philosophy as an independent branch of activity loses its medium of existence.' What follows is an analysis of Marxist political economy and the theory of value, the effort to derive the ethics of socialism from this analysis, and a discussion that deals with all the major issues of moral theory – values, rights, obligations, normative judgements, moral imperatives, notions of 'good', 'right' and 'wrong' and so on. (The discussion is interspersed with an effective critique of bourgeois ethics whose theories, even otherwise, are, at best, exercises in 'ideology', as the term was originally used in classical Marxism. Ideology, Engels had said, 'is a process accomplished by the so-called thinker consciously, indeed, but with a false consciousness. The real motives impelling him remain unknown to him, otherwise it would not be an ideological process at all'.) Ash negotiates his way through a complex, rather tricky philosophical territory making a competent and judicious use of his knowledge of both classical Marxism and the relevant non-Marxist thought on the subject. Ash's argument here as elsewhere, notably in the chapter, 'Alienation and Political Change' is exceptionally rich in its philosophical-theoretical texture and there is much that a socialist can learn from it.

Ash does focus on Marxist political economy and the theory of value as the basis of his inquiry into the ethics of socialism. But his argument is not to be reduced to *only* this, for it often goes beyond itself to touch upon or deal with other important and urgent issues of theory and politics, notably Marxist understanding of society and the consequent necessity of socialism, which makes *Workers' Politics,* more than a book on ethics a work on the more comprehensive themes of Marxist theory, socialism and socialist politics. As Ash himself in his Preface to the book states what is possibly the most important implication of his argument: The moral necessity of a socialist understanding of society as the basis for united action to end the exploitation of working people by capitalist corporatists and begin the establishment of a free, peaceful and truly democrative world.

Ash's Preface to *Workers' Politics,* with its critical assessment of recent historical developments, global and local, including American domination of the world and the Blair government's 'Thatcherite' policies and the discussion in 'Alienation and Political Change' of diverse issues of Marxist theory and socialist politics including 'socialism in practice' of the Soviet Union and allied countries, which make its reading an exciting and rewarding experience, point to the comprehensive nature and larger relevance of *Workers' Politics* as a Marxist intervention in behalf of socialism in these ideologically 'dark times'.

Ash's argument on the ethics of socialism has its validity. Critics will of course find it wanting and may even reject it altogether. The more ignorant and prejudiced among them may even question that workers' politics can have an ethics to it. All others may look askance at Ash's effort itself and invoke the 'naturalistic falling' against it. It can even be claimed that its validity notwithstanding, Ash's argument yields less an ethics of socialism and far more a basis for a better, more effective pursuit of socialist politics.

I cannot here discuss all this for the simple reason that being away from the academy for more than twenty-five years, I lack the required familiarity with contemporary philosophising on the subject. I no longer have the kind of need or interest in the subject which as a practising academic I once had, when concerns of peer-group scholarship had to be, necessarily, my concerns too. In fact my credibility as a teacher depended on a genuine and acknowledged familiarity with the mainstream discipline, my reservations about it notwithstanding. I no longer have the interest or compulsion to keep up with any peers; hence my inability to engage in a proper discussion of Ash's argument. (There is also an additional physical disability which currently limits my ability to read and write). However, as I commend Ash's argument to the readers, I would like to support or supplement it by offering three sets of relevant observations culled from what I have written earlier, which individually and collectively are suggestive of other routes of inquiry into the ethics of socialism.

To begin with there is the straightforward Marxist view that our morals or moral principle are natural to human beings, natural not in any transcendental sense, validated by the charms of abstract ideals or some superhuman source or authority, but in the sense of being produced and ordained by them in response to social needs, above all their need for a humane social existence. (Human nature, a product of our interacting biological and sociological inheritances, is essentially modifiable and has been changing from one epoch to another. And this changing, reflected in the growth of our moral principles, ideals or values, has also meant human nature all the time becoming more *human*.)

In the conventional view our moral or ethical principles are assumed to be or treated as 'good' in themselves, which is simply not the case. Our morals, ideals or ethical principles do not exist in themselves, in their own right, independently of nature and history, rooted in God, gods or goddesses, or scriptures or in some way possessing an eternal, absolute, authoritative reality of their own. According to a naturalistic view of man and his world, now accepted by most scholars of ethics and by anthropologists, psychologists and scientists in general, all mental, moral or spiritual phenomena are genuine functions of living organisms at the human level of development (just as life itself is a mode of behaviour of matter at a particular level). It is thus argued that the evolutionary process has risen higher than its source, nature has evolved humans with their morals, ideals or ethical principles. These emerge from the requirement of social life and derive their validity from their usefulness. Hence they are also subject to modification according to circumstances and may, under certain conditions, be suspended.

This view accommodates not only the varying interpretation or practice of ethical principles, their modification, adherence or abandonment, but also their presence and growth through different phases of human history and thus also the notion of class and other history-bound moralities. Pointing out that feudal morality, bourgeois and proletarian morality have much in common because they represent three different stages of the same historical development, Engels had then written of the social origins of class morality:

> 'Men, consciously or unconsciously, derive their moral ideas in the last from the practical relations on which their class position is based – from the economic relations in which they carry on production and exchange . . . Morality was always a class morality; it has either justified the domination and the interests of the ruling class, or as soon as the oppressed class has become powerful enough it has represented the revolt against this domination and the future interests of the oppressed.

Underlining the Marxist understanding of the social origins of moral principles, Marx had said:

> ' "Right" whether it be equal right or any other kind, can never be higher than the economic structure of society and the cultural development thereby determined.'

I may here add that, arguing along these lines, John Lewis has suggested the following for analysing moral standards in a capitalist society:

(1) There are permanent elements of morality that belong to all forms of social organization, primitive, feudal, capitalist and socialist

(2) These however may be interpreted and modified in the interests of cretain groups, classes and races. We all believe in justice and up to a point mean the same thing by it, but beyond that point the socialist and the capitalist, the African and the White South African interpret it differently.

(3) In certain societies, or when contradictions develop within a declining form of society, it becomes increasingly difficult to practise even the accepted morality and in consequence there is a growth of hypocrisy, casuistry, and the distortion of morals to suit vested interests, or in the last resort an open and eynical repudiation of morality.

(4) But alongside an accepted morality reflecting the general interest we may have not only an emphasis, a modification, an interpretation, reflecting class interests, but a special code of morals and the claiming of special rights, which arise directly out of the position, privileges and functions of the ruling class (e.g. the sacrednes of property).

(5) Finally, once again alongside the more general morality and in opposition to the morality of ruling class rights, there will be a special code of morality arising among the oppressed and rebellious which challenges ruling class morals, and advances its own ideals and standards, its own moral condemnation of ruling class morals and the conventions of the times – the morals of a revolutionary class.

My second set of observations is a long excerpt from a review of W.J. Stankiewicz's *Approaches to Democracy* (1980) focused on the issue of *relativism* which is a staple of bourgeois social and moral theory, surfacing in it again and again in one form or another – the latest example being its centrality in the post-modernist theory:

> Stankiewicz, I think, is absolutely right in rejecting *relativism*, in stressing the importance of norms and seeking to put them on a more adequate or firm basis, and, above all, in insisting upon the need for political theory to face and sort out the relevant problems in this area. He even warns us that if the needful here is not done by "specialists in the field" then "naive theorizing" or "naive pseudo-theorizing" will take over, leading inevitably to "unnecessary conflict, confusion and muddling through" etc. Yet the "theorizing" Stankiewicz himself does on this subject, I am afraid, is of little help towards developing the much-needed "adequate normative scheme", that is, a more valid normative theory, for either politics in general or "the democratic system" in particular. Despite repeated references to "reason" and to the need "to incorporate a rational element into normative behaviour", and several sympathetic nods in the direction of "natural law", he can find no better or more secure basis for such "political theory" than that provided by the everyday understanding of "the common man", by what Stankiewicz

himself now defines as 'commonsense'. He writes: "The strength of political theory is that it has always rested on the 'commonsense' view – suggested by introspection and empirical evidence – that we have conception of a self extending in time; that we can choose to act in different ways; that we try to choose in accordance with self-interest; and that we use norms as statements about our self-interest. This attitude is general. No matter what philosophy has to say about the 'commonsense' view, philosophers themselves act upon it". Again, "Normative political theory makes the 'commonsense' assumption that there are certain principles of behaviour – norms – of whose ultimate origin or nature we are not sure, but which in a way provide some general descriptions of behaviour. They not only make statements about things as they are, but also offer 'explanations' of men's behaviour and can serve as tools for making predictions".

Now almost every one of the propositions advanced here by Stankiewicz or attributed by him to "the 'commonsense' view", utter banality of some of them apart, is open to serious objections on empirical as well as philosophical grounds. Most revealing is the unmistakable *bourgeois* flavour of Stankiewicz's 'commonsense' (with its overriding concern with self-interest, and with property as the passage quoted earlier shows). And with all the progress made in the field, who today will accept such a simplistic view of men's behaviour, treat norms as such simple, direct and effective determinants for purposes of description, explanation and prediction? It is indeed amazing that Stankiewicz offers us, in the year 1980, a virtually "norms" theory of history – after the universally recognised revolution in historiography that has occurred in our times consequent upon the pioneering achievement of Kari Marx. I cannot undertake a discussion of these issues here. More relevant to our immediate purpose is to point out the further fact that even as Stankiewicz recommends his 'commonsense'-based political theory as the way out of the situation created by relativism, he notes its difficulties, that is, the difficulties involved in using such a theory for concrete decision-making in a democratic system. And these, among others, relate to "uncertainty about the scope of norms", uncertainty or lack of knowledge about "what position its norms (such as liberty and equality) occupy in the normative hierarchy" and, above all, the fact that "political philosphers have not made it clear how the theory can be applied without reflecting the subjective preferences of the theorist", etc.

All this hardly adds up to any kind of alternative to relativism. Far from being a new guide,it looks very much like yet another variant of relativism itself. We seem condemned to "unnecessary conflict, confusion and muddling through"!

As part of his general argument, and in seeking "to escape relativism", Stankiewicz does in one place try to establish a more valid basis for norms. But his argument remains unelaborated – it covers barely a page of his book – and in its implication it is, to say the least, extremely problematic. Interestingly enough, while repeatedly stating, *a l'mode,* that "none of us can 'prove' the validity of the norms we hold" and that they are "not verifiable by the methods of science", Stankiewicz, in effect, argues that the validity of "good" (norms) can be established by a procedure essentially similar to that which, according to him, is used for validating "truth" (science).

Arguing that in both cases you need "a central point of reference" which "must obviously be fixed or 'abolute' ", he tells us that "there is only one thing that fulfils this condition: the standard of 'good' is the same as that of 'truth' – namely the 'self'." This by itself would imply pure relativism, even solipsism, but for the fact that "we demand that all statements about truth be verifiable: they must always yield the same obserations under the same conditions", and in this "the self gives the observations of the other about the 'it' of objective reality a weight equal to its own". Science thus avoids relativism or solipsism and can validate itself "because it rests on two fundamental propositions: the *self-it* distinction and the *self-other,* and the latter is vital to its defence of objective truth". Stankiewicz thus sums up his argument: "Science, then, escapes solipsism through a self-other dichotomy. If it has validity in converting relative truths to absolutes, there is no reason not to use the same principle to convert relative 'goods' to absolutes, as in fact mankind appears to have been doing throughout history". In other words, "the 'self' accepts as a standard of 'good' its own welfare, just as it accepts as a standard of 'truth' its own perceptions and converts these from relative standards to absolutes by means of substantiations or verifications; the latter are made possible by the self-other identification", Stankiewicz concludes : "If we deny the validity of this technique our science becomes solipsistic and our ethics relativistic. If we accept it, then both 'truth' and the 'good' are verifiable".

One careful look at Stankiewicz's agrument will make it clear that it does not offer any real escape from relativism in the field of norms. It is only a scientific-looking defence or justification of that which is commonly observed and accepted, only a rationalisation of what *is.* If an escape, it is one from some abstract relativism of theory into the concrete relativism of the 'commonsense'! Far from providing any genuine basis for validation of norms, of "good", this kind of argument, if rigorously pursued, would depriven even "truths" of science of their validation or verification. In its passive empiricistic emphasis, by focusing exclusively on the commonly shared observation of "it" by the "self" and the "other", and refusing to move beyond it, Stankiewicz's argument obscures the more basic premises of veriflcation of truth in science, namely, an independently exsisting objective reality that we *know* in science, and the primacy science accords to *practice* in the knowing of this reality, in the discovery of *its* truth. In science, as Marx pointed out, we move from "the appearance", the commonly observed, to reality, "the nature of things". (The sun is commonly observed to rise every morning, but does it?) Science is a language for talking not about perception, or observation, or experience, but about the world.

If Stankiewicz's treatment of relativism born of the usual scepticism concerning the validation of norms is most unsatisfactory and fully revealing of the basic inadequacy of his idealist-rationalist approach, with its social underpinning of bourgeois individualism, the situation is no better when he comes to deal with another kind of relativism to which also he gives a great deal of attention. The adversary this time is *determinism.* While his attack covers the behaviourlist version of it also – in so far as "modern behavioural sciences have adopted the postition that the science of human behaviour must be consistent with the methodology of the physical sciences which is based on determinism" – the main target is what Stankiewicz describes as "historical determinism", particularly of the sort which, according to him, Marxism represents. As he puts it: "The Marxist school of historical determinists are compelled to stop their analysis when they have established the relation between the historical conditions and the norms; by their own assertions norms are products of social conditions and this view excludes the possibility that these products could now affect social conditions. If they allowed the norms to acquire an existence of their own – such that they could influence behaviour – they would be forced to give up their historical determinism". Or, again: "The point is that historical determinists argue that the relation is one way: norms are the product of circumstances but cannot themselves produce new circumstances without violating the premise about the nature of norms".

With Stankiewicz his opponents' position and therefore his own argument demolishing it are both quite simple. He writes: "Given determinism, is it possible to hold a genuinely normative position, the answer is negative". For "the problem with seeing any norms as historically determined is that universals become excluded". Since "the concept of determinism implies involuntary change" and thus rules out any deliberate or conscious "ordering" or "re-ordering of society", "*any* deterministic school of thought is in fundamental conflict with the individualism and freedom on which democracy is premised". We are also told that "determinism (is) incompatible with political - or ethical - theory"; in fact "it is not possible to be both a political theorist and a determinist". More specifically, we are informed that Marx, as a determinist, "ignores the individual and focuses on the fact of society", that for him "man's sense of 'freedom' is an illusion", that historical determinism "entails anti-individualism, for the capacity of the individual to make right choices is taken from him". In fact "determinists and non-determinists are fully aware that the concepts of reason and freedom put them in opposite camps". So goes on Stankiewicz, repetitvely, to win an easy victory. For who wouldn't like to be in the camp of reason and freedom with Stankiewicz and, hopefully, with "political or ethical theory" too?

Anyone even remotely familiar with the theoretical and political work of Marx will recognise that what is being presented here is a gross caricature. This is neither new nor surprising, for such vulgarisation of Marx and Marxism has been for long a staple of academic and not-so-academic writing on politics and philosophy in the Anglo-Saxon world. (Witness, for example, the mutually exclusive caricaltures of Marxism as the most dangerous "historicism" and an equally dangerous "rationalism" in Popper and Oakeshott respectively). More interesting and significant is the fact that Stankiewicz, so concerned with "the individual", "individual's freedom", "his capacity to make right choices", etc., is yet so completely oblivious of the discussion that has been raging all around him in the West on Marx's theory of alienation. I wonder what sense Stankiewicz would make of Marx's own life and struggles, the clear-eyed free choices he made for himself and the sacrifices he made as a revolutionary in pursuit of those choices, or of Marx's ethical theory whose central concern is *always* the individual and the posibility of a free, unalienated, truly rich human life for him, from that early warning: "What is to be avoided above all is the reestablishing of 'Society' as an abstraction *vis-à-vis* the individual. The individual *is the social being*. His life . . . is therefore, an expression and confirmation of *social-life*" (*Economic and Philosophic Manuscripts of 1844*); through his passionate plea for reconstituting society as "an association in which the free development of each is the condition for the free development of all" (*Communist Manifesto*), to his final argument, towards the end of his life, on behalf of "the true realm of freedom" which makes possible "that development of human power, which is its own end" (*Capital,* Vol. III), etc.

I have no intention of making a detailed comment on Stankiewicz's understanding of Marx or Marxism. It would suffice to note that his argument on the subject of "historical determinism" is vitiated by three inter-related, and rather elementary, errors or confusions.

In the first place, to deny an independent origin or development to norms, to deny that norms or ethical ideals can be explained entirely or even mainly in terms of a genealogy of their own or to argue that they are social products and that social or historical conditios exercise a powerful selective and formative influence over the norms or ideals dominant at a particular historical period – all this is not to deny norms and ideals their role and influence in the historical process, their ability to "affect social conditions", "give rise to historical situations", or "produce new circumstances". In fact, the real issues here, far from being closed by it, arise only *after* "historical determinism" has been taken note of. As Engels put it: "Once an historical element has been brought into the world by other elements . . . it also reacts in its turn and may react on its environment and even on its own causes". An effect, norms or ideals can and do function as powerful causes also–though their power is not absolute but limited by, dependent or conditional upon, the given historical situation or circumstances. The relation here far from being "one way" is really, and always, dialectical in nature. No doubt, norms are extremely important. In fact they are among the specifics of the *human* situation. But they arise and are effective only *in* history.

In the second place, to point out the historically conditioned nature of norms or ethical ideals is not to deny them, or deprive them of their validity in any way. In fact the question of their origin is essentially irrelevant to the question of their validity. This is settled according to altogether different criteria. All morality arises in history, as part of the process of social and historical development; norms are created by men on the basis of their needs and experience in pursuit of their ends. But the question of their validity or adequacy, at a particular point of time, is settled by other, different, criteria. For example, norms *freedom* and *slavery* have both arisen in history, they are indeed "historically determined" and the latter was even upheld by men of great reason like Plato and Aristotle. But we are today, as always, and in a fully meaningful sense, free to choose between them, free to reject slavery and uphold freedom. And we do so for good reasons, which have really nothing to do with the social or historical origin of these norms, with any "historical determinism", but everything with criteria based on and derived from *man's essential, and growing, humanity.* [Just as science and superstition, ideas true as well as false, all arise historically, but science or truth is established by criteria (subsumed under the scientific method) which are *essentially* independent of their origins, of history.]

In the third place, Stankiewicz's treatment of the problem of *determinism* and *freedom,* despite a couple of half-hearted cautionary hints in the right direction, is confused, if not positively misleading, and essentially evasive of the real issues. It is neither possible nor necessary to disentangle his argument here and examine its implications in detail; only a couple of observations will do. On the one hand, his general argument against 'determinism' which, according to him, permits only "involuntary change" and therefore means a denial of freedom to man, tends to obscure the fact that freedom, in an important sense, depends upon, is the recognition of, determinism, that "determined" character of man's world, *given man's knowledge of it,* is precisely what gives him the possibility and the opportunity of exercising his freedom, of doing or achieving what he wants to do or achieve. In a truly "non-determined" world, where *anything* can happen, men will have no freedom at all in any meaningful sense. ("We cannot command nature except by obeying her", Bacon had rightly asserted in a similar context). On the other hand, Stankieicz's specific argument for "non-determinism" which he regards as a necessary premise of freedom if rigorously pursued, will demand finding freedom in some truly "non-determined" choice, which would be an extraordinary choice indeed, something entirely arbitrary, even irresponsible, an uncausal cause producing some existentialist or metaphysical freedom-in-itself. Such a free or non-determined choice simply does not exist; it is meaningless and impossible. The real issue to be faced here is that, in any given situation, men can and do make choices, genuineoy free and rational choices in the only sense they can do so, without having to reject "causation" or "determinism", and that men are rightly held responsible by their fellowmen for the choices they make. Describing the argument that if an action is law-governed or determined then it is not free, as "highly dubious". Professor Alasdair MacIntyre has written; "when we count an action unfree or non-rational, as we do the compulsive behaviour of neurotics, we do so if the action is outside the agent's own rational control, if it cannot be altered in the light of relevant deliberation. But for this to be the case it is not enough that the action be caused; what mattters is whether the causes of the action in question are such as to render the agent incapable of rational control, immune to rational considerations. If the agent's own rational deliberation *is* the cause of his action, this is a paradigm case of free and rational action. Hence it is not . . . whether an action is or is not caused and law-governed that matters; it is the character and the content of the causes and the laws in question".

Against the idealists[3] and the earlier materialists' imaginary and mechanistic counter-posing of "determinism" to "freedom", dialectics of the real human situation was well expressed by Marx when, rejecting such materialism, he wrote: "the materialist doctrine that men are products of circumstances and upbringing, and that, therefore, changed men are products of other circumstances and changed upbringing, forgets that it is men that change circumstances and that the educator himself needs educating". And men do this changing or "educating" through choices, which even when historically conditioned, law-governed or otherwise subject to "causation" – all this is amenable to knowledge – are yet genuine human choices, more or less free and rational and are rightly treated as such by social and moral theory.

Man as a product of natural evolution is an animal but one with a difference, for he alone has the capacity among other things, for science and for ethics. Thus he functions, actively and creatively, in relation to his environment, the two continuously making and remaking each other. As man he is neither totally determined by his environment and, therefore, unconditionally subject to it, nor totally free in relation to it and therefore its unconditional master. Between the ideal extremes of "determinism" and "freedom" he builds his real world, with his science and with his ethics, his knowledge being both the means and the measure of his freedom.

Such being the case, Stankiewicz is only spreading confusion and pursuing false trails by raising the issues of "determinism" *versus* "non-determinism", by situating what he calls "a genuinely normative position" somewhere outside history or society, by abstractly opposing "freedom" to "determinism" and seeking it in the metaphysics of some truly "non-determined" choice, etc. Importance of norms for all human behaviour, so emphasised by Stankiewicz, is obvious enough and is really denied by none. Far more important and relevant is to insist that norms, while historically evolved and rationally validated (as briefly indicated above), should be relative to the needs and possibilites of the given objective situation, neither demanding more, as utopianism has always done, nor offering less, as the liberal-conservative political theory does today. Besides, "it is because morality is always and in all places relative to circumstances", as Professor Muirhead once wrote, "that it is binding at any time and in any place". In other words, even as it rightly rejects the actual or finds it wanting, the ideal should be possible too, the "ought" must, in this sense, be a derivative or function of "is". In this sense, again, given their essential *humanist* premises, the more our norms are dependent upon or determined by the facts of the case, by the consideration of the circumstances, the limitations and possibilities of the

> objective conditions, the more effective and powerful they will be. I might add that to take circumstances or conditions into account does not eliminate personal choice or reponsibility. In fact it is the only way to make the right choices, to make these choices meaningful and effective, and to act responsibly. "Men make their own history", Marx wrote, "but they do not make it just as they please. They make it under circumstances directly encountered, given and transmitted from the past".
>
> Having long since moved away from the search for universals, in science as well as ethics, as something absolute, rooted in some transcendental source, or in some way possessing an independent, authoritative reality of their own, we have come to recognise them as the achievement of human beings in the course of their social and historical development. Therefore, what we need is an approach which, even as it knows these universals to be grounded in history, can yet find its way to verify or validate them. In other words, we need a theory which establishes the truths of science and the validity of morals, even while recognising them as living, concrete categories of real, continually moving, continually changing human existence, which can conceptualise these universals as constantly evolving unities of the absolute and the relative and, thus, provide for the growth of truth and the growth of morality in a manner as to enable us, at any particular point of time, not only to speak of ideas being more or less true and of ideals being more or less right but also assert that our truth though relative is none the less objective truth in terms of an independently existing reality, and that our morality though relative is nonetheless valid morality in terms of the needs and possibilities of the objective human situation.
>
> But it is possible to develop such an approach or theory only on the basis of a philosophy which is both materialist and dialectical in its treatment of the issues of science and ethics. The eclectic idealism of the bourgeois-rationalist variety that Stankiewicz works with does not even let him ask the right questions or pose them in the right manner.

My third set of observations are passages excerpted from my recently published *Crisis of Socialism – Notes in Defence of a Commitment* focussed on Marx's ethical-aesthetic critique of capitalism which can be a good starting point for our inquiry into the ethics of socialism:

> Socialism as negation of capitalism of course means a thorough-going transformation of property relations and abolition of private profit as the

organising pinciple of production, a genuine, not merely formal or juridical social ownership of the commanding heights of the economy and democratically planned use of social-material resources for human welfare. These are, however, necessary rather than sufficient conditions for socialism, and certainly not description of socialism. For Marx the negation involved very much more than such necessary transformation of economic arrangements, 'the subordination of (people's) common social productivity as their (own) social power', as he put it.

'The mode of production', according Marx, 'must not be considered simply as being the reproduction of the physical existence of the individuals. Rather it is a definite form of expressing their life, "a definite mode of life" on their part'. Capitalism as a mode of procuction, for example, completely subordinates human needs to the reproduction of exchange-value in the interest of capital's expanded self-realisation, which makes it pre-eminently a system not only of accumulation, but of commodification as well, which in its immediate working and ultimate outcome seeks to commodify every aspect of social life or human exstence. In socialism, as Marx wrote in *The Poverty of Philosophy,* humans must change 'from top to bottom the conditions of their industrial and political existence, and consequently *their whole manner of being'*. Central to this changed 'manner of being' is the end of a private-property-governed and commodified existence, the 'unfreedom' of capitalist social order and the beginning, in Marx's words, of 'free individuality based on the universal development of the individual' in a socialist society. In other words, socialism is a society ensuring the 'free development' of its members, 'the asociated producers', enabling them to realise their human powers, needs and capacities in as rich, untrammelled and all-round manner as possible. It is by the unleashing of actual productive forces that these human powers and capacities are bred and only by transformation of the social relations of production that the conditions in which they can flourish all-round can be created.

This draws our attention to an aspect of Marx's argument concerning capitalism that we need to notice for the light it throws on his idea of socialism, rather the *revolutionary humanist ambition* of his idea of socialism. This is the ethical and aesthetic-cultural dimension of his critique of capitalism, expressing a concern that everything Marx wrote is suffused with, and is in fact a distinctive feature of his social theory. Though this dimension never came to be theorised by him – unlike the economics of capitalism Marx's humanist concern is an ever-present motivating force in his work as a thinker and a revolutionary.

Underlying Marx's humanist concern is his view of man, of man's *essential* humanity, his intrinsic being or immanent nature, the evolution-produced special property as a human being that, beyond the mere bodily' or 'mundane' activity and needs which in his own way he shares with other living beings, distinguishes man from them, his 'species-being' as Marx called it. Marx expressed this *differentia specifica* of man in such phrases as 'conscious life-activity directly distinguishes man from animal life-activity', 'free conscious activity is man's species character', 'freedom is thoroughly the essence of man', conscious and purposive activity that 'distinguishes the worst architect from the best of bees', etc. This is how Marx viewed human nature in general, which then comes to be modified in each historical epoch, his species-distinctive capacity being determined and developed but more often also limited, curtailed, mutilated or perverted in the course of his socio-historical development, more specially under capitalism.

Speaking of Marx's *Capital,* Che Guevara had once pointed out that 'the magnitude of this monumental achievement of human intelligence is such that we are often oblivious to the profoundly humanist (in the best sense of the word) nature of its interests'. In other words, Marx's humanist concern was an integral part of his critique of capitalism as an economic system. Apart from several brillianty insightful passages on the human condition under capitalism, *Capital's* vocabulary on the subject is characterised by an indignant and relentless use of such terms as 'brutalizing', 'alienating', 'monstrous', 'savage', 'ghoulish', 'besitial', 'inhuman', and so on. Marx's humanist concern is equally well experessed in several sharp passages of the *Communist Manifesto.* But this concern – what is man?, how capitalism limits, distorts or damages his essential humanity? and what can man become? – is somewhat more elaborately stated in his early writings. Its most explicit expression is in Marx's *Economic and Philosophical Manuscripts of 1844*, with its focus on human condition, the alienated existence of human beings, in capitalist society. And Marx's argument of 150 years ago today stands more than vindicated. Witness to it is the extraordinary interest *Manuscripts* have evoked, and the endorsement its argument has received in our times, especially in the countries of advanced capitalism, making *Manuscripts* one of the half-a-dozen most discussed writings of the post-Second World War period. Apropos non-Marxist western scholars' interest in this and related writings of Marx, it is interesting to note that while some of them have indeed shown a real desire to understand him and written with sympathy and perception, not a few have sought, some of them so very desperately, to so focus on these writings as to separate Marx from himself and from Marxism

– to separate the young Marx from the old, the *'idealistic'*, 'freedom-loving' Marx of *Economic and Philosophic Manuscripts* from the supposedly cynical and disillusioned Marx of *Capital,* Marx the humanist from Marx the revolutionary and an advocate of class struggle, Marx from Engels, and, of course, from Lenin and Mao Tse-tung and any radical movement; he was now their own humanist and 'Western' Marx, having nothing to do with revolution or 'the East'.

At the heart of Marx's ethical and aesthetic-cultural critique of capitalism lies his deep concern for humanity, its present condition and possible future. Central to his argument is the idea (particularly expressed, along with *Manuscripts of* 1884, in his other early writings such as *On the Jewish Question, Contribution to the Critique of Hegel's Philosophy of Right, The Holy Family,* etc.) that man, stripped of his human essence when he first fell into the class of exploited, faces 'the destruction of all humanity' in him under capitalism. The process of Capitalist exploitation, with its attendant 'greed and the war between the greedy – competition', not only holds the entire society, the capitalist as well as the worker, in its irresistable compulsive grip and at the mercy of 'the blind forces' of the market, it also transforms free creative self-activity of man into alienated labour, and reduces man himself to a commodity. It 'estranges man from nature, from himself, his own active functioning . . . from his *essence* . . . It makes his *essence* into a mere means for his existence . . . (and results in) the alienation of *man* from *man.*' Capitalism tears up 'all genuine bonds between men' and replaces them by selfishness, dissolving 'the world of men into a world of atomized individuals, hostile towards each other'. It leaves 'no other nexus between man and man than naked self-interest, than callous "cash payment"' and resolves 'personal worth into exchange value'. The very things which were once 'communicated, but never exchanged; given, but never sold; acquired, but never bought – virtue, love, conviction, knowledge, conscience, etc,' – now become marketable and pass 'into commerce'; 'the *divine* power of money' overturns and confounds 'all human and natural qualities' in the marketplace. There comes to be generated a savage lust for money and property, a maniacal obsession with the accumulation of capital, a veritable fanaticism of appropriation. Amassing wealth becomes the supreme object of human endeavour and the final criterion of human success. The emphasis is on acquisitiveness and the only success that matters is the success of the market-place, resulting in 'that whole system of appetites and values' which 'with its deification of the life of snatching to hoard, and hoarding to snatch' leaves, as Tawney wrote, 'a taste as of ashes on the lips of a civilization which has brought to the conquest of its material environment resources unknown in earlier ages, but which has not yet learned to master itself'. And all this leaves man, even the so-called rich man of capitalism, 'ever poorer as a *man',* robbed of real life and crippled in his inner being.

Marx in line with his mode of thinking, took a historical view of the growth of needs and desires of human beings as one aspect of the general development of human nature, which is also the subjective aspect of the growth of human powers and capacities. With the development of our powers and capacities new needs emerge; and the growth of new needs spurs the development of new powers. As Marx saw this process, it is 'the absolute working out of (man's) creative potentialities, with no presupposition other than the previous historic development', which makes 'this totality of development', i.e. the development of human powers as such 'an end in itself', not to be measured on any *predetermined* yardstick. Human development in this perspective is the growth of human capacities and powers, the actualisation of human potentialities, the self-development and self-realisation of human beings. This however must not be understood in any utilitarian or hedonistic manner. Central to the growth of human powers and capacities is the development of the specifically human faculties, the creative, aesthetic faculties of human beings, their 'glorious human senses'. For Marx, like the evolution-produced five physical senses, these too are 'the work of all previous history'. Marx wrote: 'The most beautiful music has *no* sense for the unmusical ear, because my object can only be the confirmation of one of my essential powers . . . . For the same reasons the *senses* of social man are *different* from those of non-social man. Only through the objectively unfolded wealth of human nature can the wealth of subjective *human* sensitivity – a musical ear, an eye for the beauty of form, in short, *senses* capable of human gratification – be either cultivated or created.'

This is surely suggestive of an infinite future of creation and cultivation of 'the wealth of subjective *human* sensitivity', of specifically human senses, which is really the same as human nature all the time *becoming more human.* And the important point is that, for Marx, the exercise of these naturally and historically produced specifically human senses – the sense for music and poetry, art, science and history, love, justice and compassion, and so on – constituted the very essence of a truly human appropriation of life and nature, a genuinely rich human life. That is how, in pointing out the alienating, depersonalising and dehumanising consequences of capitalism, Marx particularly focused attention on the fact that for all the glorious human senses, whose active and concrete exercise alone constitutes the true content of a genuinely rich human life, capitalism substitutes a single abstract sense, the sense for property, a particular, historically transient, substitute sense which plays havoc with human personality and plunges man, in the words of Ladislav Stoll, 'into the terrible inner sickness of a dehumanised world'. Marx wrote: 'In place of *all* these physical and mental senses there has . . . come the sheer estrangement of *all* these senses – the sense of *having.* The human being had to be reduced to this absolute poverty in order that he might yield his inner wealth to the outer world'. 'The more you *have',* said Marx, 'the less you *are'.* Hence his insistence that 'the transcendence of private property is therefore the complete *emancipation* of all human senses and attributes'. He spoke of communism,' the *actual* phase necessary for the next stage of historical development in the process of human emancipation and recovery', 'as the positive transcendence of *private property as human self-estrangement,* and therefore as the real *appropriation of the human essence* by and for man; communism therefore as the complete return of man to himself as a *social* (i.e., human) being – a return become conscious, and accomplished within the entire wealth of previous development.' Marx added: 'What is to be avoided above all is the re-establishing of "Society" as an abstraction *vis-à-vis* the individual. The individual *is the social being.* His life . . . is therefore an expression and confirmation of *social life.'* Marx is an individualist in the basic sense that his ultimate vision was a society where, as Marx himself put it, 'the free development of each is the condition for the free development of all'.

What this 'free development', the above-mentioned 'transcendence of human self-estrangement' means, what Marx meant when early in his life he wrote (in *Economic and Philosophic Manuscripts of* 1844) that 'communism equals humanism', and towards the end spoke (in *Capital,* Vol. III) of 'the true realm of freedom' which makes possible 'that development of human power, which is its own end', what vision of the genuinely rich juman life lay behind his life-long struggle for socialism – this has been well expressed by Ladislav Stoll. Pointing out that 'in place of many-sided, active, concrete appropration of life and the world, through which the individual says not only "I see, I hear, I smell, I taste, I touch", but also, "I work, I study, I love, I admire, I struggle for a happier tomorrow" – in place of all this wealth of emotion capitalism makes one single emotion supreme: "I *have!*"', Stoll writes:

> The truly human way of appropriating the world's riches is that by which man really overcomes the world, in other words, with all his senses, for unlike the animals man has a whole series of glorious human senses, not only the senses of sight, hearing, smell, taste and touch, but also a sense for music, a sense for poetry, a sense for the plastic arts, a sense for science,

> a sense for mathematics, a sense for history, crystalography, etc. It is only when a man begins to satisfy the needs of these glorious human senses, which one and all are the product of historical development, that he can appropriate to himself all the beauties of the world and become genuinely rich.

In a related comment on Marx's *Manuscripts of 1844*, Erich Fromm has written:

> Socialism, for Marx, is a society which permits the actualization of man's essence, by overcoming his alienation. It is nothing less than creating the conditions for the truly free, rational, active and independent man; it is the fulfilment of the prophetic aim: the destruction of the ideals . . . For Marx, the aim of socialism was freedom . . . based on man's standing on his own feet, using his own powers and relating himself to the world productively.

Again, on the same theme:

> For Marx, the abolition of capitalism and the establishment of socialist economy does not by itself usher in a 'truly human society', it only makes it possible. Material fulfilment is for him only the condition, the necessary basis, and not the sum, of man's 'spiritual', that is, 'truly human' fulfilment. The vision which underlies his whole work from the early 1840s to the end is the vision of 'human emancipation'. His life and struggle was a plea to replace the pitiable, fragmentary and self-alienated existence, which is man's lot in a class-divided and exploitative society that is capitalism, with a truly rich human life; it was an assertion of life abundant against mere existence. Socialism opens up the possibility of this abundant life. More than ending the economic exploitation of a capitalist market system, it will make for direct cooperative socio-economic relations between people such that they cease to be alienated from the product of their labour, from nature and their fellow human beings, and from themselves. And as socialism transits to communism, with the productive forces further developed, all the springs of collective wealth flowing freely, labour become not merely a means but prime necessity of life, and the personalty-diminishing excesses of division of labour eliminated, the way will be open for the full flowering of man's creative potentialities, his glorious human senses, for 'the unfolding of man', 'the all round development of the individual', as Marx put it.

Early in his life, this is how Marx saw this 'unfolding' or 'all round development', or looked beyond the reduction of human work to dictated 'mindless detail task' that division of labour under capitalism entails:

> as soon as the division of labour comes into being, each man has a particular, exclusive sphere of activity, which is forced upon him and from which he cannot escape. He is a hunter, a fisherman, a shepherd, or a critical critic, and must remain so if he does not want to lose his means of livelihood; while in a communist society, where nobody has one exclusive sphere of activity, but each can become accomplished in any branch he wishes, society regulates the general production and thus makes it possible for me to do one thing today and another tomorrow, to hunt in the morning, fish in the afternoon, rear cattle in the evening, criticize after dinner, just as I have a mind, without ever becoming hunter, fisherman, shepherd or critic . . . (No longer a human being needs to be) exclusively a painter, sculptor, etc. . . . In a communist society there are no painters but at most people who engage in painting among other activities.

In another celebrated passage, now towards the end of his life, Marx saw socialism in its transition to communism as humankind's transition to 'the realm of freedom' which according to him lies beyond material pursuits, beyond all activity geared to economic needs. He wrote:

> . . . The realm of freedom actually begins only where labour which is determined by necessity and mundane considerations ceases; thus *in the very nature of things* it lies beyond the sphere of actual material production. Just as the savage must wrestle with nature to satisfy his wants, to maintain and reproduce life, so must civilised man, and he must do so in all social formations and under all modes of production. . . . Freedom in this field can only consist in socialised man, the associated producers, rationally regulating their interchange with nature, bringing it under their common control, instead of being ruled by it as by a blind power; and achieving this with the least exenditure of energy and under conditions most favourable to, and worthy of, their human nature. But it nonetheless still remains a realm of necessity. Beyond it begins that development of human power which is an end in itself, the true realm of freedom, which, however, can blossom forth only with this realm of necessity as its basis.

The aspiration or vision that Marx here sets forth is in fact as old as civilisation; it is there, for instance, in Plato and Aristotle, though its realisation, then and afterwards, was seen possible only for a few. Marx put more substance into this aspiration and sought its realisation for *all* human beings. In other words, economic activity was, throughout, deemed to have meaning only if it serves something other than itself. For Marx this is activities 'valued as an end in themselves' (as he phrased it in the *Grundrisse*), which for him is indeed 'the true measure of wealth'.

A first condition for such a shift of balance in human activity from 'the realm of necessity' to 'the realm of freedom' is obviously a reduction in socially necessary labour time that economic activity involves. Society would have to be able to produce sufficient to satisfy the necessities of material existence withot absorbing all the time and effort of its people. Marx saw this becoming a distinct possibility, for the first time, with the productive achievements of capitalism (and those he visualised under socialism). Compared with the means these achievements put at our disposal, 'the theft of somebody else's labour time, on which wealth now rests, appears a miserable base', wrote Marx. To take 'working time as the standard of wealth,' Marx argued, 'is to base wealth on poverty, . . . reducing time as a whole to working time and degrading the individual to the simple role of the working man, dominated by his labour.' This was becoming no longer necessary, and the possibility existed for moving towards a qualitatively different society in which, as Marx put it, 'the surplus labour of the masses will no longer be the condition for the development of general wealth as the leisure of the few will cease to be the condition for the full development of the human brain'. Herein lay the hope and promise of the future, a real basis for Marx's vision of a transition from the realm of necessity to the realm of freedom where there is 'free individuality' and 'the development of human power is an end in itself'. Here at last, in Marx's famous 1859 formulation, the 'pre-history' of humanity ends and its 'history' begins. For Marx, it is this beginning that socialism represents.

It has been fashionable in a society vitally interested in persuading its victims to underreach themselves, to decry and dismiss Marx's vision of socialism as something 'utopian', a 'romantic' or 'millennial' dream. One can only ask such critics or sceptics to shed their myopia and look at the world around them with a little less prejudice and more courage, for utopian or not so utopian for his age, Marx was remarkably prophetic for us; his vision is very much a realistic proposition today with the magnificent possibilities now being opened up for humankind by the scientific-technological revolutions of our time – provided, of course, these revolutions are used not for stoking up the furnaces of private profit and privilege, or making wars, as it is bound to be under capitalism, but for the benefit of humanity at large which socialism may not guarantee but certainly makes possible.

Of 'Consumerism':

An aspect of Marx's analysis of capitalism, which deserves to be specifically noticed, is his brilliant anticipation of what we have come to recognise as 'consumerism', an increasingly dominant and deeply disturbing and destructive bane of life in contemporary capitalist societies, which Marx castigated as the 'true norm' of capitalism. Marx saw human nature as modifiable in history. He had written: 'Our desires and pleasures spring from society, we measure them, therefore, by society and not by the objects which serve for their satisfaction. Because they are of a social nature, they are of a relative nature'. And however arisen, they continue to be modified, gain or lose in importance, with changing social conditions. Take, for instance, such pathological phenomena as greed or selfishness. Capitalism did not invent them; they are deep in human nature, related as they are to elementary infantile structures and the overall determining situation of *scarcity* which has characterised civilisation throughout and so far. But capitalism has undoubtedly magnified their role in ordinary life, and, unlike its predecessor feudal or other pre-capitalist social formations, which had the (Christian or analogous) grace to condemn greed or selfishness, capitalism even celebrates them. For Marx, therefore, 'consumerism' is not a matter of human nature as such, of its so-called insatiable appetites, but of a human nature desired, moulded and manipulated by capitalism as a market-based system of private property and profit-making. Capitalism invariably tends, via profitability in the marketplace, to drive a wedge between human *needs* and human *wants,* and to proliferate the wants in a manner that, as Baran once said, 'people steeped in the culture of monoply capitalism do not want what they need and do not need what they wnat'. Capitalism irresistibly gives rise to 'consumerism' which is essentially the artificial market-determined and mediated stimulation of consumption for private profit under capitalism. In an extended comment, with an opening reference to socialism, Marx wrote in the *Manuscripts of 1844*:

We have seen what significance, given socialism, the *wealth* of human needs has, and what significance, therefore, both *a* given *new mode of production* and a new *object of production* have: a new manifestation of the forces of *human* nature and a new enrichment of *human* nature. Under private property their significance is reversed: every person speculates on creating a *new* need in another, so as to drive him to a fresh sacrifice, to place him in a new dependence and to seduce him into a new mode of *gratification* and therefore economic ruin. Each tries to establish over the other an *alien* power, so as

> thereby to find satisfaction of his own selfish need. The increase in the quantity of objects is accompanied by an extension of the realm of alien powers to which man is subjected, and every new product represents a new *potency* of mutual swindling and mutual plundering. Man becomes ever poorer as man . . . . *Excess* and *intemperance* come to be (capitalism's) true norm . . . the extension of products and needs falls into *contriving* and ever-*calculating* subservience to inhuman, refined, unatural and *imaginary* appetites . . .

Marx added:

> and no eunuch flatters his despot more basely or uses more despicable means to stimulate his dulled capacity for pleasure in order to sneak a favour for himself than does the industrial eunuch – the producer – to sneak for himself a few pennies . . . He puts himself in the sevice of the other's most depraved fancies, plays the pimp between him and his need, excites in him morbid appetites, lies in wait for each of his weakneses . . .

Of 'development':

> Yet again, there is the overarching question as to what kind of society we, as *human beings,* want to have. Surely it is people and not 'economic growth' or 'productivity' that must come first in such a society. It has to be a humane society that fosters cooperation, solidarity and respect for universal ethical values, and makes for a non alienated, 'truly rich human life' that Marx spoke of. Of course such a society is impossible without basic material security and need satisfaction. But to believe that you can assure need satisfaction through greed, private acquisitive drives, universal competition and strife – the values of capitalism – and yet hope for a humane society of cooperation and solidarity is utopianism of the worst kind. Subordinating humanity to economics, to imperatives of the market, capitalism commodifies life and undermines and rots away the relations between human beings which constitute societies. Its ethos of the marketplace – competition, egoism, aggression, alienation, univesal venality, in short the rat race – creates a moral vacuum in which nothing counts except what the individual wants and can grab, here and now. At the end of it all, even when wants are satisfied, the people are ever more subordinated, ever less free, ever more flattened and made passive by the dictatorship of consumerism that arbitrarily shapes values, imposing on them the heavy burden of uniformity. The values of difference, individualisation (not individualism), all-sided development

> of man, of human freedom itself, disappear in the market-place which is proclaimed to be free. As *human beings,* people simply don't fit into capitalism. For a truly humane society to come into existence, capitalism has to go.

Finally a passage on 'socialist utopianism':

> 'Utopian' is the charge that continues to be made against socialism. In a sense, any political project is the affirmation of something that is not here, something, in short, imagined and therefore amenable to the charge of utopianism. But, obviously, this is not what the critics mean. Their real objection is to the nature of the socialist project, the transcendence of capitalism it seeks. There are those for whom any effort to move beyond the confines of capitalism is utopian – a position not too difficult to understand. As Arnold Thurman once put it : 'It may be asserted as a principle of human organisation that when new types of social organisation are required, respectable, well-thought-of, and conservative people are unable to take part in them. Their moral and economic prejudices, their desire for the approval of other members of the group, compel them to oppose any form of organisation which does not fit into the picture of society as they have known it in the past . . . . Nothing seems clearer than that the attitudes of any given ruling class are so set that all arguments in the world will not change them'. But this obviously does not make the charge of 'utopianism' valid. There is, however, another argument which has a wider acceptance. It questions and rejects the socialist project of a viable, classless and stateless, socialised property-based free and humane social order as an impossible ideal, something that does not and cannot exist, something never done or realised before; we simply cannot do without private property or classes, without a capitalist market or class-structure to make the economy work. This argument does carry weight with the ignorant and the unwary, the so-called 'average' citizens in thrall to the conventional bourgeois ways of thinking. But it is nevertheless a straw argument.
>
> Our growing knowledge in the fields of ethnography and anthropology, about humans' present and past, has much in it that shows this argument to be seriously flawed. Australian aborigines have reportedly maintained for millennia a society in near-perfect ecological balance, with no wars, ruling classes, or expolitation of each other, and with minimal material wants satisfied with a minimum of work and a maximum of creatively used 'free time'. Evolutionist anthropology has generally suported the view that there

were thousands of years of classless, stateless, non-patriarchal agricultural societies, some large and complex, before the origins of private property. We can indeed be said to have had the experience of socialism or 'primitive commnism' far longer than we have of class societies. This experience, in its absence of private property and classes, had a humane quality to it, something worth reappropriation, of course, in necessarily new forms – which suggests more than just viability of a socialist future for humankind. In one of his images of the society of the future this is indeed how Marx saw it. Marx thought of socialism/communism in terms of a 'process of human emancipation and recovey', 'as the complete return of man to himself as a *social* (that is, human) being – a return become conscious, and accomplished within the entire wealth of previous development'.

This apart, it is a form of myopic conservative prejudice to think that everything which does not exist cannot exist. With the same 'logic' one could have stated that slavery was the only possible form of large-scale agricultural and handicraft production (in the first century AD); that monarchy was the only possible form of goverment (in the fourteenth and fifteenth centuries); that parliament could only be elected without universal franchise (in the eighteenth century), etc. Yet slavery finished by being abolished. Republic appeared while monarchies disappeared in their majority. Universal franchise ended by becoming general in all countries opting for a parliamentary system. Not to see what is developing without being already realised is a form ideological colour-blindness often based upon wishful thinking; you don't see what you don't want to see.

Ernest Mandel has argued:

> The platitude that "Marxian socialism" does not exist anywhere in the world tody is tirelessly repeated, as in effect an argument against all human progress. But was it utopian to fight for the abolition of slavery, which existed on a large scale for more than a thousand years? . . . Religious oppression, including the burning of hereties at the stake, was a "fact of life" for at least five centuries. Was it then utopian to try to establish freedom of conscience and freedom of thought? . . . Why should it be utopian today to try to do away with wage labour and gigantic state bureaucracies, which after all have been central structures of society for no more than two hundred years? . . . Utopia, in the broad sense of the word, has been one of the great motors of the eventual achievement of historical progress.

Any serious student of history would know that every significant social

> advance in history has at some point had to conquer the notion that it was impossible or that it had never been done before. Utopias are what have moved people throughout history to make it a better world. So it is now with socialism.
>
> Theoretically, the possibility of socialism arises from within the contradictions of capitalism. Morally, opposition to capitalism is its own justification since capitalism is today poisoning human survival itself, let alone human happiness. The resolve to overturn this globally dominant system and build socialism does indeed involve 'utopian surplus', as Ernst Bloch once called it. The utopian dimension of the socialist project of course must not translate itself into either 'teleology' or 'messianic eschatology'. We must not be starry-eyed about the future and also need to divest ourselves of the hubris of tying our own mortality to its construction. But we must also not let the historically limited and capitalism-blighted vision of our enemies settle the question of possibilities of the future. 'Utopian' is a compliment and a challenge we should be willing to accept.

Workers' Politics argues for Marxist understanding of society and the consequent necessity of socialism. Ash sees this necessity not as something pre-determined or inevitable but as a possibility that we need to struggle for. As Marx once put it:

> (The) circumstances cry out: Things cannot remain that way, they must become different and we ourselves, we human beings, must make them different.

This is indeed how Marxism has always viewed the necessity of socialism. Contrary to what the critics have regularly alleged or tried to foist upon it, Marxism of Karl Marx is not a determinist doctrine. Whatever determinism there is in his Marxism, is a most conditional one, which accords primacy to human praxis, to revolutionary politics. If attention was drawn to the economic-structural necessities underlying the historical processes, it was for enhancing the freedom for *praxis*, for not foreclosing but liberating human practice, for freer choices by humans, free not in some abstract or metapysical sense, but in the only possible *human* sense of men and women choosing and acting with the fullest possible knowledge and consideration of the necessities of the objective material situation or circumstances. Such is the dialectics of freedom and necessity in Marx.

Thus there are no inevitabilities in Marx and no guarantees of victory either; only alternatives. Even as he insisted in the *Communist Manifesto* that 'the history of all hitherto existing society is the history of class struggle'. Marx had immediately added that this struggle 'each time ended, either in a revolutionay reconstitution of society at large, or in the common ruin of the contending classes'. Again, he had hailed the productive achievements of capitalism – 'it has been the first to show what man's activity can bring about', creating 'more massive and more colossal productive forces than have all preceding generations together' (*Communist Manifesto*). But he had also pointed out not only the damage that capitalism regularly inflicts upon humans and nature but also its long-term destructive potential – 'its accumulation process', Marx wrote in *Grundrisse,* can have 'the consequences even for the total destruction of humanity' – a prognosis which Rosa Luxemburg later summed up as the alternative: "socialism or barbarism".

Incidentally, these alternatives to socialism – the threat of 'common ruin of the contending classes', and 'the total destruction of humanity' are already a part of the reality of our world today.

(It was Marx's prognosis that capitalism in its ultimate consequences could spell even 'the total destruction of humanity'. But giving capitalism a short lease of life, Marx never explored this distant possibility. The distant possibility is now an imminent threat hanging over the future of humankind. As noted above, Rosa Luxemburg had summed up Marx's prognosis in her famous poser: 'socialism or barbarism'. Capitalism living beyond its historical time indeed spells a future of barbarism for humankind. It could be a nuclear holocaust that its politics has threatened for more than half a century or the almost certain ecological disaster which – noise over so-called 'sustainable development' notwithstanding – capitalism's logic of accumulation now portends. This makes the struggle for socialism all the more imperative and urgent today.)

It was Marx's analysis and critique of capitalism that led him to argue for its negation in socialism, for the necessity (and possibility) of a socialist negation of the capitalist social order. As Marx foresaw, capitalism has grown and expanded to become a *deadly* serious business. Constituted, essentially, by class exploitation, capitalism is today more than just a system of class oppression, of economic inqualities and iniquities. It is a ruthless totalising process which seeks to shape our lives in every conceivable sphere, everywhere, in the relative opulence of the capitalist North as much as in its impoverished peripheries, subjecting all social life, through the manifold power of capital, to the abstract requirements of the market, commodifying life in all its aspects. This makes a mockery of all our values, all our aspirations to autonomy, freedom of choice and democratic self-government, all that is good, decent and worthwhile in life. Marx had noticed this at the very beginning of modern capitalism and warned us. Today his warning rings more true than ever before. Hence also the necessity as never before, of a socialist negation of capitalism.

Nothing that has happened since the days of Marx, including what has happened in the erstwhile Soviet Union, vitiates or refutes Marx's analysis and critique of capitalism and his argument for socialism. The current crisis of global capitalism which has simultaneously exposed globalisation's reality as capitalism and the crisis-ridden reality of capitalism only further confirms the continuing validity of Marx's analysis and argument.

Of course, as in the past, bailed out by the state at the cost of the common people, capitalism will survive this crisis too but this survival, by itself cannot be seen as an argument for the desirability of the capitalist order, much less as any sort of 'triumph' of capitalism. 'That position', says Paul Baran, 'is no more defensible than would be the view that an inability of the human body to resist tuberculosis, however caused, furnishes a proof of the harmlessness or even usefulness of that illness'. Capitalism will survive but only to get into deeper crises in the future. That is, in the absence of a successful challenge, capitalism may continue to survive in a state of 'depressed continuum', as Meszaros has called it, which also means capitalism's survival as a failed system. At the end of its five centuries-old existence, global capitalism is indeed a very much failed system today. The evidence of this failure is starkly visible in every part and aspect of contemporary capitalist world. It is visible in the impoverishment and immiseration on the rise just about everywhere in the world; in the official statistics on rates of unemployment, poverty, homelessness, and hunger; in the sullen slums of major cities of Western bourgeois democracies, proliferating urban ghettos of the gritty capitals of former Soviet bloc countries and the warrens of teeming tumbledown shanties of the peripheral South; in the gross inequalities of the world, the wretchedness of the impoverished and excluded within the rich Western societies and the huge mass of misery in the poorer countries; in the morally intolerable and socially unnecessary suffering – what Bourdieu has called *la misere du monde* – produced by capitalism everywhere.

As I have written elsewhere:

> The 'actually existing socialism' – which was not Marx's socialism whose possibility remains open – has of course, failed. But, surely, the 'actually existing capitalism' – which is the only kind of capitalism possible – has not been the succes it is made out to be. In any objective judgement, capitalism too has been a failure in our times. Other considerations apart, capitalism has been a failure, in terms of possibly the most legitimate criteria for assessing the performance of a social system: 'fullness of employment' and 'goodness of employment' of the actual and potential resources available in society. Never before in human history has the gap between society's potentiality and society's performance been so immense as it is today in capitalism's current stage of deveopment. Evidence is there in the extraordinary productive capacity that three successive industrial revolutions have put at the disposal of humankind and the poverty and illiteracy, squalid slums and homelessness that are the lot of millions of families in the wealthiest countries of the capitalist world and the hunger and misery of hundreds of millions of people, living out their empty and barren lives in the hovels of the peripheral or semiperipheral poor countries of the third world. The third world today is indeed a monument to the failure of capitalism in our times . . .

This, however, is not to suggest any collapse of capitalism, now or in the future. Systems don't collapse like that. (Possibly the only exception in our times is the system in the Soviet Union which indeed 'self-destructed', something explained by the *sui generis* nature of the class exploitative system that the deformed Soviet socialism had ultimately degenerated into.) In other words, crisis or failure as mentioned above, is not to be confused with any so-called 'breakdown' or 'impending breakdown'. Capitalism will not collapse by itself. A nuclear war or a environmental disaster may lead to barbarism or worse. Otherwise the rule of capital will end when it is overthrown by the people. Hence uncertainties of the situation notwithstanding, the need is for socialists to put class struggle at the centre of their politics. And to be truly anti-systemic, it has to be a struggle for both reform and revolution, with the former subordinated to the latter as enjoined by Marx. 'An anti-systemic movement,' as Wallerstein has argued, 'cannot neglect short term defensive action, including electoral action. The world's populations live in the present, and their immediate needs have to be addressed. Any movement that neglects them is bound to lose the widespread passive support that is essential for its long-term success. But the motive and justification for defensive action should not be that of remedying a failing system . . .' Apart from seeking to prevent the system's negative effects from getting worse in the short run, defensive action (or the struggle for reform) should be so conducted as to subserve the long-term revolutionary aim of a transcedence of the system itself.

The world is acknowledgedly in deep trouble today, plagued by a myriad problems. Insofar as it is the world of global capitalism, Marxism remains indispensable for those who would confront these problems with any hope of success. I will only add that this world is populated not only by lovers of capitalism, or its mere victims, or by 'cheerful robots' as C. Wright Mills called them, but also, and increasingly, by some very angry human beings, those still fighting under the darkened skies for a world fit for everyone. Socialists of course have no illusions that the struggle for socialism is going to be easy or expeditiously successful. After the first failure it will be far more difficult in many ways than before, it is going to be a long detour to socialism next time. But they have no reason to feel gloomy about the prospects either. The material conditions are more favourable and objective compulsions far stronger than appeared possible a few year ago, and the constituency for the socialist cause can only grow as capitalism shows itself increasingly incapable of coping with the crises it produces . . .

Apropos the post-Soviet capitalist triumphalism, Paul Sweezy and Harry Magdoff had written: 'Capitalism's victory settles nothing. In its global form it encompasses ever more people and intensifies their exploitation and oppression. History shows that there have been alternatives in the past, and reason tells us that there will be others in the future . . . It is of the greatest importance to keep the radical tradition alive and vigorous, ready to undergrid and give direction to the revolutionary struggles that lie ahead'. Since then, euphoria over 'capitalism's victory' long over, the struggles that lay ahead are already on the agenda of the peoples everywhere. As suggested earlier, this is where I locate the relevance of William Ash's *Workers' Politics – the ethics of socialism.*

Randhir Singh,
August 2009.

Chapter 1
Values — The meaning of Value Judgments

INTRODUCTION

When we ask a philosophical question like 'What is value?', there are really two problems involved. In the first place there is the challenge to find a satisfactory answer to such an inquiry when past attempts to do so have already filled many volumes. And in the second place, arising from this very fact, follows the further consideration: 'How can there have been so much confusion about what we mean by our own concepts?' A concern with such questions as why we are puzzled by the idea of 'value' or why completely contradictory opinions about it have been held at the same time and place or why the same arguments about its true meaning have recurred at quite different times and places - questions like these inevitably force us to broaden the scope of our study beyond the confines of academic philosophy and approach the subject from a social and historical point of view. The justification for attacking the problem on a wider front is that often to understand how or why a certain question can be asked is a major step in the direction of being able to answer it.

The guiding principle of this whole inquiry into the nature of ethics is Marxist. What is meant by that? On Marx's tomb in Highgate cemetery is inscribed: 'The philosophers have only interpreted the world in different ways; the point is to change it.'[1] Marxism is not just one more interpretation of the world. It is a methodology for analysing society in such a way that its working class victims can organise themselves to change it. Many who write or lecture about Marxism, including a number of those who describe themselves as Marxists, treat it simply as another interpretation to be explained, another theory to be expounded. As such it can be compared and contrasted with various interpretations of the past and present and even combined with them. By mixing Marxism with a bit of Freudianism or existentialism or structuralism, for example, it can be composed into a fine French stew to satisfy a wide variety of palates - which is the sort of philosophising that prompted Marx to say: 'Where speculation ends - in real life - there real positive science begins; the representation of the practical activity, of the practical process of the development of man. Empty talk about consciousness ceases, and real knowledge has to take its place. When reality is depicted, philosophy as an independent branch of activity loses its medium of existence.'[2] It's what led Mao Tsetung to say: 'Liberate philosophy from the confines of the philosopher's lecture rooms and text books and turn it into a sharp weapon in the hands of the masses.'[3]

Marx justifies this emphasis on real life by pointing out that it is not the consciousness of men that determines their existence, but, on the contrary, their social existence that determines their consciousness. People have to produce the means of their sustenance in order to be able to think about themselves at all. Thinking about society is not a self-sustaining activity: it is bound to be influenced through and through by the preconditional necessity of entering into social relationships for the purpose of maintaining life. When the division of labour which is the basis of social classes does permit certain people to be 'thinkers', to the very extent that they are freed from the necessity of physical work by other people's efforts, their ideas may be 'freed' from relevance to reality.

To argue that the existence of men in society conditions their consciousness is to assume a materialistic as opposed to an idealistic point of view. It accepts the scientific evidence for the existence of an objective world long before there was any conscious life on it and rejects the religious view that a kind of human consciousness originated the process of reality instead of being a product of it. Awareness, therefore, has been conditioned by the physical context in which it developed; and this fact is crucial for a valid theory of knowledge. The question of how we can know the world around us is not unlike the question of how it is that the food our environment provides happens to agree with our stomachs. Either can become a mystery if we ignore the fact that minds, like stomachs, originated in and have been conditioned by a pre-existent natural order.

Marx is a materialist but not a determinist. How could he be when his entire work is coloured by the profound belief that through understanding the way society really functions those suffering from class exploitation are free to organise and liberate themselves! 'The materialist doctrine that men are products of circumstances and upbringing, and that, therefore, changed men are products of other circumstances and changed upbringing, forgets that it is men that change circumstances and the educator must himself be educated...The coincidence of the changing of circumstances and of human activity can be conceived and rationally understood only as revolutionary practice.'[4]

A materialistic point of view means starting with the real rather than the ideal. From Descartes on, the emphasis on the individual in the rise of the bourgeoisie led to a fundamental ontological mistake - reducing absolute certainty to the self-conscious, thinking ego (cogito ergo sum) and then trying to reconstruct the universe around one from that 'certainty'. Separating oneself from the world and society and then trying to reconstruct them from one's own impressions, feelings and ideas inevitably leads to the question of whether one has got it right or not. But as Marx says: 'The question whether objective truth can be attributed to human thinking is not a question of theory but is a practical question. In practice man must prove the truth, that is, the reality and power, the this-sidedness of his thinking. The dispute over the reality or non-reality of thinking which is isolated from practice is a purely scholastic question.'[5]

Many philosophers calling themselves empiricists like Russell, Wittgenstein, Ayer and others have been involved in the Cartesian game of trying to construct a material world out of such idealist constituents as sense impressions, concepts, language. Language, for example, instead of being about reality becomes reality. A statement like 'The world is everything that is the case' really means that one creates the world in making true pronouncements about it! In other words, while they have disposed of objective idealism. individualistic liberal philosophers tend to turn themselves into subjective idealists, all solipsistically balancing the world on their noses like a lot of trained seals.

Marxists like Althusser are similarly engaged in 'constructing' society mentally, even if they use Marxian categories as their building blocks. Ideology becomes a kind of neo-Kantian screen through which all of us, workers and capitalists alike, have to squint at reality. And there is the dominating structuralism of 'over-determination' to complicate any collective effort at emancipation. The society thus 'created' can be thought and written about but could not be acted on effectively in order to change it - which is about as unMarxist as it is possible to get!

If the point of Marxism is not simply to interpret the world but to change it, how can ideology, how can theory do this? Obviously not simply by complaining about how badly exploited people are treated; but what force can ideas about such bad treatment have? Marx answers: 'Clearly the weapon of criticism cannot replace criticism of weapons, and material force must be overthrown by material force. But theory also becomes a material force once it has gripped the masses.'[6]

And how does one arrive at theories which can grip the masses? Not by any egocentric Cartesian route. It is like the man who, in answer to the question of how does one get to Dublin, replied: "If I wanted to go to Dublin, I wouldn't start from here". If you want to arrive at practical truths about human society which can 'grip' those who must change it to survive, you do not start with self-consciousness as an isolate and then try to build human society out of the subjective side of your relationships with things and people. You are not going to get to objective truth starting from the subjective myth of a disembodied mind ruminating on the reality of what surrounds it. 'Practice, knowledge, again practice, and again knowledge' as Mao Tsetung says.

Ethics is the most practical branch of philosophy. It is immediately concerned with people's actions, and since people's actions are largely directed toward securing a livelihood and providing for the continuance of human life, ethics is closely associated with the economic basis of society. In communities like our own, factory and market place are the great concourses of human activity; and the relationships people establish in the process of first producing and then exchanging the goods on which life depends are bound to affect deeply their conception of ethical conduct. It is no mere verbal coincidence that terms like 'values' and 'goods', though with somewhat different connotations, play such an important part in the considerations of both political economy and moral philosophy.

But does not the fact that ethical concepts reflect the economic basis of society cast doubt on the moral validity of our consideration of such questions as: What is value? What is its relationship, if any, to usefulness? What is the function of value judgments? In saying that ethical concepts reflect the material conditions of life, it is not meant to suggest that this reflection is passive and mirror-like. It is dynamic, reacting dialectically on the human situation originally imaged.

Marx may seem to give some substance to such doubts when he says in the Preface to *Capital*: 'I paint the capitalist and the landlord in no sense 'couleur de rose'. But here individuals are dealt with only in so far as they are the personifications of economic categories, embodiments of particular class relations and class interests. My standpoint, from which the evolution of the economic formation of society is viewed as a process of natural history, can less than any other make the individual responsible for relations whose creature he socially remains, however much he may subjectively raise himself above them.'[7] 'Here', in *Capital*, Marx is providing as objective an analysis as is possible of the way the capitalist system works; but there is never any question that this analysis is not intended to serve the normative ideal of the *Communist Manifesto*.

And even though for the most part, in *Capital*, Marx is dealing with a level of abstraction at which such moral considerations as individual responsibility do not apply, it does not mean, as many philosophers have tried to argue, that Marx rejects any idea of the mediation of a normative ideal in the changes in society brought about by an exploited class. There is no way that the very word 'exploitation' can be deprived of normative significance. On ethical grounds he dismisses utilitarianism for 'its absurdity of merging all the manifold relations of people in the one relation of usefulness.' He goes on to say: 'This apparently metaphysical abstraction arises from the fact that in modern bourgeois society all relations are subordinated in practice to the one abstract monetary-commercial relation...The utility relation has a quite definite meaning, namely, that I derive benefit for myself by doing harm to someone else.'[8]

This is a profoundly moral statement which enables us to begin to understand the nature of Marx's morality. Lenin provides a clear expression of it: 'Of course there is such a thing as communist ethics... But we repudiate all morality derived from non-human and non-class concepts...We say that our morality is entirely subordinated to the interests of the class struggle of the proletariat...Our morality serves the purpose of helping human society to rise to a higher level and to get rid of the exploitation of labour.'[9]

In the course of this book we shall have many more statements by Marx and others demonstrating what Marxist morality is; and, more important, we shall see how it works in practice.

What, then, is value? One way of trying to understand the nature of value is to see how the most general value word in our language, 'good', is actually used and to attempt to define from such instances what we really mean by the attribution to anything of 'goodness'. Let us first see how philosophers past and present have dealt with the question of value in these terms.

VALUE AS DESCRIPTIVE

Now when we say that a thing is 'good' we might mean that it has some objective quality which can be so designated or that someone has an attitude toward it which can be described as favourable. In either case a factual proposition could be substituted for the sentence containing a value word without loss of meaning. This naturalistic account is rejected by many philosophers who deny that descriptive statements about the thing itself or about the mental state of someone who approves of it really express the full significance of calling it 'good'. According to non-naturalists, value words do not have so purely empirical a reference.

If the naturalists were correct, value words would raise no problems because they could be translated without loss into factual expressions. Everything that could meaningfully be said could take the form of descriptive propositions about objects or states of mind. To verify the objective use of 'good' we would need only examine anything so described to make sure it had the requisite natural property. The subjective use would be proved by ascertaining whether anyone asserting a thing's 'goodness' actually had a favourable regard for it. In each case the meaning of 'goodness' would be explained by the respective methods of validating sentences containing it.

But is 'goodness' a property that objects as such can have? Obviously it is not an immediately discernible property like 'roundness' or 'hardness' or 'yellowness'; and such first-order properties in themselves are quite irrelevant to the question of an object's 'goodness'. Qualities like 'durability' or 'handiness' or 'brilliantly coloured' do seem to have some bearing on a thing's value; and to call an object 'good' may be a kind of shorthand expression for various characteristics of this latter type. If a watch is accurate, sturdy and convenient to carry, then it is a good watch, and no more is meant by the word 'good' than the sum of these descriptive phrases.

But although such qualities as 'efficient', 'durable' or 'handy' are all observable, they can be distinguished from physical properties in that they only belong to an object by virtue of the use or enjoyment someone can get from it. This distinction may be denied by idealists who take first-order properties also to be dependent on the observer; but that is a step onto a slippery logical slope which can only end in impractical isolation from reality. Stones in a creek bed would have their specific sizes and shapes if the earth were uninhabited; but only if a person were looking for something to make into a tool would certain of the stones come to be designated as 'good'. It is the purpose a person has in mind which differentiates good stones from useless ones.

On reflection it seems that nothing is ever good intrinsically, merely because it is what it is quite irrespective of a subject who judges and approves it. We would not say, for example, that a thing was a particularly good apple because it particularly clearly satisfied some scientific test of its appleness but because it particularly agreeably satisfied some demand as to its taste, nourishing character or pleasant odour and appearance - all qualities involving its enjoyment by someone; and even if an electronic device is imagined for sorting good apples from bad, the standard of selection built into the machine is based on differentiating between ripeness and rottenness according to a human need. This characteristic of serving a purpose or satisfying a need as essential to the nature of 'goodness' forces us to abandon the attempt to find the meaning of value in existential propositions about objects as such.

If 'good', then, cannot be taken as simply qualifying an object, does it refer instead to the state of one who derives satisfaction from an object? Value would thus be purely subjective and we would not desire a thing because it was good: it would be good because we desired it. To say that something was 'good' would mean merely that at one time or another by at least someone it was wanted, approved of or favourably regarded.

But when the question of degrees of goodness is considered,

some of the difficulties with this subjective account of value begin to appear. Since we desire some things more than others, we would presumably say that those things for which we have a greater desire are better. But desire for something increases to the extent that we are deprived of it and under certain circumstances a crust of bread can be the most desirable thing in the world. Yet it appears very odd to hold that, since a thing's value can depend on its not being available, the greater the scarcity of good things in the world the more value there would be. Furthermore, we often disagree over whether one thing is better than another for a particular purpose and argue about our differences. Such an argument makes sense if it concerns a conflict of opinions about the relative merits of two objects as candidates for preference; but as a dispute about whether we really have the respective states of mind we say we have, it would be utterly pointless. Comparative judgments of this kind seem to lead us back to the object again as the referent of value judgments; but we have already failed to find any objective property to attach them to.

Perhaps, then, 'goodness' might refer neither to object nor subject in themselves but to some causal relationship between properties of the object and qualities of feeling in the subject. Certainly this account avoids some of the difficulties met with in simpler versions of the descriptive explanation of value. On the one hand, we are no longer confronted with the problem of how a thing can have value irrespective of an evaluator and, on the other, we have eliminated the absurdity of having to assign maximum value to a world where satisfactory things are scarcest. What we have now is a naturalistic formula by which value resides in the relationship between certain observable properties of the object like durable, handy, efficient or tasty and certain recognisable reactions on the part of the subject like wanting, enjoying, liking or approving - in much the same way as knowledge might be taken to be the result of the action of an objective physical property like 'yellowness' on a percipient sensitive to rays of light.

Because, of course, any naturalistic account of value words means that there is no distinction between value judgments and factual statements, that questions about value resolve themselves into epistemological questions concerning our knowledge of reality. The view that value is simply a property of the object is equivalent to naive realism which airily denies that the acquisition of knowledge presents any problem at all; the belief that it merely qualifies the feelings of anyone who enjoys or desires the object represents subjective idealism; and the opinion that it is to be found in a causal relationship between the two is a form of mechanical materialism. According to this last interpretation, just as natural objects impinge on our passive awareness and give us our ideas of reality, so things with certain qualities can satisfy our desires and by giving us pleasurable sensations earn the designation 'good'.

It is this causal account of the production of pleasurable states which underlies the utilitarian ethics of the English empiricists. Since 'goodness' is considered to be a pleasurable state brought about by the provision of objects which induce such happy feelings, then the supreme good can be expressed as the greatest possible happiness for the greatest number of people and this can be advanced as the proper goal of personal morality or government policy.

But there are difficulties with this value relationship between good objects and pleasurable feelings which are analogous to certain problems encountered in connection with the empiricist theory of knowledge. Perceptual illusions can make us suspicious of a mechanical production of knowledge by way of the senses; and even if these errors are corrigible by reasoning based on the evidence of other sense impressions, the process is more sophisticated than would be allowed for by a theory of the mind as passively receptive and knowledge itself as the mere result of the association of ideas. Similarly, there are psychological phenomena which cast doubt on the efficacy of our formula for the production of value by pleasurable reactions to objects described as 'good'. Not only can the same object arouse in us quite different feelings at different times but, more generally, the very search for happiness by multiplying satisfactions can prove self-defeating.

Epistemologically this discrepancy can lead to a development in empiricism by which we are assumed to know directly not things themselves but our ideas of things. Sense data are imposed between ourselves and the world, shutting us off from it; and what began as an objective, materialistic theory of knowledge ends in subjective idealism. In the same way there is a tendency for the utilitarian account of value, which seemed to steer a middle course between objective and subjective extremes, increasingly to derive the goodness of things from our feelings about them rather than to assume that because a thing has certain qualities we are bound to want it. There is a basic instability in the causal formula by which value tends to become more and more subjective and ceases to link in a direct relationship our states of feeling and specifically good objects. There is also, as we shall see, a reason why this shift toward subjectivism occurs.

But the main objection to the naturalistic explanation of value is that it does not permit us to go on to make the kind of statements which are characteristically ethical. If the supreme good is the greatest happiness of the largest number of people, we expect it to follow that as between possible courses of action we ought to choose the one which most contributes to the maximum realisation of happiness. But the utilitarian definition of 'good' does not warrant such a prescriptive conclusion. If 'good' merely describes certain objects or certain reactions or a certain relationship between them, we can only derive from such accounts of the matter statements which are themselves merely descriptive of human behaviour. We could say that people do tend by and large to seek out things which induce pleasurable sensations and even that they may take pleasure themselves in contributing to the pleasure of others once their own pleasure has been sufficiently gratified; but we could not say that they ought to act so as to bring about these effects. We could say that some forms of pleasure are higher or more lasting than others; but we could not say that anyone ought to choose them.

The reason for this is simply that, logically, nothing can be extracted from a definition which was not, at least implicitly, given in that definition to begin with. The naturalistic interpretation of value reduces sentences containing value words like 'good' to factual propositions. 'You ought to choose this' or 'You ought to like that' are not factual propositions. There is no existential state of affairs which they simply describe; and therefore they cannot be derived from an account of 'good' which is purely descriptive. The attempt to do so has been called the naturalistic fallacy. It is like saying 'There is a pin sticking in you and you really ought to try to feel it.' The empiricist philosopher, David Hume, who formulated this principle as 'no ought from an is' provides in 'A Treatise of Human Nature' one of the most notorious examples of this very fallacy: 'Reason is, and ought only to be the slave of the passions and can never pretend to any other office than to serve and obey them.'[10] A similar example is provided by Jeremy Bentham's well-known statement: 'Nature has placed mankind under the governance of two sovereign masters, pain and pleasure. It is for them alone to point out what we ought to do, as well as to determine what we shall do.'[11]

VALUE AS PRESCRIPTIVE

If, then, the philosophical attempt to make descriptive sentences cover the whole field of experience seems either to deny us the use of characteristic value terms or to try to convince us that when we do use such terms we do not really mean by them what we think we mean, let us look at the problem from the other end. Starting with prescriptive sentences including value terms let us see how description might be logically accommodated also. Unless a place for descriptive sentences is somehow maintained, of course, reason can play no part in value judgments and our prescriptive utterances will be purely arbitrary.

Among the sternest critics of the fallacy by which utilitarians pass without logical justification from defining 'good' in terms of some descriptive aspect of object or subject to a use of value words for persuasion or recommendation are the intuitionists like G.E. Moore. They try to avoid the difficulty themselves by denying that 'good' is definable at all. It is a simple notion with which we are directly acquainted, an ultimate term which cannot be analysed into some other property like 'being desired'. Just as 'yellowness' is immediately perceived as what we see, so 'goodness' is immediately intuited as what we value, as what ought to be. It is a non-natural quality and, indeed, a thing need not actually exist to be accounted good in this sense of ought-to-beness. The intuitionists would, in fact, argue that the very attempt to make value judgments conform to the sort of proposition which links two things that exist instead of recognising them as expressions of 'seeing' something in a special light is to commit the naturalistic fallacy.

Intuitionists can thus speak legitimately of good things as those we ought to prefer because the 'ought' is, according to them, inherent in our apprehension of a thing's 'goodness'. But do we actually have this faculty of simply intuiting what ought to be preferred? If so, there should be the same general measure of agreement about what is good as about what is yellow or round and, just as differences of opinion about physical properties can be settled by accurate testing of the object or by checking against a common standard an individual's perceptive sensibilities, so in arguments about degrees of goodness there should be some criteria for testing our special apprehension of the ought-to-be-chosen. But the moment such an appeal to some basis of comparison is allowed, like suitability for a purpose or pleasure-giving capacity, 'good' has been defined in terms of something else and the whole intuitionist case is lost. If, on the other hand, differences about relative degrees of goodness are simply accepted as irreconcilable, 'good' ceases to be objective and the postulation of a special kind of awareness by which we can be acquainted with the special quality 'goodness' loses any point.

But even if the intuitionists fail to validate their conception of 'good' as an undefinable, directly apprehensible quality, they do demonstrate an important aspect of the way a value word like 'good' actually functions. If we say that a watch, for instance, is 'good' simply because in keeping accurate time it satisfies a need of its possessor, we find that there is one sense of the word that we cannot account for. In attributing goodness to a thing we mean to commend it, but nothing can be commended for merely being what it is. Commendation implies that something need not have been what it is; and this idea cannot be conveyed by any factual proposition about the observable properties of the object, the current state of anyone's feelings about it or any immediately recognisable relationship between the two. It is not a question of analysing characteristics of watches or of feelings about watches and, above a certain level of accuracy or beyond a certain degree of acceptability, adding 'good' to the other modifying adjectives. In ascribing 'goodness' to something we not only wish to say that such and such a thing with particular qualities is, in fact, approved by someone or other but also that it is worthy of approval - a use, as we have already noted, that can never be adequately explained on the basis of a naturalistic interpretation of value words. Descriptive sentences are a passive recognition of what is the case, while the prescriptive use of 'good' is a way of actively advocating what it is thought should be the case.

This active role of value words in commending something or urging others to approve of it Kant would account for by associating goodness not with passive feelings but with the dynamic will. For him the only thing which is good absolutely is a good will, and by a good will he means one which acts in accord with rational principles irrespective of any inclination toward sensuous gratification. Since the human will is not free from such inclinations, the dictates of reason take the form of commands which the will is obliged to obey in order to be designated good. To call any object 'good', therefore, implies the injunction 'choose this' - not because the choice will bring personal satisfaction but because it conforms to the universal maxims of pure reason. Value does not reside in what is desired; it is a characteristic of the will which is directed toward what ought to be chosen.

But what is the source of these universal maxims which must guide our acts of choice? They cannot be abstracted from our experience of what things in the past have been conducive to happiness or useful for attaining practical ends because that would mean that value sentences, as the naturalists contend, are ultimately reducible to factual propositions. Kant's answer to this question follows the same line as his proposed solution to the problem of how we can know the world around us. Just as the so-called empirical laws of nature cannot themselves be discovered empirically but must be deduced from the logical categories without which there can be no sensible experience, so the categorical imperative which is reason's demand on the will can only be derived from the self-conscious principles of pure rationality itself, regardless of any consequences such an imperative may entail in the ordinary world of desire and satisfaction. Because people have a kind of double citizenship in both the sensible world and the world of the understanding which it epistemologically presupposes, the practical will can be subject to those maxims of reason incumbent on all rational beings as such. As belonging to the sensible world the will is influenced by natural desires but as belonging also to the intelligible world it is free to act only in such a manner as to be able to prescribe the principles of its action as a universal law. Therefore, willing reasonably can be expressed as an 'ought' and a general rule can be laid down for the selective conduct in respect to a good watch of anyone anywhere ever needing to measure time.

Kant realised, of course, that even if we accept as valid his method of establishing the cogency of universal maxims of choice on the same basis as his deduction of a natural principle like the law of causation from the categories of thought, it is still legitimate to ask why the individual will should conform to these maxims. His work on ethics consists largely of a sincere but hopeless quest for a third term connecting with the rigour of natural law the categorical imperative with the good will. This is another way of saying that he was trying to discover a direct relationship between the world of the understanding whence value judgments obtain their full prescriptive force and the sensible world where only descriptions of things are possible. Without such a relationship there is no way of explaining why anyone ought to choose what is good in the Kantian sense: with it choice loses its unique reference to the concept of duty as such which Kant wished to maintain as the distinctive characteristic of 'ought' sentences.

The seriousness of Kant's attempt to define the relationship between prescriptive and descriptive sentences, between 'good' as a value word and 'good' as a property of things or of people's attitude toward things, is attested by his never abandoning the thing-in-itself. A more thoroughgoing idealism like Hegel's which cuts itself free of the material world even in so attenuated a form as the thing-in-itself has no difficulty in establishing the non-natural character of value words. Since we have the idea of value as that which is worthy of choice and since ideas are the ultimate reality, then the worthy of choice obviously exists. The only problem is that on the basis of these idealistic assumptions our descriptive statements become non-naturalistic too and all watches, good or bad, become merely the outward appearance of ideal time pieces.

Non-naturalist theories of value imply at some stage or other the possibility of non-empirical knowledge. This may take the passive Platonic form of deriving our knowledge of things from pre-existent general ideas like 'yellowness' or 'roundness' or 'thingness' itself and using this priority of the ideal to explain our direct apprehension of a quality like 'goodness'. Or it may take a more dynamic form of assuming that the human mind enters actively into the process of experiencing the world by contributing the logical categories which are a condition of that experience, thus providing us with an analogy by which we can understand the value we find in the world as something we put there ourselves through possessing a value-creative will.

Even though non-naturalistic interpretations of value do not simply resolve themselves into epistemological theories as must happen, by definition, with any naturalistic account, they do involve epistemological considerations. The ethical question of how value judgments which are not to be reduced to statements of fact can yet have a content that is in some sense true or false is very much like the epistemological question of how any proposition can be at once deductive and informative. Logically speaking, the whole non-naturalist case is closely associated with the validity of synthetic a priori propositions which tell us something but are not derived from experience. If such propositions are possible and meaningful, it is reasonable to suppose that there are also judgments which can cogently ascribe a non-natural property like 'value' to objects existing in the natural world.

VALUE AS NEITHER DESCRIPTIVE NOR PRESCRIPTIVE

Logical positivists divide all meaningful propositions into analytic a priori, which are purely formal tautologies like the laws of thought or the rules of mathematics, and synthetic a posteriori, which are empirical hypotheses like our ordinary descriptive statements. The former are certain but do not tell us anything we did not already know implicitly; the latter are informative but have only an inductive probability.

Since no other kind of proposition is admitted and since value judgments are obviously not formal tautologies, they must either be reducible to descriptive statements, as naturalists like the utilitarians suppose, or else they are not propositions at all. A.J. Ayer argues against the reduction of value to non-value statements on the ground that it is not consistent with the conventions of our actual language. Value words, as the intuitionists maintain, have an intrinsic significance which prevents us from translating sentences containing them into empirical propositions. But since, as a positivist, Ayer cannot accept the possibility of non-empirical propositions, he must deny that value judgments have the propositional characteristic of actually stating anything -either about objects or situations or even about the minds and attitudes of people who make them. A word like 'good' may imply certain descriptive features such as, in the case of watches, accuracy or compactness; but in so far as it is used in an ethical sense of ascribing value to a thing as that which ought to be chosen or preferred, it is a pseudo-concept which adds nothing to the meaning of a sentence within which it occurs. Instead of saying 'This is a good watch' we might as well have said 'Watch!' with a special emphasis. The evaluative function of 'good' is merely an emotional sound of approval on the part of the speaker which could have been conveyed as well by the tone of voice or by writing an exclamation point after the object word.

The contention that this emotive theory of value is simply a form of subjectivism is countered by the insistence on the difference between asserting and expressing a feeling. To argue that a thing is 'good' because we like it is to determine the validity of value judgments by the nature of our feelings; but a shout of joy has no validity, asserts nothing and thus escapes the objections to a subjective theory of value. In this way logical positivists can claim to have avoided an illegitimate use of value words - by the extreme expedient of emptying all meaning from the idea of value! And as we shall see, there is a reason for this move.

And yet people go on making what seem to be value judgments and appearing to mean more by them than they would by a groan or a chuckle. They give every impression of arguing about values and they could not do this logically if an emotive theory of value were true. Positivists may insist that such people are really arguing about facts; but this is scarcely the case when they debate whether a watch is really worth what it costs or whether promise-keeping ought to override all other considerations. People apparently believe that values can be inculcated and it would be difficult to maintain that what they actually mean is teaching the young when a sigh or an expletive is appropriate. In short this positivist account is no more consistent with the conventions of language than the naturalist account.

Linguistic analysis plays a part in the development of the logical positivist argument and much recent philosophy has been concerned with treating problems as the result of confusion about the language in which such problems are expressed. But the very philosophical divisions a linguistic approach was supposed to circumvent break out afresh. Some argue from an idealistic point of view that there are no facts apart from the propositions asserting them, that language, like the Kantian categories, conditions all experience and that the rules of grammar are a kind of logical framework of the universe or that language, like the Hegelian idea, is itself the real in its most comprehensible manifestation. These find no difficulty in establishing a non-naturalistic account of value - but at the cost of any straightforward explanation of our factual knowledge since the material world has vanished in the Word. Others bring an empiricist attitude to bear on the expressions people actually use; but not by way of providing a critique of popular forms of speech nor a study of how a social product like language developed historically nor a comparison of the characteristic expressions of one type of society with those of another or of one section of the same society with those of another section. Their empiricism consists rather in taking everyday language as a sort of datum from which they can generalise about how a particular language works but never why it works that way.

VALUE AS EITHER DESCRIPTIVE OR PRESCRIPTIVE

When we consider the actual use people make of a word like 'good', we do find that it may be descriptive, referring either to the suitability of an object or to its being wanted; but it may also be prescriptive and play a persuasive or commendatory role. Sometimes one thing is meant and sometimes the other. Depending on what one is trying to say, or the purpose behind speech, 'good' can have a predominantly factual meaning or it can have the evaluative force of an implicit injunction. To state that a watch is good may mean simply that it has certain characteristics which make it an object of approval; or it may mean that it ought to be approved, that it exemplifies the right way to make watches or that it must be included in any general list of valuable things. Sentences incorporating these distinctive usages behave quite differently; and since neither entails the other logically, they represent quite different realms of discourse. And there some contemporary philosophers, like R.M.Hare in *The Language of Morals* would have us leave the matter. Once we have cleared up the confusion caused by employing the same word for two such various ends, we can just accept that we are naturalists when we make factual statements about useful things and that we are non-naturalists when we make value judgments.

If we ask for an explanation of this linguistic phenomenon, we are very likely to be fobbed off with yet more examples proving that 'good' really is used in these two different ways. The method of inquiry precludes the possibility of looking at what language is describing to discover why it takes the form that it does; just as logical positivists cannot account for their division of meaningful propositions into formal tautologies and empirical hypotheses without offending against their own classification. And just as we fail to see how these two types of propositions could ever combine to give us valid knowledge unless there were some relationship embracing both, so it seems unsatisfactory to accept any final distinction between descriptive and prescriptive sentences.

It is no use asking neo-pragmatists or post-modernists for any help in this matter. Their ultra-relativist rejection of any truth going beyond what is currently accepted as 'good in the way of belief' would rule our question about the relationship between factual propositions and value judgments out of court. There are only the conceived consensus beliefs of particular 'interest groups' or 'interpretive communities' and no grounds at all for the kind of determinate historical truth-claims we are looking for to solve our problem.

The idea of separate realms of discourse for factual propositions and value judgments is not really very different from the Kantian conception of membership in the two different worlds of sensibility and understanding. We inhabit both worlds: there must be some link between them. The theoretical world which appears in our descriptive propositions about useful objects and our attitude toward them must bear some relationship to the practical world in which we advise people about the feelings they should have toward various things, commend certain objects as being better than others and, even, state categorically that this thing or that ought to be regarded with approval.

What we are looking for is a connection between the utility of the objects we call 'good' and their value. We cannot derive the latter from the former without committing the naturalistic fallacy. We cannot deduce the former from the latter without assuming an idealism that defies our commonsense acceptance of the basic nature of sensuous experience. But if neither can be defined in terms of the other, may it not be that each is a distinguishable aspect of some comprehensive whole in which their relationship could be understood? Are we not, perhaps, victims of our own analytic methods in having taken something apart and then forgotten the nature of whatever it was we began with?

The problem of accommodating 'facts' and 'value' within the same realm of discourse without loss in what each essentially means is like the problem of other sets of terms which remain isolated, irreconcilable and ultimately inexplicable as long as they are not seen as part of a larger whole in which they are related as different moments in the same process. Empiricism and idealism, for example, have been taken as opposite poles around which philosophers have collected like children taking sides in a game. The sensing of physical reality, the empirical moment, and the combining and re-ordering of sense impressions to formulate propositions and draw inferences, the ideal moment, are two stages in the total process of knowledge which is only completed with the submission of such logical hypotheses to the test of social practice. Otherwise we are simply left with an empirical induction which never has a right to its conclusion and an idealistic deduction which never has a right to its premise.

A dead, static universe could be studied analytically and disjunctively; but the vital process of change and development in its universal sweep has to be seen historically and dialectically. If one logical system is more suitable than another, depending on whether we are pigeon-holing a statically-conceived reality or comprehending a reality in which there is movement, growth and change, then the very laws of thought cannot be said to be without content and must be recognised as in some degree synthetic. As will be seen, there are social circumstances in which internal relations tend to be obscured: the lively links between human beings and nature and among human beings themselves are distorted to the point of seeming to have broken altogether and reality appears to be made up of discrete objects and individual human beings best handled by a classificatory logic. The laws of thought themselves are rooted in social experience.

ECONOMIC VALUE

The meaning of 'good' seems to split apart into a description of a thing's suitability to satisfy human needs and an evaluation of a thing as somehow worthy of choice. It is this latter sense which has proved philosophically troublesome. If a thing satisfies a desire or serves a purpose, it can be described as 'good' and why should that not be the end of the matter? Why have we developed an evaluative language at all? Factual statements can describe a thing's useful qualities; emotive utterances can express degrees of personal satisfaction. How has the terminology for conveying the idea of a thing's worthiness ever come to be devised? It would be pure fetishism to suppose that we wished to praise objects themselves for gratifying our desires; but what else can be meant by regarding objects as value-bearing?

The answer to this question will involve us in a historical quest for the social origins of our value language which, because of the internal relationships of all fields of knowledge, will be interdisciplinary in scope - with particular reference to economics. However, it must be pointed out that the term 'economics' is used by Marx in its broad sense of covering the whole historically-developed process of producing and distributing for consumption the goods by which human beings live. It is economics in this sense that is going to help us in our investigation of the nature of value. To draw conclusions from certain partial aspects of economics, like the apparently mechanical operations of individual choice in a so-called free market, is generally deprecated as 'economistic' - just as the equally partial 'isolated consumerist' point of view of the philosophers we have noted kept them from providing us with an adequate explanation of a value word like 'good' because they were rather like individual shoppers wandering among goods with prices on them they could not account for.

Now the close similarity between the philosophical argument about a natural or a non-natural interpretation of value and a discussion about the nature of objects belonging to a different field of study altogether may already have been noted. If it is said of a particular class of articles that 'they have two forms, a physical or natural form, and a value form', and that 'value represents a non-natural property of the object', we might suppose that it was a continuation of our old ethical debate about the definition of 'good'. In fact, these quotations are taken from Marx's analysis of a commodity in the first chapter of *Capital*. And if there is an analogy between defining 'good' and defining 'goods', if there is a connection between things qualified by our most general word of appraisal and the articles which are exchanged in the market, it might prove useful in an investigation of the nature of value.

Just as we found that the word 'good' combined two distinct meanings, so we find that a commodity has two quite different aspects - its use value or utility and its exchange value or, simply, its value. Every commodity has certain recognisable properties which qualify it to satisfy some human want. This aspect corresponds with the utilitarian, naturalistic, descriptive sense of 'good'. But in the act of exchange this same commodity reveals a quantitative character by which it proves commensurable with all other commodities. This non-natural property of having a fixed place in an orderly scale of goods is a consequence of the social conditions of production and is not directly perceptible in the isolated object itself. This is its value, and it is this aspect of the commodity which corresponds with the prescriptive sense of 'good' in value judgments.

One of the difficulties about defining the word 'good' is that it can be applied to a vast variety of things which apparently have nothing in common - not even the fact that they are all continuously wanted. In much the same way commodities of every different kind can be exchanged against each other in the market. This is possible because, however various such goods may be, they all embody measurable quantities of the same thing - the human labour that produced them. It is in the operation of exchange that economic value reveals itself as 'a congelation of undifferentiated human labour'. 'Value is labour', Marx says; 'it is materialised labour in its general social form.'[12] The fact that this human labour in the abstract not only creates all values but, as a power which can be rendered in units, is also the measure of all value, accounts for the equivalence obtaining among varying proportions of the most diverse commodities. This relationship among objects which enables us to apply the same standard to the whole multifarious range of marketable articles reflects a relationship among people as mutual contributors to a fund of labour power which is their common capital in all dealings with their environment. Since the connection between the labour of any one individual and that of the rest appears as a connection between commodities, Marx describes the relations of producers to each other as, paradoxically, 'material relations between persons and social relations between things'.

We can see why economic value is a non-natural property and remains imperceptible. It is not an intrinsic characteristic of objects as such but represents the social history of an object in the context of all other value-bearing objects on which human effort has been expended. The act of exchange by its very nature involves an evaluation; and this evaluation, in effect, releases the human story of associative production which is locked up in commodities.

Can this labour theory of value, borrowed from the field of economics, help to solve a philosophical problem encountered in attempts to define the nature of 'good' as a value word? An active, dynamic quality was noted in value judgments which distinguishes them from the passive, informational role of statements of fact and which could best be rendered as imperatives of choice. Is this not because value judgments, like the price tags hung on commodities, refer ultimately to some purposive human activity behind those things which are judged to be good? In a value sentence such as 'This is a good watch' are we not, in fact, commending the workmanship which went into its manufacture? Is it not this causal connection between an object and successful human activity in the past to which attention is drawn in prescriptive judgments rather than some immediately discernible property of the object itself or some psychological effect the object has caused?

The economic value of goods does not refer directly to the immediate desires people have for them, else the prices of foodstuffs would fluctuate wildly before and after meal times; and value judgments have this same objective character of not varying according to how much anyone at the moment actually wants what is called 'good' - though, of course, an article which no one could ever want at all would not have been produced to begin with. It has already been remarked that a non-naturalistic interpretation of value seemed to depend on our having put value into the world ourselves, in much the same way as an idealistic theory of knowledge depends on our having put meaning into the world. It now appears that we have put value into the world - not subjectively like an idealistic philosopher but objectively in the very practical sense of physical changes wrought in our environment by our own efforts.

While an explanation of value generalised from its economic sense may seem reasonable enough in judgments like 'good watches' or 'good motor cars', it might appear odd to interpret an expression like 'good apples' in terms of past activity. And yet apples are no mere gift of nature: they represent many generations of selective cultivation, quite apart from the work of picking, packing and transport which must all enter into their being available for consumption in an optimum state. Indeed, it will be found that few things encountered in ordinary civilised existence are unmixed with human labour, 'man's universality manifesting itself practically', as Marx puts it, 'through his capacity for appropriating nature as his inorganic body'.[13]

Those things on which people have not acted at all, such as stars or oceans or mountain ranges, are not usually referred to in our ordinary speech as 'good' because we do not normally pat nature on the back for her efforts. We are more likely to call them 'sublime'.

'awesome' or 'beautiful' in reference to the feelings they invoke in us. If we should disagree about our responses to these phenomena, it is not possible to argue about such differences as it is possible to argue about whether a watch is good or not. As applied to things like virgin forests, deposits of minerals or the creek-bed stones of an earlier example, 'good' is evaluative in the prospective sense of what human effort can make of them. At the other extreme from entirely natural formations are those things which represent an expenditure of human labour but turn out to be useless. We might wish to commend the effort behind some contraption that failed to work, as for example 'a good perpetual motion device', meaning a good stab at such an impractical undertaking; but we would not intend 'good' to be taken as descriptive of the object itself. Most of the things met with in our day-to-day living fall within these limiting cases and, being at once useful and the result of purposeful activity, can be qualified as 'good' in both its descriptive and evaluative senses.

In Marx's words 'Value in general is a form of social labour'. People's labour through the ages has transformed the objective world to satisfy their needs; and the sum total of changes in that world as a result of their productive efforts, 'putting their life' into the objects around them, is the measure of value in the world.

VALUE AND THE DIVISION OF LABOUR

It is obvious why the analysis of a commodity yields the two distinct aspects of utility and value. The social fact of the division of labour implies a separation between productive effort and enjoyed satisfactions with some form of exchange providing the link between them, and this split between production and consumption is reflected in the double nature of every marketable object.

Unlike Robinson Crusoe on his island or the directly associated labour of the most primitive communities, human exertion in commodity-producing societies is not aimed immediately at satisfying desires but at creating exchange values. Utility results from the concrete labour of various workers making this or that specific article; but before such articles are used they appear on the market as values - that is, as quantities of abstract labour which can be measured against each other in terms of the universal commodity, money. Only by purchase can these articles, whose essential characteristic as values is their temporary removal from the area of human use, be converted into objects of personal consumption.

Thus the same commodity can be seen at different stages as either utilisable or valuable, but not both at the same time. We are forced to think about the matter dialectically because commodity production and exchange itself, like any process, cannot be dealt with by a purely disjunctive logic without producing philosophical anomalies.

Is it not this same social division of labour which accounts for the two different meanings we found in analysing the word 'good'? Once the effort of producing goods has become separated from their acquisition for use, there is a consequent polarisation of the concepts relative to each phase. Ideas like the value of human effort, the necessity of working for a living and the justice of a fair return are found in connection with production, while in respect to consumption one is concerned with enjoyment, with human needs and desires and the things which can satisfy them. Furthermore, production is social and objective in the sense that people pool their resources in the fabrication of objects embodying value, while consumption is individualistic and subjective.

Each set of concepts is valid for one moment of a process which includes both the laborious provision and the pleasurable use of goods; but each on its own tells only half of the story. The utilitarian, subjective aspect of 'goodness' expresses people's dependence on nature for the satisfaction of their wants: value as an objective measure of the exertion employed in supplying our needs expresses people's dominion over nature. It is this division between passive enjoyment and active effort which is reflected in the distinction between a descriptive and prescriptive use of the value word 'good'.

But is it reasonable to suppose that a simple economic fact like the division of labour could sink so deep into human consciousness as to determine our very use of concepts and affect our ways of thinking? We can ask such a question because the social process by which we satisfy our needs in an indirect manner is so familiar that it seems perfectly natural; but ordinary human beings in the early stages of commodity production must have required a long period of adjustment to get accustomed to this idea that the things they made by their own efforts were not theirs for immediate use. Even now, we can imagine how odd it might seem to anyone who had not grown up in our kind of society to see people working to produce types of goods they will never themselves be able to use in any way or moving among displayed articles of use and, even in the most pressing need for them, regarding all but that tiny portion for which they have artificial counters to exchange as strictly taboo or, more horribly, to see Indians in their hundreds dying of starvation on the streets of Calcutta in 1943 in front of restaurants within which the normal purchase and consumption of meals by rich banias and British officials was going on as usual!

The interdiction of use, on which the emergence of value as distinguishable from utility depends, must have made a tremendous impact on the awareness of those who had first to accommodate themselves to the divorce between satisfactions and work done. This is attested by the whole weight of primitive myth and religion required to back up the extension of the earliest biological division of labour within the family to the beginnings of an economic division of labour within the whole tribe. Taboo, totemism and the very tribal clan structure were all associated with the simple fact that our ancestors had to learn not to devour things the moment they killed or found them.

And in the same way that this must have conditioned their mental and moral outlook, we ourselves are similarly conditioned today by the social organisation which has developed out of that original division of labour. Whether, for us, reality is simply what we experience immediately through our sense impressions or whether it is what we understand through thinking out the inner relationships and ultimate constituents of things is closely associated with the distinction we make between the qualitative aspect of the goods we consume and the quantitative aspect of those same goods as abstract value created by human labour. Moral philosophies based on hedonism and those based on concepts of duty and obligation are also related to that same distinction. Nor could our conception of time have remained unaffected by the need to think in longer periods than the short cycle of desire and fulfilment in pre-commodity life. The whole enormously increased range over which human purpose is free to act effectively can only have developed under the influence of the roundabout methods of production originating in that early division of labour.

But if historical economic facts like the division of labour and the rise of commodity production can help us to understand the nature of value in its widest sense, why have not philosophers availed themselves of this key? Why have they not explored the relation between the economic and the ethical significance of value instead of insisting on distinguishing them?

Part of the answer to this question is provided by the way the division of labour itself may be carried to ridiculous extremes, as in the rigid compartmentalism of various teaching disciplines. Economists deal with theories about the practical ordering of society; philosophers deal with the ideas and concepts about life which people in society have; and if there is any relationship between these two areas of study it will not be found by the professionals on either side who remain strictly within their own academic territory.

More profoundly, the division of labour, particularly the division between manual and mental labour, also determines the experience of the economic process professional philosophers in our society have. Not directly involved in production itself, nor even for the most part having so much as seen the inside of a factory, they are influenced in their attitudes by their role as consumers and tend to be more concerned with the end results of the system, the goods made available for use, than with the activity which produced them. Take up any recent book on ethics and consider the illustrative examples offered. Many will be about the act of choice involved in buying one thing rather than another or about the way in which we order our subjective preferences for things: few if any will be about the associative labour process which brought such things into being. The productive activity of people in their relations to each other, to the means of production and to the objective world not only provides the goods on which life depends but also conditions the concepts on which valid thought depends. A consumer's eye view of society in slighting such basic activity is prone to miss the full significance of concepts whose origin and development are largely determined by the way in which commodities are produced and exchanged.

This consumer's attitude can lead naturally to a utilitarian bias in which 'good' is identified with whatever aspect of an object makes it suitable for individual use, and value is either defined in terms of such suitability or left altogether unaccounted for. A subjective view of this kind is the obvious response of a shopper who is not interested in how various articles have appeared on the shelves but merely wishes to arrange in a private order of priority the satisfactions which can be afforded. These same goods would appear in a very different light to a worker involved in the manufacturing process which made them available; but ours is not on the whole a society in which industrial workers get books of philosophy published.

Suppose professional philosophers do realise that this utilitarian account is not adequate, that it by-passes the essential problem of value instead of trying to solve it. They may be aware that the enjoyment of goods implies some kind of effort; but if their own experience has never included any acquaintanceship with the productive activity on which all value is ultimately grounded and if they continue to approach the question from a consumer's point of view, this effort is likely to appear to them, idealistically, as the moral exertion by which people become worthy of the good things of life. Value thus pertains to things not in respect to the actual labour of their makers but out of regard for the spiritual aspirations of their prospective users.

In this way the non-naturalist, ignoring a thing's utility, arrives at a view of value so utterly detached from any context of human satisfaction that choice seems 'free' in the sense of being purely arbitrary or else appears to be motivated in the empty terms of duty for the sake of duty. What has actually happened in this derivation of the sense of value is that by stressing, however unconsciously, that moment in a commodity's history when it is under the interdiction of use as a mere quantification represented by its price, the non-naturalist sees value as belonging only to the abstract idea of an object. As simply marketable, objects have no natural properties and are as unchanging and timeless as Platonic archetypes. Therefore goodness by this account can come to be regarded as 'The Good', an ideal conception which has lost all connection with the world of actual human effort and can only be sought in some 'remembered' realm of pure thought.

Both kinds of errors about value, either explaining it away altogether or turning it into something transcendental, are the result of an unconscious bias rooted in the mistake of starting from the wrong end of the production process - from the consumer's end. As Marx says: 'If you proceed from production, you necessarily concern yourself with the real conditions of production and the productive activity of men. But if you proceed from consumption...you can afford to ignore the real living conditions and the activity of men.'[14] That is why Marx's definition of class is based not on criteria of consumption like arbitrary levels of income, the possession of status symbols or the ideas people may have about themselves as a result of such considerations, but on the objective social fact of people's position in the productive process, of their relationship to the means of production.

Naturalists in failing to grasp the dialectic of the whole process from production through distribution to consumption cannot account for a thing's being both useful and valuable: non-naturalists in seeing this process, if at all, as a dialectic of ideas tend to make value other-worldly.

Value, in fact, stamps an object as what Marx calls a 'social hieroglyphic' and it can only be deciphered by reference to the productive relationships of a commodity exchanging society. Value is the language of people's economic intercourse with each other which has for its subject the constructive changes effected in the world by their associative efforts - just as factual propositions are the language of people's scientific communications about the world as presented. All language is a social product and must be accounted for ultimately in terms of the type of society in which it functions. The language of value has the peculiar characteristics we have noted because in our own type of society it reminds us, however indirectly, that everything we call 'good' in a prescriptive sense is the result of human activity. It is the means whereby tribute is paid to the productive labour of human beings.

THE RELATION BETWEEN VALUE AND UTILITY

It has been shown how the descriptive and prescriptive senses of 'good' are an ideological reflection of the distinction within a commodity between utility and value, a distinction resulting from the division of labour which gives rise to commodity-exchanging societies. In order to show how these two senses of 'good' are related to each other, it is necessary to trace the kind of relationship that obtains between the commodity as an object of use and the commodity as a value-bearing object.

The economic law of value derives the worth of commodities from the labour incorporated in them and thus fixes their values in terms of the relation of each to all others. How, then, does this law relate the value of these commodities to human needs? What, in other words, is the connecting link between things exchangeable at determinate ratios and people who bring to the market their personal demands for satisfaction?

Now this is to approach from the opposite direction the problem Marx describes as confronting the possessor of capital who wishes to make a profit from the buying and selling of commodities. In conditions of free competition any trade in commodities whose value relationships are fixed by the amount of incorporated labour will always leave him right where he started. He is actually looking for a special kind of commodity whose usefulness consists in its being value-creative. Since only human labour can create value, his requirement is met by the appearance on the market, as a commodity, of the labour-power of free workers' - free in the double sense that they can dispose of their labour-power at will and that they have been 'freed' of anything else to dispose of.

We are looking for a human relationship which by taking the form of commodity exchange will reveal the connection between utility and value, the link between what human beings want and the worth of their efforts in making things. And this relationship is, of course, that same contract between the purchaser of labour-power and the labourers themselves who thus turn their own capacity to work into a commodity. The value of labour-power is determined, like that of every other commodity, by the labour time necessary for its production, which is only to say that the value of labour-power is the value of the means of subsistence required for labourers to maintain and reproduce themselves. The means of subsistence are simply commodities whose utility sustains the labourers and their families and whose value expresses the worth of their labour-power. It is, therefore, through the act of exchange whereby a human quality, labour-power, becomes a commodity among commodities that the law of value establishes a causal relationship between work done and needs which can be satisfied. It is because so much labour-power has been sold that an equivalent amount of goods can be acquired for use.

The appearance on the market of labour-power as a commodity is the basic social fact of the capitalist system and the key to understanding how, in human terms, that system works.

The historical conditions of capitalism's existence are by no means given by the mere circulation of money and commodities. It can spring into being only when the owner of the means of production and subsistence meets in the market with the free labourer selling his labour-power. And this one historical condition comprises a world's history. Capital, therefore, announces from its first appearance a new epoch in the process of social production.[15]

The alienation of the workers' capacity to produce value so that it can be bought by the capitalist who thereby acquires the products the workers' make is the relationship Marx explores so illuminatingly in the Economic and Philosophical Manuscripts of 1844, showing how alienated labour on the workers' side is private property on the capitalist's side. The workers' who once owned their own tools become themselves tools in the hands of the capitalist and, having fulfilled their work contract, buy back for their own use that portion of the product which is the accepted equivalent of the labour-power they have sold.

While the law of value of which this transaction is an expression relates acquired satisfactions to work done, it by no means equates human labour and the reward which might be considered its due. The law of value in no way prevents the dealer in labour-power who is the dominant partner in all labour contracts through his possession, as private property, of the means of production, from exacting value-creative work beyond the worth of the labourers' own needs. Although an employer only pays for labour-power, a commodity with a fixed market rate, he acquires the use of labour itself, the creative source of all values whatsoever.

That portion of the labourers' output produced in working beyond the time necessary for supplying the substance of their personal needs Marx calls surplus-value which, as a result of the labourers' alienation of their value-creative capacity in the contract they make with an employer, becomes the property of the employer. In his definition of the value of labour-power Marx does not accept the 'iron law of wages' theory whereby this value can never rise above a bare subsistence level. 'The number and extent of the labourer's so-called necessary wants, as also the modes of satisfying them, are themselves the products of historical development, and depend therefore to a great extent on the degree of civilisation of a country.'[16] The law of value does not fix the precise amount of goods workers' receive in terms of what will barely keep them alive any more than it fixes the exact price of goods in terms of their incorporated value: it establishes the area in which wages and prices can move without breaking the relations of production which make the capitalist system what it is.

Nor does the law of value, as we shall see, prevent such cancerous growths in capitalist society as commodity fetishism, money idolatry or profit as an end in itself, which are all expressions for the way the alienated labour of workers' changes, under control of the capitalist, into a hostile thing standing over against its original creators. For our present purpose, the law of value simply provides a clue, by means of rough equivalents, to the way alienated labour, or value, passes through various transformations in commodity-exchanging societies from production through distribution to consumption, thus serving as a link between the socially sundered operations of making things and enjoying them. The value form commodities assume as 'congealed abstract labour' can be compared to a kind of deep freeze into which all utilisable goods pass, with the guarantee that what the members of a commodity-producing society take out bears a socially determined, but by no means necessarily equitable, relationship to what they respectively put in.

It has been shown that the difference between naturalistic and non-naturalistic interpretations of a value word like 'good', the distinction between 'good' as a description of usefulness and 'good' as a prescriptive evaluation, is rooted in the material conditions of life in a society based on a market economy and reflects the social division of labour which gives rise to such societies. We are now in a position to see how the economic law of value which governs exchanges in societies of this type can help us to understand the nature of value judgments in general.

If this law has the economic function of relating the utility of commodities to their value, and if the two different senses of 'good' are grounded in the double nature of commodities, then it is reasonable to argue that value judgments have the logical role of indicating the connection between the descriptive and prescriptive uses of value words. By referring to the labour of adapting things for use and also to the enjoyment of using these things, such judgments enable us to weigh the objective cost in human effort of our subjective preferences. They give us in highly abridged form the history in human terms of any object presented for our appreciation.

Value judgments, in effect, restore us momentarily to a pre-commodity situation in which the active labour of making or acquiring something and the passively-felt desire for it are still united in a single comprehensive reflex. 'This is a good watch' thus means not only that it has certain qualities such as accuracy and compactness which can make anyone requiring a time-piece regard it favourably, but also that a person ought to admire its craftsmanship, to respect the knowledge implicit in its manufacture and to imagine retrospectively the human effort and skill it represents - all in selecting it or recommending it to others as an object of choice.

It may seem strange that value judgments could perform such a task without our being altogether aware of it each time we attribute 'goodness' to something; but then the economic law of value itself, operating as a characteristic of objects, as an exchange ratio of commodities, appears to people not as the rule of their own isolated acts but as an external necessity inherent in the nature of things. This same false consciousness engendered by commodity exchange which transforms social relations into relations between things both creates the logical need for value judgments and obscures their true function. In a social order where, as a result of the alienation of human labour, things arrogate to themselves the kind of relationships which can only really pertain to persons we need to be reminded, however obliquely, of the connection between useful objects and the human effort embodied in them. This value judgments do, thus making the act of choice, in the highly complicated circumstances of commodity-exchanging society, rational.

Economic value can only be understood in terms of the buying and selling of labour-power. Value judgments in general must also be considered in conjunction with the way work is performed and paid for in society, since every evaluative use of a word like 'good' is ultimately an appreciation of someone's labour or skill.

In the context of class-divided society the economic law of value, by revealing a huge discrepancy between contributed labour and distributed satisfactions, lays bare the fact of surplus-value. This is the levy the class in control of the means of production, which are simply the objectified form in the present of labour-power purchased in the past, exacts from the class owning nothing but its capacity to work.

Once the true function of value judgments is grasped, it may be seen that they, too, are not silent on the scandal of this exploitation which hides behind commodity operations. Indeed, some philosophers, in glossing over this sort of depredation by the class which dominates the society in which their mental labours are employed and in possibly resenting the verbal tribute they pay to the class of manual workers whenever they make a value judgment, may be suspected of a certain disingenuousness in cloaking the whole subject of value in a pall of obscurantism.

OBJECTIONS TO THE LABOUR THEORY OF VALUE

As corroboration of the argument that value judgments are closely related in function to the economic law of value, it can be pointed out that the attempts of certain philosophers to empty the concept of 'value' of any real meaning and the attempts of certain political economists to refute the 'labour theory of value' follow precisely similar lines. It can hardly be a coincidence that in the same place and at the same time the Viennese Circle of logical positivists and the Austrian marginal utility school of economists were endeavouring to explain away value in either an ethical or an economic sense. This intellectual task seemed socially necessary because any realistic account of value risked calling attention to surplus-value and the way in which it was appropriated. The task was carried out by deducing from the tendency toward atomisation in capitalist society, of which these intellectuals are both masters and victims, a philosophy of extreme individualism and then using this assumption of discrete, individualistic egoism to deny objectivity to a social product like value. Since knowledge itself is a social product, it, too, was robbed of objectivity by the same mental process; but that was not considered an excessive price to pay for sterilising value of any dangerous implications by making it purely subjective.

In general, attacks by the apologists of capitalism on the labour theory of value as developed by Marx from classical economists like Ricardo have taken the form of misrepresenting him in order to refute him. By pretending that Marx refined and developed the theory in order to account for individual prices instead of, as was actually the case, using it to explain the fundamental dynamism of the whole economic process of capitalism, they can claim to have caught him out when, later on, as a detail in the overall structure, he gives a price-of-production analysis its due place. And this price-of-production itself is firmly based on the original formulation of the theory of value since the element of profit depends on the difference between the value of labour-power and the value of finished commodities, involving, of course, the appropriation of surplus-value.

The analysis of a particular mode of production in Capital sets before us a working model of a whole society with all its interlocking relationships. In constructing this model abstracted from reality, Marx begins with a world in which there are goods which have been adapted or created for human use. All these goods represent the labour and ingenuity which people have expended in transforming their natural environment into a better-stocked and more suitable home for themselves and their descendants. Value is the measure of this effort and serves the economic purpose of enabling us in a commodity-producing society to trade very different things against each other in terms of the human effort they incorporate; and, generally speaking, the prices of these things are proportional to the amount of labour-time required at a particular stage of social development to produce and distribute them. The very distortions resulting from natural or man-made scarcities imply a basic standard from which prices can temporarily depart. Value also serves the ethical purpose of reminding us, each time we judge some article useful and worth acquiring, of what we owe to the activity and skill of fellow human beings.

But the equivalence which value establishes among different goods in terms of incorporated labour and between those goods and the claims on them the workers who created them are entitled to make also reveals the social fact that another class of people, whose ownership of the means of production entitles them to profit from the labour-power of workers, enjoy material wealth and political power far beyond any contribution in energy or skill which they have made to the production of goods.

This broad picture of capitalist society with all its ethical implications is not challenged by pointing out limitations on the labour theory of value as a means of predicting what a feather boa will cost in three month's time. Objections usually take the form of setting forth difficulties in computing labour-time as an exact measurement, involving such problems as distinguishing between productive and non-productive or skilled and unskilled labour, as differentiating between hours actually spent on a job and socially necessary labour-time, or as separating labour expended over a given period from the value given up in the same period by capital goods in which labour has been embodied in the past. All these difficulties arise in connection with misapplying the theory to try to determine the price of a specific article instead of using it to provide an explanation of the approximate price-relationships over the whole range of goods - relationships which may fluctuate with changes in productivity but can only be accounted for in any given period by the labour theory of value operating with the social norms of productive work relevant to that time.

Critics of Marx's objective theory of value may bring an enormous subtlety to bear on questions of consumption; but by practically ignoring production except as an investment possibility, they can profess to find no need for any principle which links the two together and accounts for the eventual distribution of goods in terms of the values they acquire in being produced. Marxists would not object to the use of a marginal utility calculus as an adjunct to centralised planning, in societies where such planning is, in fact, possible; but they would rightly deny that any mere description of propensities to consume could obviate the need for a theory of value. The tendency of latter day economists in the capitalist world to combine a cunning analysis of the superficial aspect of things with an obstinate, or perhaps terrified, refusal to look beneath the surface may be compared with the philosophy of phenomenalism. Just as phenomenalists ultimately reduce the whole science of reality to certain pointer readings, so the marginal utility school finds the only significance of the economic process in price movements. The only reforms which could be envisaged on such a superficial reading of social organisation would be very minor schemes of redistribution.

Ideological motivation in terms of class interest is often no more conscious than the rationalisations of behaviour offered by a patient on a psychiatrist's couch; but this is not always the case. In the early stages of the attack on the classical school of political economy from which Marx had taken and further developed certain basic concepts, writers on economics like Boehm-Bawerk were quite open in admitting that they were inspired to denounce the labour theory of value by their dislike of socialism. Philosophers approaching the question of value in general have occasionally been as frank. W.D. Lamont, for example, in *The Value Judgment* appreciates the relevance of economic analysis to the whole problem of value but in accepting the utility theory of the supply-and-demand school he can give only a superficial account of the value judgment which he describes as forward-looking, not backward-looking, and as therefore having nothing to do with past effort but only with future utility. This we can now recognise as an expression of the consumption bias of those who assume unquestioningly an automatic flow of commodities on which they can confer 'value' simply by deigning to consume them.

The bourgeois ethic of utilitarianism is the official moral philosophy of capitalism's academic apologists. If one wants to see this 'morality' in operation, better than consulting their books is watching the world of television commercials which provides a perfect paradigm of the way this consumerist system works. Advertising, on the pretence of giving us what we want most, makes sure that we will want most what it is most profitable and often harmful to give us. The motives appealed to are the typical selfish capitalist ones of envy, greed, individualistic display and self-aggrandisement. Our surprise if we should ever hear an advertisement exhorting us to use such and such a product because it would incline us toward helping our fellow human beings or would make a useful contribution to the life of our times exposes the true nature of this philosophy. Margaret Thatcher, when she was Prime Minister of Britain expressed the ethics of capitalism very clearly when she said 'There is no such thing as society'; there are only individuals proving themselves by how much they can grab hold of and hang on to.

Marx points out that:

> this ethic of utilitarianism came to the fore with Hobbes and Locke, at the same time as the first and second English revolutions, those first battles by which the bourgeoisie won political power... Political economy is the real science of this theory of utility with its absurdity of merging all the manifold relations of people in the one relation of usefulness. This apparently metaphysical abstraction arises from the fact that in modern bourgeois society all relations are subordinated in practice to the one abstract monetary-commercial relation...
>
> The utility relation has a quite definite meaning, namely, that I derive benefit for myself by doing harm to someone else (exploitation de l'homme par l'homme)
>
> ...and this is precisely the relation of utility. All this is actually the case with the bourgeois. For him only one relation is valid on its own account - the relation of exploitation; all other relations have validity for him only insofar as he can include them under this one relation; and even where he encounters relations which cannot be directly subordinated to the relation of exploitation, he subordinates them to it at least in his imagination. The material expression of this use is money which represents the value of all things, people and social relations. Incidentally, one sees at a glance that the category 'utilisation' is first abstracted from the actual relations of intercourse which I have with other people... and then these reflections are made out to be the reality of the category that has been abstracted from them themselves, a wholly metaphysical method of procedure. In exactly the same way and with the same justification, Hegel depicts all relations as relations of the objective spirit.[17]

Such attacks by Marx on utilitarian ethics are often taken by anti-Marxists as attacks on ethics as such. But that this is not the case is shown by his criticism of the supposedly self-regulating character of a system based on self-interest. 'The factory owners' strenuous opposition to those clauses (in the Factory Acts) which compelled them to spend a little money upon protecting the limbs of their workpeople...throws once more a glaring light upon the free-trade dogma that, in a society where antagonistic interests are at work, everyone favours the welfare of the community when he seeks to promote his own personal advantage.[18] When Marx says 'Law, morality, religion, are just so many bourgeois prejudices behind which lurk in ambush just so many bourgeois interests'[19] he is not urging the working class to get rid of law and morality. He is urging the working class to get rid of the dominance of the bourgeoisie and their interests thus redeeming law and morality from the influence of their selfish greed.

VALUE AND THE MARXIST THEORY OF KNOWLEDGE

We have already noted that theories of value and theories of knowledge do not belong to separate mental compartments and that adopting any particular form of the one has implications for the other. The problem of the relationship between prescriptive and descriptive sentences proves, in fact, to be a question of the epistemological accommodation of value judgments. We have seen that empiricism in general finds it impossible to account for evaluation without either explaining it away or committing the naturalistic fallacy. The various schools of idealism, on the other hand, appear to do more justice to concepts like 'value' but at the expense of an acceptably realistic explanation of factual knowledge. How does the Marxist theory of value fare in respect to its own theory of knowledge?

As has been shown Marxism maintains an objective theory of value which, somewhat like the intuitionists, takes certain non-natural qualities of a thing as the subject of value judgments while, at the same time, its materialist approach to the problem of knowledge seems closer to the empiricists. How is this logically possible? It will be remembered that in Marx's analysis of a commodity he shows that it has both utility and value but that these two aspects are mutually exclusive and can only qualify an article successively. This characteristic of commodities is grounded in the dialectical nature of change in general and of the productive process in particular. Marxist epistemology, being grounded in these material conditions, is itself dialectical and can therefore accommodate both prescriptive and descriptive sentences which are related to each other in much the same way as the value and utility of a commodity.

Indeed, the production of valid knowledge exactly reflects in its phases the production and distribution of valuable goods. The making of a thing within the natural limitations imposed by the qualities of the raw material and the skill of the maker is like physical perception; the stripping of the object of its particularity to appear on the market as a mere quantification of value is like the process of thinking in abstract terms whereby internal relationships are discovered and possibilities of change and development are grasped; and the re-acquisition of the commodity to satisfy human needs is like putting ideas and theories arrived at abstractly back into the world to be tested and proved right or wrong in social practice.

Statements may be distinguished according to which of the three moments in the process of knowledge they belong to. Those belonging to the first phase correspond to the natural environment they immediately reflect; those in the second, abstracted from the first, cohere logically among themselves; and the whole process is finally verified by virtue of the fact that the third phase simply is the practical re-application of duly deliberated sensuous information. Lenin makes the point that idealism is one phase of the process of knowledge and only becomes absurd as a movement of thought out of this context.

Philosophical idealism is only non-sense from the standpoint of crude, simple, metaphysical materialism. From the standpoint of dialectical materialism, on the other hand, philosophical idealism is a one-sided, exaggerated development of one of the features, aspects, facets of knowledge into an absolute, divorced from matter, from nature, apotheosised.[20]

And Mao Tsetung in 'On Practice' sets out the whole process clearly:

> The first step in the process of knowledge is contact with the things of the external world; this belongs to the stage of perception. The second step is a synthesis of the data of perception by making a re-arrangement or a reconstruction; this belongs to the stage of conception, judgment and inference...But the process of knowledge does not end here...The third step is the practical application of theoretic conclusions.[21]

The mass line, 'from the people, to the people', which we will have occasion to refer to often, is simply this same Marxist theory of knowledge applied to social practice.

> Take the ideas of the masses (scattered and unsystematic ideas) and concentrate them (through study turn them into concentrated and systematic ideas) then go to the masses and propagate and explain these ideas until the masses embrace them as their own, hold fast to them and translate them into action.[22]

Statements belonging to different moments in the process of knowledge cannot simply be resolved into each other - any more than a plant, say, can be at once seed, flower and fruit; but though distinguishable these various types of statement are yet related to each other in the total act of knowledge. Empirical propositions are based on sense impressions; but reasoning cannot work with these particular impressions as such. It requires concepts which are abstracted from the facts of sensuous experience: even to compare two objects it needs universals like 'roundness' or 'hardness' which are not mere passive reflections of anything in nature. And after the combination of abstract ideas in inferential judgments which remain arbitrary constructs until tested comes verification in social practice, theories and hypotheses validated by the shared experience they lead us to expect.

The great act of human abstraction by which people projected value in the form of a circulating currency about the fifth century B.C. In Greece, India and China stimulated a vast upsurge of philosophical thinking in those places, beginning with the proto-scientific search for a substance which could be the ultimate source of all natural objects on the analogy of money which can manifest itself in the form of all human-made articles and then going on to a proto-sociological concern with the relations of people in society prompted by the effects of the disruption of old tribal forms of organisation by new class distinctions.

Descriptive sentences, in which 'good' appears as an adjective qualifying either the object to be enjoyed or the psychological state of the enjoying subject, are perceptual propositions belonging to the first moment of thought. Prescriptive sentences, in which 'good' has an evaluative force, draw upon insights from the second or speculative moment to become injunctions belonging to the third or practical moment. In this dialectical account theory and practice are not separated and, therefore, the link between theoretical propositions of suitability and the practical imperatives implicit in value judgments is always there to be discovered by peering beneath the superficial phenomena of commodity exchange.

HUMAN VALUE AND CAPITALIST DISVALUE

Value, of course, is not only the measure of physical effort resulting in the production of objective goods, though that is its most patent form. The mental effort which produces a new type of tool or a useful scientific formula is also measurable in terms of values of an intellectual order. Those forms of human artistic activity which have become more and more detached from the actual productive process - song, dance and music, the graphic arts and orature - are all extensions of the basic equivalence between human effort and valuable goods. The very mental and spiritual climate we breathe is as rich an atmosphere of people's imaginative creations as the cities in which we dwell are vast memorials of their physical labours. Ours is a world full of value, material, mental and spiritual, which our fellow human beings, past and present, have put there by their exertion over the whole field of human endeavour.

The recognition and appreciation of value and the desire to contribute to that store of value in the world are the characteristics of civilised human beings. That is why in countries which are trying to establish socialism all young people are expected as part of their training to labour at hard physical tasks in factory and field, so that they can learn through sweat and tired muscles that fundamental equation between work done and goods produced in which all values are grounded. That is why those citizens whose service takes them into offices, lecture halls, laboratories or libraries also spend some time each year at manual tasks to re-affirm the basic physical comradeship of all who labour together with their hands for the general good.

With this attitude can be contrasted the early efforts to enforce the division of labour and to defend the institution of slavery by regarding all physical labour as utterly contemptible and those who perform it so depraved as to deserve no better fate. It must have required the same sort of continuous pressure over a considerable time to win people over to this view of manual work as had been required to make them observe interdictions of use on consumable goods so that those goods could appear in the market for exchange. Plato puts a taboo on all such labour as far as freemen are concerned and strongly admonishes any citizen who should stray from the path of virtue by soiling his hands in hard work. Platonic values are completely detached from anything so degrading as physical effort and become instead the abstract universals with which the mind works in the second phase of the process of knowledge where, for

Plato, all understanding is arrested in eternal contemplation of the ideal.

A priorism is the philosophical device for justifying the division of labour by showing that some people are quite naturally endowed with the intellectual qualities to control and direct while others are born to be society's slaves - a kind of service performed for the ruling class today by such 'thinkers' as the Eysencks and Jensens. In the past this service was performed by those like Carlyle whom Marx explicitly criticised for treating historically-created class differences as eternally ordained natural differences which people were supposed to 'recognise and revere by bowing before the wise and noble ones in a cult of genius'.

In socialist China an ideological campaign was waged by the people against this kind of contemptuous idealism by attacking the reactionary views of Confucius, Plato's approximate contemporary, who also supported a caste society based on slavery and was opposed by relatively progressive 'legalists' who, like the Greek 'sophists', have usually been presented in a bad light because of the influence down the ages Plato and Confucius have enjoyed as useful to successive ruling classes.

In commodity-exchanging societies, of which capitalist countries are the final and most extreme cases, mental and spiritual values, productions of the intellect and creative imagination, are themselves commodities. Designers, inventors and artists sell their skill in exactly the same way as workers sell their labour-power, and in the same way what they produce is determined by what is profitable to the purchaser of their talent, not by what might be useful and inspirational to the public. Even such a value as justice, created out of the struggle and sacrifice of countless martyrs in the past, becomes a commodity which has to be bought and paid for.

To appreciate what has happened to value and our understanding of it in present-day capitalist society we have to look at the basic presuppositions of capitalism as a mode of production influencing the way of life of a vast proportion of the world's population. The utilitarian 'ethics' of capitalism has been succinctly stated by Adam Smith when he writes:

> It is not from the benevolence of the butcher, the brewer or the baker that we expect our dinner, but from their regard to their own interest. We address ourselves not to their humanity but to their self-love, and never talk to them of our own necessities but of their advantage.[23]

This is to look at the whole human co-operative process of producing the values which sustain the quality of human life and assure its continuance into the future from the point of view of shop keepers trying to make a profit and bargain-hunting individuals driven by their selfish desires. Values do not enter into their scheme of things - just prices.

As has already been noted there is a tendency for professional thinkers, university professors and intellectuals generally, who have had little or no experience of working with others to make things for human use, to consider questions of value from either a completely idealistic point of view as unconnected with the ordinary business of life or from an individualistic consumer's point of view of putting in some order of personal priority goods which may be on offer. They tend to leave out of account the collective activity by which human labour made those valuable goods available. Consumption is selfish and individualistic: no one else can satisfy my hunger for me. Production is co-operative and social: we can all work for each other. Capitalist utilitarianism is based on self-interest, the ethics of consumerism.

During the Proletarian Cultural Revolution in China this ethical bias of capitalism was fought by calling on the people to 'Fight self-interest! Proceed in all cases from the interests of the people and not from one's self-interest or from the interests of a small group.' When revolutionary zeal led them to say that 'public interest and self-interest cannot peacefully co-exist: we must not allow even a speck of the dust of self-interest to enter our minds' they were going too far, of course, and practically turning themselves into the ascetic desert fathers of early Christianity. There has to be co-operative production and individualistic consumption: public interest and self-interest. The Albanian socialist Ramiz Alia puts it thus:

> To give priority to personal interests means to give priority to the individual not to the collective, to partial not to basic interests, to the interests of the moment not to those of the future, to material not to moral stimuli, to national egotism not to proletarian internationalism...Self interests are objective interests, entirely legitimate and rational. Society is not something abstract but composed of people (with all their individual needs), just as general interest is not something abstract but is made up of all the vital interests of workers. Therefore our fight is not against the very existence of self-interest but against placing it above general interest. We are for combining and harmonising them by subjecting personal interests to the interests of the working class, of the people, of revolution and socialism.

In theory the principle of bourgeois morality, individual selfishness, was supposed to work in such a way that all the individual wills selfishly competing with each other would cancel out for the general good. The theory was that the capitalists in the course of seeking their own private profit would incidentally feed, clothe and house all those who brought their labour-power to market. In this way an acceptable relationship between values produced and goods consumed would be maintained in spite of a reasonable degree of exploitation. In fact, the idea that the capitalist system could dispense with morality and that its more or less equitable functioning could be a by-product of a profit-motivated market economy is a colossal and tragic example of the naturalistic fallacy on a world-wide scale!

Nor can those countries which have had a working class revolution dispense with democratic social morality and rely solely on material incentives to bring about automatically the further development of socialist human beings. Revisionism is simply bourgeois economics and social attitudes disguised as Marxism and it incorporates the same fallacy of a de-valued ethics.

Not only is it impossible to reconcile the profit-seeking of the few with the general good of the many, it is not even possible to reconcile it with a properly functioning economy having a reasonably constant rate of growth. The tendency of capitalism in Marx's words to 'establish an accumulation of misery' at one pole, 'corresponding with the accumulation of capital at the other', whether within the metropolitan capitalist country itself or, even more disastrously, within its economic empire, cannot possibly make for stability. The erratic, unplanned development of profit seeking, the attempts to control the market by monopolisation and cartelisation and the efforts to keep wages low by mass unemployment all have the effect of preventing the law of value from functioning in such a way as to maintain a proper balance either between different kinds of production, like consumer goods and goods to promote the further growth of production, or between the employment of value-creative labour at its market price and the effective market demand for goods that have been produced.

This results in a periodic destructive decline in the economy until it has sunk to a more primitive level at which the law of value comes into play again. Much-heralded solutions to these capitalist contradictions usually consist of governmental intervention to use more or less socialist means, not to move toward socialism, but simply to save capitalism - like the Keynesian answer to under-consumption by deficit financing and pump-priming which lead to other contradictions just as intractable, like massive indebtedness, trade imbalances and world-wide inflation. Or like state control of an industry too big for private ownership to launch or too despoiled by private extraction of profit without investment to survive which can then be financed by tax-payers and built up to the point where it can be profitably privatised or reprivatised!

Since 'value' as having both an economic and an ethical meaning serves as a middle term relating the material base of society to its ideas of morality, we can describe this malfunctioning of the law of value in moral language. The critical economic dislocations to which capitalism is prone amount, ethically speaking, to a growing disjunction between the efforts of those whose work is value-creative and the goods they can expect or even the respect they enjoy. Honest toil and skilled craftsmanship lose their value in the quite practical sense that they are inadequately rewarded and may well be denied any opportunity for employment at all. In a society where this disjunction has occurred there is, to begin with, a diminishing correlation between social merit and economic recompense; and, eventually, at a more advanced stage of deterioration, there is even a negative correlation. Not only does genuinely constructive work in any particular field cease to receive its due acknowledgement but a monetary premium is placed on the most anti-social forms of activity. The dignity of human labour is mocked when it is so obviously the parasitical and destructive elements which flourish under a system increasingly characterised by waste and speculation and activated by appeals to people's basest motives.

Quite simply it takes too many starving millions at the bottom of the capitalist system to pay for the relatively few affluent people at the top. While capitalists grab for themselves the riches of private profit the working people all over the capitalist world have to pay the huge social costs of wasted raw materials and ecological despoliation. As George Thomson puts it:'The free play of market forces must be brought under control if our civilisation is to be saved from self-destruction, and that can only be done by the deprived and the dispossessed. When they take their future into their own hands, they will cast off their backwardness, and by releasing new forces, material and spiritual, raise civilisation to a higher level.'

Even if it were possible for the capitalist system to function in such a manner that there was a fairer share-out of goods among those whose efforts are value-creative, it would not meet the real point of the Marxist social critique. It is not simply distribution which is defective but production itself - the very process by which people objectify themselves in commodities that do not belong to them, that are directly determined neither in quantity nor quality by people's real needs, that stand over against their creators as an alien world of things obeying laws of profit which are utterly irrelevant to the well-being of those who actually made them. Instead of profit serving as a stimulus to the production of the things society needs, it becomes openly what it always was in intention - an end in itself to which human beings are perpetually sacrificed.

The split between duty and pleasure, between work and enjoyment which is itself a consequence of commoditisation has the effect of freeing desires from any natural context to be played upon by advertising and sales campaigns so that demands can be artificially created for goods which are profitable. Unable to absorb the values it is technically capable of producing capitalism finds it profitable to divert human effort into the production of shoddy, ephemeral and harmful objects, thus wasting our natural heritage to fill the world with things to which the name 'goods' can only be applied in irony - the production not of value but of disvalue. Criminal waste of this kind cannot but be reflected in a moral crisis as grave as the economic. All those implicated in preserving such a system inevitably tend, in Oscar Wilde's phrase, to know the price of everything and the value of nothing. The ultimate example of this perversion of people's productive ability was the search by the major imperialist power for a commodity whose only utility would be the massive destruction of human life while leaving property intact!

The full development of commodity exchange under capitalism by which human relationships become more and more a function of things, leads in time to the dehumanisation of whole societies. In no other way can we account for the cruel barbarities of those capitalist countries most industrially advanced. A system which begins with the robbery of surplus-value, cloaked behind a deal in commoditised labour, goes on to loot and massacre on a world-wide scale, often hiding such crimes behind movements in world prices. Have so many millions of people died of starvation in this or that part of the world which depends on the sale of raw materials? Too bad. The terms of trade have moved against them. It is like committing mass murder by pushing a button instead of having to hack people to pieces with a sword. Piles of human hair in extermination centres, preserved for some possible economic use, is an example of what can happen in a system which turns people into commodities in order to profit from them.

It is in connection with value and its distortion and degradation under capitalism that the basic impulse to overthrow the system is born - whether it is a question of the personal and particular injustices suffered by individuals which begin to unite them in opposition or of the general demoralisation and corruption over the whole contemporary scene which even revolts many of those who are not directly victimised. Any professed love of humanity which is not accompanied by a condemnation of this vicious, dehumanising system is pure humbug.

CHAPTER I VALUES

1 *Marx, 'Theses on Feuerbach', Selected Works, vol, II, p367*
2 *Marx, 'The German Ideology' p15*
3 *Mao Tsetung, as quoted in 'Philosophy no Mystery'*
4 *Marx, 'Theses on Feuerbach' Selected Works, vol, II, p365*
5 *Marx, 'Theses on Feuerbach' Selected Works, vol, II, p365*
6 *Marx, 'Critique of Hegel's Philosophy of Right' Early Writings (Pelican Marx Library) p251*
7 *Marx, Preface to First German Edition of 'Capital', Selected Works, vol, I, p10*
8 *Marx, 'The German Ideology'*
9 *Lenin, 'The Tasks of the Youth Leagues', Selected Works, vol, II, p667*

10 *David Hume, 'A Treatise of Human Nature' p415*
11 *Jeremy Bentham, 'Introduction to the Principles of Morals and Legislation'*
12 *Marx, 'Capital', vol, III, p795*
13 *Marx, 'Economic and Philosophic Manuscripts of 1844' p74*
14 *Marx, 'The German Ideology', p164*
15 *Marx, 'Capital', vol, I, p170*
16 *Marx, 'Capital', vol, I, p171*
17 *Marx, 'The German Ideology'*
18 *Marx, 'Capital', vol, I p480-1*
19 *Marx and Engels, 'The Communist Manifesto', Selected Works vol, 1, p33*
20 *Lenin, 'Collected Works', vol, xxxviii, p363*
21 *Mao Tsetung, 'On Practice', Selected Works, vol, I, pp290-3*
22 *Mao Tsetung, 'Some Questions Concerning Methods of Leadership', Selected Works, vol, III, p119*
23 *Adam Smith, 'Wealth of Nations', p13*

Chapter 2
Rights – The Meaning of Normative Judgments

INTRODUCTION

As was demonstrated in the previous chapter the meaning of 'good' as it appears in value judgments is ultimately derived from an analysis of the specific goods people produce. This meaning, bound up as it is with certain relations of production, can only be understood in the context of definite forms of social existence, but since the production of goods for exchange is as old as, and not unconnected with, the keeping of written records, the word 'good' with approximately the same intention has a very wide historical extension.

Having grounded the value judgment in the human activity of producing goods to sustain and enrich the lives of fellow human beings it could be appreciated as a moral tribute to the quality of value-creative work. By the same token exploiting a controlling position in respect to the productive process to foist on human beings defective or harmful 'goods' would deserve a negative value judgment which branded it immoral.

In the present section we shall be considering the meaning of 'right' as it appears in such normative judgments as 'He has a right to it because he made it or because he paid for it' or 'It is right to keep faith with one's workmates or to abide by contracts with one's employer'. This meaning, too, has to be deduced from specific rights which are grounded in the material conditions of life in this or that type of society.

As a completely abstract term existing above and independently of any specific material conditions of life and, therefore, universally applicable at all times anywhere 'right', like other ethical expressions, would prove in fact to apply nowhere and at no time. It could only maintain the absolute purity of so transcendental a character by never suffering the violation of getting involved in any concrete situation.

Morality, on this interpretation of its terms, instead of being practical would become a matter of ideal contemplation, a Platonic obsession with universal forms, a preparation for purely mental existence in an entirely abstract world, not physical existence in this one.

And yet if concepts like 'right' were not to some extent abstractions, thought could make no use of them. Therefore, in the course of investigating what 'right' means we shall also try to discover how such a concept could have arisen as a relatively detached idea. General rights like life, liberty and freedom of speech are derived from the idea of human equality. The idea that all human beings are equal is a correlate of the equalisation of 'human labour in general' as the source and measure of value; and, conversely, the notion of human equality had to acquire the 'fixity of a popular prejudice' before the real nature of value could be properly appreciated.

The co-operative production of the values sustaining human life is what is distinctive about the human species. Consumption which enables the individual to stay alive is shared by all forms of life. That is why Marx, whether explaining the nature of capitalism or the meaning of normative words like 'right', says: Do not start from consumption and expect to understand production. Start from production - production in the different historical modes through which it has developed, production in its class antagonistic form for each mode.

Rights represent claims on other people, one form of which is a claim to goods. Whenever we say that it is right to do this or that, we are recognising the legitimacy of some claim on us. 'It is right to help a friend in need' implies a respect for the claim that person has on us by virtue of that relationship. 'It is right to return a lost article to its owner' implies a respect for that person's claim to possession. This respect for claims, this respect for their legitimacy is our acknowledgement of the element of morality in the concept of 'right' by which every admitted claim involves certain things it is right for people to do, not excluding ourselves. Expressions like 'might is right' or 'possession is nine tenths of the law' describe a situation in which the idea of respect for claims is missing. Mere descriptions of what people do cannot be generalised into what they ought to do; and in themselves they invest the concept 'right' with no ethical significance.

RIGHTS AS CLAIMS ON OTHER PEOPLE

Recognised claims on others are based on certain social relationships linking people together in a particular type of society. There are considerations which children owe to parents and parents to children which must be taken into account in assessing the actions they respectively perform; the marriage tie and the bond of friendship carry with them the idea of mutual claims whose recognition is the real meaning of such relations; and membership of any community involves a whole complex of reciprocal rights.

If these relationships were eternal and unchanging, the concept of 'right' as deduced from them would have the universal quality sometimes ascribed to it. In fact, looked at historically or, for that matter, geographically, such relationships are seen to vary considerably at different times and places. Even the family relationships of mating and rearing children can hardly be the same in patriarchal as in matriarchal communities which owe their difference originally to whether the provision of food is predominantly a wide-ranging pursuit like hunting or keeping cattle or a more home-based activity like primitive agriculture. The bonds of friendship which in a feudal context can involve loyalty unto death may only imply a special concern for promise-keeping in a contractual society like ours. Robbery under certain circumstances, like 'lifting' another tribe's cattle, may be considered a social duty while in another type of society it is a capital crime to steal a loaf of bread to feed one's starving children. And, according to the same legal code, gambling on the street for pennies may be an indictable offence while gambling in commodities for millions is highly respectable. And the whole range of social relationships may be quite rapidly transformed by the changes in circumstances which accompany a change in class relations like the English Revolution which paved the way for the development of modern Britain.

Since generally conceded claims depend on social relationships and since these relationships are determined by the material conditions of life in various societies, 'rights' as what people are entitled to expect from each other are ultimately grounded on the economic base which supports this or that form of social organisation. We cannot say that there is some essential and unchanging meaning of 'rightness' which is unaffected by the material considerations of any particular society. That would be to make all particular expressions in any concrete circumstances of this completely idealised 'rightness' somehow irrelevant to it. It simply does not make ethical sense to say: 'You must do right, but nothing you do will ever be right in any real sense.' In fact, if 'right' had no specific content, non-ethical considerations like 'might is right', would inevitably fill the vacuum.

It might be thought that family relationships which are bound up with the reproduction of human beings common to all society would be distinguishable from those relationships which are involved in the production of goods for human use. Actually, variations in the forms of inheritance and the status of women, to say nothing of the conditions of family life in conditions of slavery, show that family relationships are to some extent, at least, a special instance of the general quality of social intercourse which echoes a particular mode of production.

From our original thesis that the social existence of people determines their consciousness, we can deduce the fact that religious and philosophical ideas also reflect the basic economic structure of society; and social relationships and the rights implicit in them are then accounted for in terms of these ideas. This ideological supervention can obscure the connection between such relationships and the material conditions of life which gave rise to them. As Marx puts it in *The German Ideology*:

> Men are the producers of their conceptions, ideas (expressed in the language of politics, laws, morality, religion, metaphysics of a people) - real, active men, as they are conditioned by a definite development of their productive forces and of the intercourse corresponding to these, up to its furthest forms. Consciousness can never be anything else than conscious existence of men in their actual life process...

As soon as this active life-process is described, history ceases to be a collection of dead facts as it is with the empiricists (facts themselves still abstract), or an imagined activity of imagined subjects, as with the idealists.[1]

In our historical studies we often see the influence of economic considerations on the conduct of some social group when its members were quite unaware of it at the time. To the question 'Why is it right to bear arms in the service of my lord?' a vassal in the Middle Ages would have answered: 'Because God commands me to honour and obey my liege'. We realise, of course, that such service was inherent in a social organisation based on a particular system of land tenure when land was the only form of wealth - though we may not always realise that the same applies to our explanations of our own actions.

These social relationships usually reveal their economic origin by finding their most practical expression in some form of the disposition of property - rights of inheritance, succession to titles and so forth. Rules of conduct in different societies are much concerned with such questions as what recompense in goods a man can expect for some injury or what rights a man has in the possessions of relatives or how a man must set about acquiring a wife where women themselves are regarded as property. An analysis of property can therefore help us to appreciate the derivation and meaning of the concept of 'right'.

An understanding of the way different modes of production and different class perspectives within each mode are reflected in different ideas about the rights people have or believe they ought to have does not and should not lead to the ultra relativism of the post-modernists. Since active human beings, conditioned by the state of development of their productive forces, are also the producers of their concepts and ideas, as those forces develop progressively, there will be an interconnected progressive development of their concepts and ideas of politics and morality.

RIGHTS AS CLAIMS TO THINGS

We have seen how the concept of 'value' arises in connection with the production of goods for human use. The concept of 'right', in so far as it is grounded in a respect for other people's proprietary interests, arises in connection with the distribution of those goods. All value is the result of the expenditure of human effort. That effort, at the same time that it creates valuable things or goods, also establishes rights in them. As Locke puts it:

> Whatever a man removes from the state of nature and mixes his labour with, thus joining it to something that is his own, thereby becomes his property'.[2]

This simple formula seems obvious enough in the case of individuals working on their own to satisfy their personal needs and those of their family. It could be extended to cover a self-sufficient tribal group which provides for the immediate wants of its members on a communal basis by directly-associated labour. But in such cases there is no problem about the ownership of property and therefore the question of 'rights' in the abstract could hardly arise. It is only at a socially advanced stage of the division of labour that property rights become a distinguishable aspect of human relationships, since, as Marx explains:

> The various stages of development in the division of labour are just so many different forms of property; and the stage reached in the division of labour also determines the relations of individuals to one another with respect to the materials, instruments and

products of labour.[3]

The attempt to find some development in the material conditions of life which could account for the precipitation of the idea of property rights as a relatively detached abstraction leads us to consider that stage in the division of labour when there are the beginnings of a market economy.

The law of value only makes its appearance as a distinguishable relationship when the separation between production and consumption has been confirmed in commodity exchange. Similarly, the concept of 'right' as a recognised claim to the possession of things only takes the form of an abstract principle when all property has begun to assume the character of commodities. As we have already noted, prior to the development of commodity production, rights in things can be defined in terms of obvious social relationships, like those among members of a family or tribe or, even, between masters and slaves or lords and serfs. The customary rules regulating the disposition of property within social organisations in which relations of production are recognisably human relations are quite simple and transparent as compared with the distribution of goods in the complex market economy which attains its fullest development under capitalism. Such pre-commodity rules cannot themselves give rise to an abstract bourgeois conception of 'right' as an eternal principle obtaining at all times and places because those rules are too closely tied to specific human relationships in societies still founded upon 'the immature development of man individually, who has not yet severed the umbilical cord that unites him with his fellow man in a primitive tribal community or upon direct relations of subjection'.[4]

But once the domination of one class of people by another ceases to appear as naked subjection and becomes the law of private property by which the position of the dominant class is established through ownership of the means of production, once the transaction between the hirer and the provider of labour-power takes a purely economic form as a commodity deal, there is a change from possession of things dominated by human relationships to human relationships dominated by possession of things or goods; and 'right' itself, losing its exclusive reference to claims between people, becomes more and more objectified as a stake in commodities. The Commodity has become the golden calf to which all must bow down. Just as relations between producers mutually engaged in creative work take the form of an equivalence between goods themselves, so other social relationships express themselves through rights to goods - from the international speculator who exerts a completely careless and arbitrary control over the lives of millions through his control of things to the ordinary house-holder who once a year sums up all his close relationships by the relative price of the gift he estimates each is worth.

In the early stages of commodity exchange, when direct human relationships reflecting the material conditions of simpler types of society are in the process of being transformed into functions of a market economy, rules of conduct may still be borrowed from previous forms of social organisation to regulate trading operations. Hybrid notions like the 'just price' or arbitrary injunctions against usury or profiteering are characteristic of this phase of social development. But once commodity production has attained its fullest growth and exchange relationships have extended into every sphere of society, the economic system appears to be self-regulating and to require no correction nor guidance from normative principles formulated in pre-commodity terms. Instead of invoking ideas of human relations derived from membership in earlier societies as a check on market deals, those very relations are conceived solely on the basis of people's encounters with each other in the market place as buyers or sellers of goods and as buyers or sellers of the capacity to produce goods.

This freeing of the concept of 'right' from any immediate reference to interpersonal ties to re-appear as proprietary relationships to things makes it sufficiently abstract to be codified in civil laws which seem to have an impartial universality for whole societies and even for human beings in general. When such legalised rights come into conflict with rights which are still bound up with more direct relationships, as when mother and son go to court over a will, husband and wife fall out over the question of their joint property or a person sues a friend for non-payment of debt, the human quality of the relationship is utterly irrelevant to what is regarded as a purely contractual problem.

Since sellers of labour-power and owners of the means of production are assumed to meet freely in the market place to strike a bargain whose terms are largely determined by an impersonal law of value, the agreement between them can be generalised abstractly as exemplifying one of the basic rights of humanity, the prerogative of all members of society to exchange their goods or their capacity for producing them on an equitable footing. The very translation of human bonds into terms of that commodity of commodities, money, so that no one need acknowledge any other master, can seem, by comparison with various forms of direct subjugation, to be a kind of individual liberation, like slaves buying their own freedom - as long as we do not look at the real social relations behind the veil of commodity deals.

In much the same way as low wages paid to workers can be 'justified' as the result of 'impersonal' considerations like supply and demand in the labour market so, as we have remarked before, the consistent exploitation of primary producing countries by highly industrialised capitalist countries which dominate world markets can be made to appear as a 'natural' movement in commodity prices with no evident human intervention.

As we have seen, the idea that all human beings are equal is itself a correlate of the equalisation of 'human labour in general' as the source and measure of value. To the extent that the legal expression of property rights and freedom of contract can be universalised for all commodity-producing societies, they come to be regarded as natural law, inevitable rules of human intercourse inherent in the nature of things and therefore beyond the reach of criticism or objection. Just as the law of value appears to be a providential arrangement whereby economic order is maintained in spite of the anarchic actions of individual producers and traders, so legalised property rights seem to be the practical expression of a purely abstract justice. In the guise of eternal principles of equity which ought to be respected at all times and places these property rights are invoked as the ultimate justification of existing social relations instead of being recognised simply as the consequence of those social relations being given a spurious universality through the mediation of omnipresent commodities.

But if the actions and attitudes of people in a commodity-exchanging society are to be regarded as an expression of abstract ethical principles, it is necessary to account for the fact that so many of them come to the market with nothing to exchange but their labour-power while a few enjoy a commanding position through their control of the only means by which that labour-power can be employed. The search for a moral starting point for the supposedly self-regulating system of a market economy leads to a mythical interpretation of primitive accumulation. It is assumed that in the past 'there were two sorts of people; one, the diligent, intelligent and above all, frugal elite; the other, lazy rascals, spending their substance and more, in riotous living'.[5]

Marx goes on to compare 'the legend of theological original sin' by which 'man came to be condemned to eat his bread in the sweat of his brow' with 'the history of economic original sin which reveals to us that there are people to whom this is by no means essential'! Such an economic fiction by which the primitive accumulation of capital is invested with virtue serves to conceal the naked forms of exploitation - the ruthless creation of a working class at home by stripping people of every possession and the violent conquest and looting of peoples abroad which, together, laid the foundations for capitalism. This myth serves to justify contemporary capitalists in their wealth and privileges as the notion of Karma enables comfortably-off to regard citizens their good fortune as the result of virtuous actions performed in a previous life.

From this idea of personal thriftiness as the origin of working capital is derived the notion that the continuing abstemiousness of those who control the means of production accounts for any unconsumed product on which further expansion of the economy depends rather than on the amount of unpaid-for labour extracted from workers as surplus value. Such a notion relies on the extremely dubious thesis that those who dominate society through their ownership of property are remarkable for their frugality and the totally unwarranted proposition that abstention itself is value-creative. As the law of value formulates the relationship between people as producers and people as consumers, the law of property which establishes rights in any surplus and unconsumed product expresses the relationship between people as owners of the means of production and people as owners of nothing but their capacity to work.

The concealment of exploitation behind the transactions of the market place in bourgeois society having given rise to generalised 'rights' which appear to apply with the same indiscriminate impartiality as the price of bread, those generalised 'rights' can then be used in providing the justification for the system in spite of the fact that for the working class they have become to some extent bogus rights. What freedom of speech mainly means is that anyone whosoever, be he a coal miner or a wealthy city financier, who has some millions of pounds at his disposal and credit facilities to raise as much again is completely at liberty to launch a newspaper. Similarly, any charwoman or dustman has the right to pursue a case of injustice committed by the most powerful corporation in the land right up to the highest court - if he or she also happens to be in a position to meet legal costs of some tens of thousand pounds. The even-handedness of such rights often takes the form that it is completely open to rich and poor alike to sell matches on the street corner or sleep rough under a bridge.

Such bogus 'rights' whose negotiability depends on an unstated membership of a privileged class, can be compared with the equally seeming impartiality of the law of supply and demand; but quite apart from the many ways in which monopolists can bend the law, only effective demands really count. People with demands like, for example, enough to eat or a roof over their heads which they cannot afford to pay for do not even enter into calculations about the amount of production required to fulfil society's needs.

Rights precipitated out of property relations are inevitably illusory for the propertyless; and, by and large, all workers in even the most advanced industrial societies are never more than five or six months away from a poverty-stricken propertylessness. That is why to the working class, 'law and morality' have become just so many 'bourgeois prejudices' which must be reclaimed as the principles governing the collective behaviour of the far more numerous working people rather than that of the relatively small minority exploiting them.

Owning nothing of the huge industrial machine that produces goods for modern society except their capacity to work it, the only right it has been possible for the working class to assert against bourgeois right is the right to withdraw one's labour and to organise with fellow workers for this purpose. This right had to be established in the teeth of ruling class opposition. Once it had been established, the ruling bourgeoisie took it over and tried to incorporate it among their own list of bogus rights. The 'right to strike' became one of the boasted liberties of the so-called 'free world'; but there has never yet been an actual strike in any capitalist country which was not either at the wrong time, the wrong place or called for the wrong reason; and whenever capitalism has found its profits in decline the attempt has immediately been made to render the strike weapon ineffectual by restrictive legislation.

The very principle of trade unionism, a merging of the self-interest of workers in a collective defence of their general interest against their exploitation by self-interested employers, runs counter to the whole selfish individualistic ethos of capitalism and for this reason is bound to provoke unending opposition in one form or another. This opposition grows out of the fundamental contradiction between the socialist collective attitudes of workers based on their co-operative relations in production and the liberal individualist attitudes of factory owners and employers based on their private ownership of the means of production and their appropriation of surplus value for the purpose of selfish consumption.

That is not to suggest that workers are not consumers or that owners and employers are not involved in any co-operative activity: only that producer collectives and consumer individualism are the predominant features of the experience of material conditions experienced by the working class and by the capitalist class and, therefore, most influential in shaping their respective ethical ideas.

COMMODITY PRODUCTION AND ETHICAL INTERPRETATIONS OF RIGHT

We have seen how an analysis of commodities yields two distinct meanings for a value word like 'good' - a descriptive sense which refers to an object's usefulness and a prescriptive sense which honours the human labour incorporated in it. This analysis also reveals a discrepancy between the value of the social product which human labour has created and the value of the goods actually enjoyed by those who produced them which equals the difference between the total of what labour has made and the total labour-value paid for. This surplus-value which, in fact, represents the saving of the working community is appropriated as the private property of those controlling the means of production. Profit is simply unpaid labour.

We have further seen how rights as claims to goods are derived from social relationships as determined by the material conditions of life in a particular economic ordering of society. As these relationships are 'dehumanised' by commodity exchange and transformed into relations between goods, there is a tendency for claims on other people to take the form of legalised rights in goods. The social fact of surplus value no longer appears as the exploitation of one class by another but as the 'rational' consequence of the laws of property.

This rationalisation could only have arisen in the course of development of a system of production in which human effort is not immediately directed to the satisfaction of wants but to the creation of value in the form of marketable goods. The division of labour which is the prior condition for such a development is also, as Marx points out, the institution of private property: 'in the one the same thing is affirmed with reference to activity as is affirmed in the other with reference to the product of activity'.[6]

Over the whole period of commodity exchange, which may be conveniently dated from the first appearance of a recognised currency in circulation to its fullest development under capitalism, the split between the production of value and the consumption of goods, the appropriation of value as 'legalised' exploitation and attempts to justify such exploitation have all profoundly influenced people's ethical attitudes toward their actions.

From the time when craftspeople made articles not for their own use but to barter for other things, they had begun, in a sense, to divide themselves into two beings. A person as maker and a person as enjoyer had become distinguishable within each individual person and there was a tendency for them to pull in opposite directions. The gap between purposeful effort and its due reward had the effect of driving apart reason which looked ahead to future satisfaction and feelings which made their demands in the present. This potential split in each person's integrity was inevitably deepened as the sundered functions of useful work and desirable gratifications became more and more identified with distinct classes - those who, on the whole, laboured without enjoyment and those who enjoyed without working. The same kind of socio-economic schizophrenia which characterised individuals in commodity-producing societies affected the entire community. There was a division between the collective responsibilities of production and the individual indulgences of consumption. The distinction between duty and pleasure which was to be such a marked feature of ethical thinking can therefore be seen as a reflection on the moral plane of both the split personality of the individual and the irreconcilability of class interests.

The ideological consequences of this distinction can be traced in the extreme positions various philosophers have taken on the issue of whether duty or pleasure is the ultimate motivating force in human conduct - from the opposite views of the Socratic and Cyrenaic Schools or of Stoicism and Epicureanism or, later, of Kant and Hume right down to similar oppositions in our own times.

In Kantian morality the division between reason and duty on the one hand and feeling and pleasure on the other takes so final a form that they inhabit entirely different worlds. The rightness of an act is considered to be vitiated by any motivation which does not stem directly from a purely rational regard for completely universalised maxims of behaviour; and this regard must never be confused with personal emotions of any kind - not even the most altruistic feelings of benevolence. Kantian morality is what the bourgeoisie would like the working class to be governed by.

At the opposite extreme are those thorough-going hedonists like Hobbes who argue that no actions are disinterested and that the pursuit of pleasure and avoidance of pain provide the sole impulse to all conduct. Reason is held to play a secondary role in merely suggesting how this overriding epicurean purpose may best be served. Hobbesian morality is what the bourgeoisie see in themselves. While utilitarians like Bentham and Mill subscribe to a similar pleasure-pain view of people's nature, they do not altogether deny themselves the language of duty when they attempt to move from this postulated fact of egoistic hedonism to the advocacy of acting for the greatest happiness of the greatest number. This transition from descriptive statements to normative or evaluative judgments is, as we have seen, illegitimate; but the naturalistic fallacy is an illogical expression of the perfectly reasonable belief that there should be some connection between what it is in a person's interest to do and what it is right to do.

The dissociation of a self-interested concern with pleasure from a dutiful respect for the claims of others in regard to human actions, like the distinction between utility and value in regard to goods, is ultimately rooted in the separation of consumption from production which originates in the division of labour. The division of labour is also the division of private from social property which gives rise to the realisation of individuality, of egoistic as opposed to group interests. Possession of desirable objects belonging exclusively to individuals of a particular class emphasises their selfish nature as consumers.

At that stage of the division of labour when relationships between people have been largely transformed into exchange relationships; and the rules of human conduct increasingly take the form of the economic laws of a supposedly self-regulating social system, the idea of 'right' may practically disappear from the language philosophers use to account for behaviour. They may speak of actions purely in terms of self-interest as when Adam Smith, both moral philosopher and political economist, speaks unambiguously of men acting not from benevolence 'but from their regard to their own interest' and counsels us to address ourselves 'not to their humanity but to their self-love'. Many other philosophers and psychologists thus come to look upon people as simply moved by mechanical responses of pleasure-seeking, pain-avoidance, like a human machine for which moral considerations are quite irrelevant and, also, unnecessary since individual desires all freely competing with each other cancel out in the general satisfaction of all anyway.

However we have seen what Marx has to say of the supposedly self-regulating character of a system based on self-interest in his remarks about the strenuous resistance of factory owners to those clauses in the Factory Acts which would require them to spend a little money on protecting the limbs of their workpeople. Indeed he speaks of the very attempt to expose the true nature of such a 'self-regulatory system' as 'summoning foes into battle the most violent, mean and malignant passions of the human breast, the furies of private interest.'

Still other philosophers, aware that the functioning of the economic system is only apparently automatic and that the production and distribution of goods reflect a bargain struck between capitalists and workers, feel the need to speak in two voices to classes with opposed interests and include contradictory elements in what is essentially a utilitarian account of ethics. Promise-keeping is vital to a contractual society like our own. The crucial relationship in an exchange economy is the purchase of labour-power; and the contract between capitalist and worker requires a moral sanction over and above mere market fluctuations. A writer on ethics like W. David Ross, mainly utilitarian in outlook, makes a special place in his theory for a deontological treatment of the obligation to abide by contracts. The idea of a 'free' contract between employer and employee as the justification of economic relationships may be compared with the idea of a 'free' social contract as underlying the relationship between political ruler and subjects. Of course this general attitude toward contractual agreements does not leave unaffected other social relationships even those of the family, like marriage.

Over the whole period of commodity exchange we find that philosophers can be grouped according to whether they emphasise self-interest or respect for the claims of others, hedonism or a sense of duty as the key to understanding human actions. But which of these two general attitudes toward morality may be chosen is neither an accident nor a matter of personal preference.

Moralists who identify themselves with a class which has enjoyed power and is threatened from below have an understandable tendency to stress duty and obedience as of primary ethical significance, particularly for the inferior classes; and their naturally conservative attitude makes them firmly resist change which they describe as illusory anyway, referring all expectations of happier circumstances to some ideal existence other than this present life. Pie in the sky. Moralists associated with a rising class have as natural a tendency to stress the satisfactions which will accrue to all once that new class is firmly in a position of control. The very struggle for ascendancy gives a practical materialist cast to their thought and the likelihood of a better ordering of society makes them the friends of change.

On the other hand, a decadent ruling class may adopt for itself an eat, drink and be merry philosophy of lavish hedonism. Apres moi le deluge. While a new bourgeois class in the period of primitive accumulation may express a propensity to save presently for future rewards in attitudes of extreme puritanism.

The distinction between an appeal to the principle of happiness in this world or to duty sanctioned by other-worldly considerations is thus closely bound up with the social movements of a particular time. There is no doubt that there has been relative progress in the succession of different modes of production.

'Every new class achieves it hegemony only on a broader basis than that of the class ruling previously.'[7] But the only final resolution of this constant counterposition of duty and pleasure would be a more comprehensive morality associated with a social movement holding within it the possibility of transcending commodity production and its divisive effect on our being and thinking - production geared to the needs of all instead of to the profits of the few. Marx describes it thus:

> The labour of the individual is taken from the start as social labour. Therefore whatever the specific material form of the product which he creates or helps to create may be, that which he has bought with his labour is not a special specific product, but a specific share of the communal production. For this reason he has no special

product that he has to exchange. His product is not an exchange value. The product does not have to be translated into a specific character form in order to acquire a universal character for the individual. Instead of a division of labour, necessarily ending in the exchange of exchange value, we would have an organisation of labour, which results in the participation of the individual in communal consumption.[8]

Or, in ethical terms, communist morality is not based simply on the availability of plenty, but also on the conditions of human dignity and freedom in which that plenty is produced by conscious self-expressive labour.

Of course it is not to be thought that the kind of explanation we have been considering for the adoption of this ethical attitude or that is consciously part of anyone's motivation. Apologists for a particular class may quite genuinely think they are speaking for society as a whole without qualification as to time or place - indeed, their usefulness as ideologues very likely depends on their thinking it. And even when they are aware of some class allegiance, they may, with the best will in the world, be as unreliable a guide to the real rather than the professed interests of that class as individuals often are in prescribing for their own ailments.

The very development of an individualistic outlook bound up with the institution of private property and achieving its extreme expression in bourgeois society cannot but obscure for those individuals the fundamental role of classes. Property is like a wall people erect between themselves and society until they can think of themselves as completely independent; and yet property itself is a social product and merely confirms their social being - but in a lifeless, estranged and distorted form.

The unselfconscious and spontaneous social being of primitive communism prior to the formation of classes, recalled in all legends of a golden age when people's hands were not raised against each other, is disrupted by the self-regarding, self-interested egoism born of the bourgeois revolution which develops into capitalism's extreme competitive individualism finally shattering social peace. Milton, writing at a crucial revolutionary stage of this development, could not but create the epic of bourgeois man. Satan's rebellion is a poetic evocation of middle-class revolt in the name of individual liberty against the hierarchical structure of feudalism. England transformed by the metallurgical industries is the hell he would rather rule in than serve in heaven. The departmentalism among his daemon henchmen reflects the specialisation in a society where the division of labour breaks down all communal effort. There is also colonialism, the vicious exploitation of the primitive communist society of Eden by the introduction among its innocent natives of sin and death in the course of their subjugation to Satanic imperialism. Indeed the whole history of capitalism is to be found in this magnificent poetical work from the progressive phase of the Civil War through its period of world-wide ascendancy and, afterwards, through its subsequent degeneration right down to the hissing, insinuating beastliness we see all too much of in the world around us today.

SOCIOLOGY OF KNOWLEDGE AND MARXIST ANALYSIS

General reflections on the relationship between the ethical views of philosophers and their class positions in the social conflicts of the time have enjoyed a certain vogue in academic circles as studies in the 'sociology of knowledge'; but these sociologists seldom realise that their own class position is affecting any conclusions they draw from such a study. It is, usually, an example of borrowing Marxist tools for a particular branch of social science instead of adopting a Marxist view of society as a whole for the purpose of changing it.

Let us make a little clearer this question of the way what appear to be the most abstract philosophical ideas are not only rooted in the social movements of a particular time and place but are also inextricably bound up with class contradictions. Let us consider two thinkers, Plato and Aristotle, contemporary with each other and living and teaching in the same city, in order to understand better why they should differ with each other so fundamentally on moral issues and why, with such varying relative influence down the intervening centuries, they should still have something to say to us today. Let us do this not as an academic exercise but as a way of getting to know our own society better because only in understanding our own society better can we hope to change it.

Athens in the fourth century B.C. was the scene of considerable social ferment; and this was reflected in the speeches and prose writings of the time as it had already been poetically expressed several generations before in the works of the great dramatists. Plato leaves us in no doubt that; in the welter of sectional interests, he speaks for a landed aristocracy whose rule had been challenged by a rising class of merchants and their political allies. His remedy for this subversion of a traditional order, as set forth in 'The Laws' and 'The Republic', is to freeze into a static caste system the division of labour on which a civilised society must be founded and to prevent any social mobility by the strictest control on trade and the severest penalties for amassing wealth beyond one's station. The caste system envisaged is as much like that successfully established in India as neo-Platonic thought is like Indian idealistic philosophy.

Because the social movement of the period was unfavourable to the interests of the class he belonged to, the same class his teacher, Socrates, would have liked to be identified with, Plato wanted society to turn back to a pre-mercantile stage. His ideal state is, in fact, an imaginative reconstruction of the past but with this major difference from the real past: it has been carefully restructured in such a way that this time it will not generate the unsatisfactory present. In this imaginary Platonic state land is allocated to a certain number of founding families whose rights to it are secured by a political settlement strengthened by religious sanctions. The land is worked by slaves who also perform all household chores. What little trade is permitted in this enclosed natural economy is in the hands of foreigners whose corruption by commerce is a matter of no concern. Their activities are under the strict control of market commissioners whose regulations are drafted in the interest of consumers - the founding families of course.

From this ideal state are to be excluded all who might prove in any way disturbing to its stability - poets, not because a man of Plato's sensibility lacked a taste for the arts but because poetry in the hands of dramatists like Aeschylus or, worse, Euripides had extolled the more democratic institutions of Athens or had questioned traditional beliefs; Ionian scientists, because they also cast doubt on the superstitions required to prop up this rigid social system and because the very growth of physical knowledge was closely associated with the expansion of trade which Plato deplored; and sophists, because as the teachers of the Athenian middle class they put at the disposal of free citizens generally, in exchange for a fee, the sort of education in philosophy and rhetoric which had been the prerogative of noble youths. What made the sophists particularly objectionable from Plato's point of view was their criticism of the conventional discrimination between Hellenes and barbarians, noblemen and commoners, free men and slaves on the grounds that such distinctions were not based on natural differences but on man-made rules.

With all menial work performed by slaves and all trade in the hands of a closely-supervised foreign community, the free-born citizens of the Republic have no occupation but purifying their own souls and keeping inferior persons to their proper tasks. This is not expressed as a privilege but a duty; and if any free citizens should stray from the pursuit of abstract goodness into some trade or craft, the urban commissioners are required to correct them by reproach and degradation until they be brought back into the right course. The institution of slavery on which this whole strictly-stratified society rests is justified on the basis of the natural inferiority of those who are forced to do all the work.

And why do you think that mechanical work and work with one's hands are matters of reproach? Is it not because in some people the element of the best is naturally weak and unable to rule the monsters within them?...

Well, then, is it not in order...that we say they must be the slaves of that best man in whom the divine dwells?[9]

This is the moral version of the argument which has been used countless times: 'Because these people are inferior let them work at some back-breaking task'. And how is it known that they are inferior? 'Because they work at back-breaking tasks.'

Since labour is the function of contemptible beings who deserve their slave status, we would hardly expect Plato to accord its products any value. And the goods produced by such unworthy means are not, in fact, to be highly regarded. 'Which class of things do you think has the greater participation in pure being, the class containing bread and drink and meat and food generally, or the class containing true belief and knowledge and mind and, in short, all virtue?'[10] This contempt for the material goods provided by servile effort leads to a certain strain of asceticism in Plato's thought; but just as true belief cannot of itself sustain life, so virtue is not simply its own reward. What is given away with one hand in an act of disdainful renunciation is hastily grabbed back again with the other. 'Can there now be any harm in our going further and restoring to justice and the rest of virtue the rewards... which it renders to the soul at the hands of gods and men, both in a man's lifetime and after he is dead?'[11]

It is on the basis of these socially determined prejudices of Plato's that we begin to account for his ethical ideas and even his metaphysical convictions. The attempt to use the ideal not to shape reality but to replace it is usually a sign of class frustration - like the daydreams in which individuals may indulge when the normal outlets for their ambitions are checked. The flowering of idealistic system-building in nineteenth-century Germany was partly the ideological reflex of a thwarted bourgeoisie, cheated by the absence of any bourgeois revolution of playing their proper role in the development of capitalism. So reality's progressive rejection of the class Plato belonged to meant that reality itself must be rejected.

To this must be added the natural tendency of a leisured class to see the normal sequence of events in the productive process in the reverse order. Instead of satisfactions being necessarily preceded by an expenditure of effort involving direct contact with the physical environment, the desire itself is sufficient to command the results of the labour of others. This makes it appear that the idea of the required object actually determined its existence. Furthermore, as Plato shows so clearly, the class contempt for those who do the work of society gets transferred in a sense to the very things they make. Ignorant shepherds, weavers and street-traders may have made a white cloak available in the market place; but such a cloak will become soiled in time and wear out. Only someone of superior intellect can abstract from it the pure idea of whiteness, eternal and changeless, residing in a world beyond the reach of those ordinary senses which one unhappily shares with rude mechanics and merchants. It is not actual goods which have worth but the ideal conception of their goodness - just as though the mental effort of conceptualisation could be substituted for the sweat and toil of creative labour as the true measure of value.

Of course, the freeing of concepts from their immediate circumstances is a necessary condition for logical thought which, as we have noted, is one part of the process of knowledge. The division between mental and manual labour provides a social background favouring the development of abstract thought as a correlate to the pure value form commodities take under the interdiction of use; but the rupture between theory and practice which can result from this same division of labour leads to conceptual thought becoming so cut off from the actual world in which it originates and to which it must return for verification that it assumes a fantastic and arbitrary independence. It is the prolongation of this arrested moment in the acquisition of true knowledge, as though commodities should be frozen forever in their value form and never consumed, the indefinite extension of this moment when concepts are 'free' of the restraints imposed by reality, which makes it seem plausible to deduce nature from the idea instead of the normal way about. These same freely floating concepts, detached from the real world, are the source from which idealistic ethics derives its notion of a limitless but essentially meaningless moral liberty.

The most obvious difficulty with Plato's ascription of value to universal ideas simply by virtue of their purity and immutability is that evil and pain are just as much universal ideas as goodness; filthiness is as abstract and changeless a concept as whiteness. Such a point can only be overlooked by a member of a class enjoying a sheltered existence in which filth, hunger and pain are far less prominent than cleanliness, satiety and health.

This postulating of the Idea of Good as the supreme value from which all other values are derived is one of the aspects of Platonic philosophy which Aristotle most severely criticised. Since such hypostatised 'goodness' cannot be brought into being by human effort, it must remain irrelevant to people's practical aspirations; and it is with just such practical interests that Aristotle is primarily concerned.

Though he was much influenced by Platonism during the years he studied at the Academy, yet, as the son of a physician at the Macedonian court, his social background was different from that of his aristocratic tutor. In his youth he must have learned something of the Hippocratic science and throughout his life his writings reflect a practical turn of mind and an unfailing curiosity about the objective world.

His concern with human activity prompts him to remark: 'All people value most what has cost them much labour in the production; for Instance, people who have themselves made their money are fonder of it than those who have inherited it'.[12] This is at least a step in the direction of recognising human effort as the source of value. His interest in the real problems of contemporary Athenian society keeps his 'Politics' practical rather than utopian. It is in this book that he makes a lasting contribution to the study of economics when he explains that: 'The uses of every possession are two, both dependent on the thing itself, but not in the same manner, the one supposing an inseparable connection with it, the other not; as a shoe, for instance, which may be either worn or exchanged for something else.'[13]

This is perhaps the earliest recognition of that distinction between utility and exchange value which has not only remained valid for economic thought right up to the present day but has also profoundly influenced our ideas about ethics. In his theory of money as the measure of value in exchange Aristotle realises that the problem of economic value is a question of equivalence, even if he is unable to press his analysis to the point of saying exactly what value is. As Marx observes:

> There was an important fact which prevented Aristotle from seeing that, to attribute value to commodities, is merely a mode of expressing all labour as equal human labour and consequently as labour of equal quality. Greek society was founded upon slavery, and had, therefore, for its natural basis, the inequality of men and of their labour-powers.[14]

The importance of the issue of slavery for any philosopher living at that particular time is shown by the fact that Aristotle devotes a large part of the very first book of the 'Politics' to its justification - as if no state could conceivably exist until this foundation for it had been firmly established. He takes a middle course between the Platonic view that the authority of the slave-owner is derived from his superior virtue and the Sophist view that not nature but a human product, law, makes one person free and another a slave. Aristotle argues that some people are, in fact, slaves by nature and it is only fitting that they should live in abject subjugation; but their ranks ought not to include those captured in an unjust war and certainly not fellow Hellenes!

This middle position on the question of slavery is not unconnected with his attitude toward the Athenian middle or professional class with whom he identified himself. His prescription for a happy community is one in which the citizens of middle station preponderate and have in their hands the reins of government. From this idea of certain people holding the balance in a properly-ordered society between extremes of wealth or poverty Aristotle draws his definition of virtue.

> It is a middle state between two faulty ones, in the way of excess on one side and defect on the other; and it is so moreover, because the faulty states on one side fall short of, and those on the other exceed, what is right, both in the case of the feelings and the actions; but virtue finds, and found adopts, the mean.[15]

In a society rent by class divisions, with the continuous threat of further civil strife, philosophers, particularly if their own class enjoys a temporary ascendancy, are very likely to stress the virtue of measure, an abatement of the war of opposites, as a remedy for social ills and, therefore, as the basis of ethics. The idea of 'measure' would have been precipitated anyway as an abstract concept by the commodity exchange of an early mercantile society in which the measuring out of goods according to their incorporated value would be a daily experience.

But 'measure' means something quite different to Plato and to Aristotle. For Plato identifying himself with a class already superseded is not something which exists on earth in any actual society. It is the harmony which would exist if people of various classes had been perdurably fixed in them and could never even think of moving from one to another, so that the music of the spheres would be the heavenly echo of a social order on earth in which people faithfully kept through the ages to the circle divinely assigned to them. Rightness is thus conceived in terms of the purely abstract and intellectually satisfying demonstrations of geometry, and logic is so idealistic that its perfect essence must never be besmirched by practical application to sordid reality.

For Aristotle this same 'measure' is the mean between extremes as realised in an actual community of people, a middle class which holds the balance in the opposition of those classes at either end of the social scale. Aristotle rejects the Platonic harmony as a mere abstraction, something over and above society which cannot be brought within the range of practical interests.

> (Plato) says that the legislator ought to make all the citizens happy; but it is impossible that the whole city can be happy, without all, or the greater, or some part of it be happy. For happiness is not like that numerical equality which arises from certain numbers when added together, although neither of them may separately contain it; for happiness cannot be thus added together, but must exist in every individual, as some properties belong to every integral; and if the military (in Plato's ideal Republic) are not happy, who else are so? for the artisans are not, nor the multitude of those who are employed in inferior offices.[16]

Plato wants to freeze society as, in his imagination, it used to be. Aristotle, identifying himself with a class that has arrived, in the sense of enjoying a preponderating influence and of temporarily holding the balance between extremes of wealth and poverty, wants to freeze society as it actually is. Both philosophers are opposed to social change and development; but Plato's changelessness is otherworldly, an abstract realm of idealised forms transcending reality and only accessible to mind, while Aristotle's acceptance of society as it is, with its actual social classes co-existing as separate compartments in a fixed relationship, can be associated with his 'pigeon-hole' logic - a logic suited to classifying things and assigning them to their proper places but incapable of dealing with motion, change and process without generating philosophical puzzles and anomalies.

In their respective attitudes toward right conduct these two philosophers lend support to a suggestion made before that, on the whole, a thinker who defends a threatened social order or one in the process of being overthrown tends to invoke duty sanctioned by considerations external to society as the standard of ethical conduct, while a thinker whose interests lie with an established or rising class tends to appeal to the utilitarian principle of happiness in this world as a sufficient explanation of behaviour. In spite of their contemporaneity and close association in the same Athenian school, Plato and Aristotle give quite different accounts of normative judgments. Plato would argue that such judgments borrow their validity from an ideal world of pure concepts which our exile in this imperfect world of the senses, dimly reflecting that ideal 'reality', does not altogether keep us from knowing and certainly does not relieve us of obedience to its injunctions. Aristotle would find the justification of these *judgments* in practical considerations of what makes for a happy, useful life in the world we perceive around us.

Because they put forward these very different views in the general language of value and because they expose the roots of even the most abstract ideas, like the very rules of thought, in such social circumstances as the relation of classes, they continue to have something to say on ethical questions as long as commodity exchange and class divisions are with us. At the same time their common concern with the specific source of a surplus of wealth in the Athens of their day, the institution of slavery, firmly roots them in their own period and locale. Philosophers will not always be so frank in their rationalisation and justification of the particular forms of exploitation on which the power and privileges of the classes they identify themselves with are based.

HISTORICAL MATERIALISM AND ETHICAL IDEAS

We have been considering how ideas about what is right in terms of human conduct are rooted in the fundamental economic structure of society and therefore change with changes in that basic social structure. This understanding of the way ethical attitudes and, indeed, the way we think about ourselves and our relationships generally are profoundly influenced by the form the production of goods and their distribution in society takes is historical materialism.

Using this historical materialist approach it is worth considering changes in the ethical attitude toward trading operations since the growth of commodity exchange is such an important social development for understanding the moral relations among human beings.

The social roots of barter are to be found ultimately in the most primitive form of the division of labour - clan specialisation inside the tribe with respect to gathering or killing a particular edible plant or animal, a practice reflected in totemism. Taboo, as we have already noted, originating in a prohibition against eating a certain kind of food where and when it was found in order to effect subsequently a proper interclan distribution, can be seen as the earliest instance of the interdiction of use which is an essential precondition for the simplest commodity exchange.

Further specialisation in agriculture and in the making of such objects as pots or weapons effects a greater production of certain things than the tribal community needs, leading to intertribal barter in which local chiefs exchange their surplus products for the different surplus products of another tribe. This traffic in goods results in a transformation of all social relationships. Artisans cease to be workers for the community and become workers for themselves...The chiefs cease to represent the separate interests of their clans. They are becoming a landed aristocracy united against the poorer clansmen by a common interest of class against class. The artisans on their part organise themselves in guilds formed on the pattern of the clan; but, so long as the economy remains agrarian, they are not in a position to dispute the supremacy of the landowners.[17]

The process in ancient Greece described by George Thomson by which tribal settlements, based on the equal sharing of goods by lot, were converted into city states 'governed by a landed nobility and surrounded by a poverty-stricken peasantry in dependent villages' would apply generally to human communities at a similar stage of development. As he goes on to say:

The new unit (the city state) was the expression of a new division of labour, agrarian and industrial, which, once established, promoted further divisions of labour and thereby raised human life to new levels of complexity on a slave basis...The later its date, the more pronounced was its class character...During the Sixth Century B.C. the development of commodity production precipitated, in all the advanced city states, a further revolution - the overthrow of the landed aristocracy by the merchant class.

This background helps us to understand the very different attitudes toward trade of Plato and Aristotle. As one who identified himself with the landed aristocracy Plato considered the whole business of exchange so reprehensible that in his ideal Republic it was to be kept to a minimum and only carried on at all by a despised group of foreigners whose activities were regulated by the strictest rules of 'fair practice'. Aristotle, taking a much more sympathetic interest in mercantilism, distinguished between money-making as a necessary aspect of sound house-keeping, from which the word 'economics' comes, and money-making as an end in itself. The former was natural and commendable while the latter was to be censured 'for it has not its origin in nature, but by it men gain from each other; for usury is most reasonably detested, as it is increasing our fortune by money itself, and not by employing it for the purpose it was originally intended, namely, exchange'.[18]

At the beginning of the Middle Ages, following on the collapse of the Roman Empire in the West and, later, on the shutting of the Mediterranean to European trade by Islamic expansion, most of western Europe was split up into self-sufficient manorial units fairly closely approximating the Platonic ideal of a natural economy dominated by a land-owning aristocracy; and the philosophy of Plato, with its contempt for commerce and its other-worldly values, was very suited to influence early Christian ideas about the morality of trade. Saint Augustine's description of value as purely subjective is characteristic of a point of view determined primarily by the interests of consumers; and his doctrine that no Christian ought to be a merchant accorded well enough with the conditions that were to prevail for some time.

With the revival of trade following on the Crusades, Aristotle was rediscovered, often through the medium of Arabic scholarship. In the writings of Saint Thomas Aquinas, whom Aristotle so greatly influenced, a crude form of the labour theory of value can be found side by side with a subjective theory; and the economic incentive of private property is defended on the basis of the Aristotelian argument that not the institution of property itself but the way it is used determines whether it is good or evil.

In the earlier period all commercial activity, natural in Aristotle's sense or not, had been regarded as a distraction from people's true business of purifying their own souls and contemplating eternal 'values'; and the abusive word 'usury' was applied to almost any profitable transaction. In the later period profiteering or the charging of excessive interest on money was condemned, but there was considered to be such a thing as legitimate trading whose limits were fixed by ethical notions like a 'fair return' or a 'just price'. In both cases the attitude was moral; but while one form of morality required people to turn away from the things of this world, the other attempted to order their activities here and now on an ethical basis.

Further change in these moral attitudes was bound to be brought about by the growth of towns and the expansion of trade with the European revival of mercantilism. The views of a landed nobility whose interests were largely those of consumers were being challenged by the views of a rising merchant class; and this clash of views was the reflection of the beginnings of a class struggle which was eventually, in one part of the world after another, to overthrow feudalism altogether.

The Church itself was gradually forced to retreat from its original position on the ethics of trading and to accept various qualifications of the idea of the 'just price'. By the fifteenth century Saint Antonio, while still insisting on the general notion of 'fair dealing', is prepared to recognise the 'impersonal forces of the market' with his admission that 'there was a debatable ground within which prices might move without involving sin'.[19] Similar qualifications were accepted in respect to usury by conceding that lenders might be reimbursed for losses incurred or for delays in repayment or even for the chances of gain which had been missed.

Not only does the temporal sequence of events show that a quickening of commercial life was the occasion for a transformation of ethical attitudes; but also the very locale of these changes in attitude emphasises the relationship between economic base and ideas of morality. The impetus to trade by the discovery of the New World (which did not, of course, know that it was lost!) would lead us to expect a rethinking of the ethics of mercantilism to appear first in Spain; and in the school of Salamanca, for example, churchmen do begin, early on, to modify their views of usury by distinguishing between divergence in place and divergence in time in order to justify the exchange bills which had become a feature of trade fairs.

But although theologians might make concessions to the economic needs of the time, the Church could never wholly abandon its prerogative of drawing the precepts for human behaviour from the realm of the ideal. As the gulf between precept and economic practice widened, the ideal foundation on which the precepts rested could only be saved by giving up the claim that they were directly relevant to the conduct of practical affairs here and now, referring instead to an idealised existence in some other time and place.

In spite of the secularisation of trading practices as the Church surrendered its right to legislate morally for the market place, religion still had a social function to perform. In class-divided societies some way has to be found of preserving the idea of an integrated social life to counter the centrifugal tendencies of directly opposed class interests. Religion means literally a renewed 'link' or 'bond' between people and god where god, in one form or many, represents the spirit of a social organisation. It does not try to put an end to class divisions but to bind society together and make some sort of communal life possible in spite of economic exploitation. By recalling the past when tribal communities were not yet divided into exploiters and exploited and by supposing that such solidarity can exist ideally in the present, even though the actual material conditions rule it out, or by projecting this conception of human harmony into a life after death, religion offers hope to the dispossessed while leaving everything as it is.

From the point of view of the ruling class, religion serves to distract the masses from active steps to improve their lot, to inculcate the social laws which subservient classes have to obey if the system is to continue and to provide a means whereby they themselves can enjoy easy consciences without surrendering any privileges. From the point of view of the ruled, religion is a source of consolation prior to the time when political struggle to relieve their stress is feasible. Marx likens it to flowers entwined in the chains of the toiling masses which hide their bonds from sight. It is no help to pluck away the flowers: the chains must be broken. 'The abolition of religion, as the illusory happiness of men, is a demand for their real happiness. The call to abandon their illusions about their condition is a call to abandon a condition which demands illusions.'[20] Religion, then, provides a spurious reconciliation of divided societies whereby Dives and Lazarus can kneel down together in the same communion, the one content in his earthly possessions, the other anticipating a reversal of fortune in a hypothetical life to come.

It is possible for religion to perform this function in divided societies because people themselves are divided. The dualism of commodities as useful and valuable reflects and is reflected by the dualistic nature of those who make them - as having both a physical and a non-natural character. People work to satisfy their material needs but the value of their work is incorporated in things that do not belong to them. Value thus appears to them as something inhabiting a different world from this one of sweat and toil, something only to be enjoyed in another life than this one. Some additional effort on the moral plane seems required to possess what they themselves have made. This aspiration growing out of the negation of physical satisfactions takes a spiritual form; and it is to this aspect of people, the producers whose products slip through their hands to re-appear on the market as abstract values mostly beyond their means, that religion speaks - the louder, of course, where deprivation is greatest.

In the historical development of ideas about the ethics of exchange, once we reach the stage of a full-blown, freely-competitive market economy in which overcharging for goods or for the use of money seems to be penalised automatically, injunctions against usury in any form tend to become a thing of the past. In the same way that human relationships in the productive process are transformed from personal ties into commodity deals, so the ethics of commerce is translated into a purely descriptive science of market operations. Freed from any obvious role in regulating the great issues of the creation and distribution of the goods by which society lives, morality in capitalist countries suffers a progressive trivialisation by which it becomes primarily concerned with those areas of life apparently impervious to commodity exchange - intimate relationships of various kinds within and without the family. It must not be thought, however, that even these personal aspects of life are left untouched by changes in the mode of production. Marx mentions the fate of Don Quixote as a pathetic example of what happens to anyone who thinks that a particular code of personal conduct is compatible with all economic forms of society.

This translation of the ethics of commerce into a descriptive science, 'the end of ideology' referred to by superficial observers, does not mean that the functioning of the economy has ceased to have moral implications - only that they have temporarily sunk out of sight and are no longer debated as such. It remains for political opposition to the system as a whole to bring these implications once more into the open where they can be reconsidered in normative judgments.

Through all these changes in ideas about trading relationships which reflect material changes in the basic mode of production it is still possible for the philosophers of different periods to speak to each other across the centuries. Plato and Aristotle may differ about the ethics of exchange and their views on this subject may be at even greater variance with those of philosophers writing since their time; but they all still seem to speak the same philosophical language in which their differences can be expressed.

Marxists do not explain this in terms of an essential human nature which stays the same through all social vicissitudes. Human nature, like the consciousness peculiar to human beings, is determined by social existence. Therefore, similarities in ways of thought must be accounted for by common features in the way societies at various times have been organised in respect to the material maintenance of life.

In spite of the revolutionary disjunctions in any story of human development stretching from the slave-based communities of ancient city states through various forms of feudalism right up to contemporary capitalism, all these modes of production have two things in common - the division of labour, with the division between ruled and rulers, exploited and exploiters as one of its main consequences, and the production of commodities evidenced by the existence of some form of currency. At each of these periods society was divided into classes, the mode of production simply being the form class exploitation took, and in all these periods there was production for the market. Since we have found that these two aspects of the material conditions of life are fundamental for the deduction of our most general ethical concepts, their presence over the whole historical period provides the basis of a common moral language.

A key concept in this language is value. Value, as we have seen, by virtue of being a concept common to both economics and ethics serves as the middle term enabling us to move logically from one realm of discourse to the other. Just as the law of value is the economic formula for reuniting the activities of making and enjoying which have been sundered by the division of labour, so the general idea of value is the philosophical formula for comprehending the connection between material social base and the broad cultural superstructure raised upon it. Economic value operates across the division of labour to relate man as enjoyer to man as maker: value in its broadest sense operates across class divisions to relate people as thinkers and ideologists to people as the creators of material goods.

This connection has been obscured for us by the separation between intellectual and manual tasks which has divorced thinking from doing, theory from practice; and it is by reminding ourselves that the source of all values is human effort that the connection can be recovered. This is the reason that Marxism can speak to working people anywhere and not just to intellectuals in the developed capitalist world. Since value has this peculiar importance in commodity-exchanging societies of containing within itself the clues to the real social relationships concealed behind deals in things, the views about value which philosophers profess at any time, even when they represent failures in comprehension or deliberate attempts to mislead, are themselves revealing in terms of trying to understand that particular age.

But if attitudes toward value in general give us the moral framework within which people reflect on matters of conduct, it is the form surplus-value takes which largely determines what specific ethical details shall be filled in. The idea that certain actions are 'right' holds for all societies since all societies have certain common basic features; but in any particular society the actual type of conduct advocated as 'right' and the reasons adduced for its 'rightness' depend on how the surplus product in that society is created and appropriated.

In a tribal economy which has advanced beyond the mere

subsistence level but in which the means of production like land are held in common, all right is group right and the morality of the tribe consists of group loyalty. Every member of the tribe is a brother or sister; everyone outside the tribe is a potential enemy. There is no question of individual rights because there is no such thing as personal property. Ceremonies and rituals serve to ratify the bonds holding the tribe together and the threat of ostracism - of being excluded from the life of the tribe, meaning moral if not physical death - is a sufficient sanction for ensuring compliance with traditional practice.

Once tribal expansion and conquest laid a foundation based on slavery for a greater surplus product appropriated by a landed aristocracy, loyalty to the group as a whole is superseded by class loyalty. Thinkers who belong to or identify themselves with that aristocracy, whose very name begs the question of their right to rule, are considerably concerned, as we saw in the case of fourth century B.C. Athenian philosophers and as was to be the case with eighteenth century A.D. English divines, with defending and justifying the institution of slavery because slave-worked mines were an obvious source of a surplus for the one and the slave-trade a major source of primitive accumulation for the other. Discussions about the actual numbers of slaves in ancient Athens or the exact proportion of primitive accumulation netted by trade in slaves in pre-industrial England are not entirely relevant to this issue. What counts is whether a particular area of the economy is where exploitation is most intense and in yielding the greatest surplus deserves the largest effort in justification.

Under feudalism there is a hierarchy of obligations, corresponding to a mode of production in which serfs tied to the fields they till are constrained to fulfil by services or dues the economic demands of an overlord, and overlords owe fealty to that king or conqueror who is the source of assigned rights in the land. This social organisation is reflected in such metaphysical ideas as a scale of beings from humans, up through various ranks of angels to god himself, the grand seigneur - each creature with a duly allotted place establishing proper relations with those above and below. Production is more for use within natural feudal units than for exchange and this explains the relative permanence of this economic mode. As Epicurus says, natural wants are limited by nature while idle imaginings stretch to infinity. The commodity, money, as the equivalent of all created values, gives such idle imaginings a concrete form and, where it circulates freely with a quickening of commercial activity, carries a propensity to greed with it. Marx expresses the same idea when he points out that in societies where not the exchange value but the utility of the product predominates, surplus-labour is limited by a given set of wants and there is no boundless thirst for additional surplus-labour arising from the nature of production itself.

It is this absence of the drive for maximising surplus-value on the part of overlords which gives feudalism its stability and resistance to change. Conquerors come and go; overlords fight among themselves to engross more land and the labour attached to it; but the economic units of feudal society, self-contained and more or less self-perpetuating communities ruled by tradition and custom, remain largely untouched - until mercantilism introduces the universal solvent, money.

We have seen how the equalisation of labour in the establishment of the value of exchangeable commodities gives rise to the idea of the equality of human beings. 'All human beings are born equal' becomes the foundation for the Enlightenment doctrine of the universal right of individual liberty. In his attacks on the ethical views of Thomas Hobbes, Adam Smith, John Stuart Mill and their contemporary disciples Marx certainly is not attacking the right of individual liberty - only those philosophers and political economists who pretend to defend individual rights but in fact do not. He is criticising those thinkers who, whether or not they realise it, speak not for the creators of value but for the bourgeoisie who exploit them and deny them their equal rights. Marxism hails the French Revolution which freed the working masses from serfdom; but it realises that capitalism replaces one form of exploitation with another, translates serfdom into wage slavery. The individual rights of all become the right of the individual owners of the means of production to extract surplus-value from all - all who possess nothing but their labour power. Under capitalism and the full growth of commodity production, which transforms human ties into economic relationships and appears to liberate people from having to acknowledge any master but money, individual rights, in theory, attain their maximum expression. But actually, as we have seen, the creation of a surplus depends on the exploitation of workers through the purchase of their labour-power, and the pretence that these deals in the worker's capacity to create value are fairly struck sets the tone of this ethical system based on promise-keeping and contractual agreements as one of fundamental dishonesty. It is this fraud at the heart of capitalism that makes it the least stable and the shortest-lived of all modes of production.

It is at the capitalist stage that classes reveal themselves as what they always were, stripped now of any status trappings, birth rights or claims to natural superiority -simply the relationship social groupings in an antagonistic exploitative situation bear to the means of production. Ownership of the means of production is the basis of exploiting non-owners, the dispossessed. Where the means of production is still mainly the individual's brute force, this possessive power takes the form of ownership of the people themselves -slavery. Where the means of production are mainly tillable land, it is rights in land which define the ruling class and give them power over those who work it. Where the means of production are capital goods, it is the possession of capital which gives the dominant class its rights in the labour of others and what that labour produces. Slavery, serfdom and wage labour are the keys to an understanding of what the different modes of production, ancient conquest-based, feudal and capitalist, are in essence and also keys to understanding the changes in moral attitudes which reflect changes in these material circumstances.

If the moral consciousness of the mass declares an economic fact to be unjust, as it has done in the case of slavery or serf-labour, that is a proof that the fact itself has been outlived, that others have made their appearance, owing to which the former has become unbearable and untenable.[21]

Engels should have made this correct observation about the moral consciousness of the ruling class rather than about that of 'the mass'. Although material circumstances underlie all thinking about ethics, the experience of material circumstances varies considerably for the exploiters and the exploited. During the Civil War in the United States the British working class sympathised with the Union demand for the liberation of the slaves while the British capitalist class supported in every way possible the slave-owning South which supplied the cotton for their textile mills. It is certainly not Marx's view that slavery could be called just when it was still in use and only became unjust when it was outlived as an economic fact. At the capitalist stage of production classes have revealed themselves to Marx's analysis as what they always were - those who were exploiters and those who were exploited as determined by their respective relationships to the means of production. We are able therefore to appreciate the exploitative injustice of slavery and serfdom even if this was hidden from those living at the time when they were common forms of labour. It was not, of course, hidden from the slaves and serfs themselves who expressed their moral condemnation in slave revolts and peasant uprisings. Marx also shows that ethical questions cannot be decided on the basis of the relative progressiveness of successive modes of exploitation when, in discussing the opium trade, he judges pre-capitalist China as ethical and the capitalist policies of England as profoundly unethical.

Applied to capitalism this scientific analysis goes beneath the surface to grasp the essential reality of relations of production and shows that the exchange between capitalists and workers which at the level of appearances may seem perfectly right and proper is in essence the downright exploitation of the working class. The motivation of Marx's monumental investigation of the capitalist system could not be more plainly stated than this: 'When a communist stands in front of scrofulous, overworked and consumptive starvelings he sees the necessity and at the same time the condition of a transformation both of industry and the social structure.'[22] In Capital Marx is quite explicit about the emancipation of the working class to be gained by this transformation. 'Freedom in this field can only consist in socialised man, the associated producers, rationally regulating their exchange with nature; and achieving this with the least expenditure of energy and in conditions most favourable to, and worthy of, their human nature.'[23] This is to contrast the individualistic and devious morality of capitalism with the collective and non-exploitative morality of socialism.

However Marx does not rely on appeals to this collective socialist morality to correct the injustices of capitalism. He calls instead for the actual transformation of society into what will become the socialist economic base of the new collective morality with its new values. Preaching the new collective morality to the bourgeoisie would not do much good. The transformation of society will establish the conditions for the new morality. 'Communists preach no morality at all...They do not put to people the moral demand: Love one another, be not egoists, because they know very well that egoism is under certain conditions the necessary form of the individual's struggle for survival.'[24] This is not, as it has sometimes been taken to be, a rejection of morality as such. It is the recognition that a moral code applicable to one mode of production may not be appropriate to another: it is the rejection of the abstract, universal morality taught by religion which shows no understanding of the kind of class exploitation rendering much of their moral teaching vapid and hypocritical.

The transformation of society is brought about by the revolutionary struggle of class conscious workers. Once the venders of their labour power recognise with all its economic and political implications that the products they have collectively made ought to belong to them collectively, just as once slaves realise that they are human beings who ought to be treated as such and once serfs become convinced that land ought to belong to the tiller, the death knell of those particular exploitative systems has sounded. It is the effort to put an end to the exploitation of one human being by another which is profoundly moral and transcends the ethical principles of any particular exploitative mode of production. That is the essence of Marxist morality. 'Our morality is entirely subordinated to the interests of the class struggle of the proletariat. Only the proletarians, fired by a new social task to accomplish for all society, to do away with all classes and class rule, are the people to break the instrument of that class rule - the state, the centralised and organised governmental power usurping to be the master instead of the servant of society.'[25]

Few serious writers on the history of human thought deny that there is a connection between what people are thinking at any particular time and the socio-economic conditions in which they find themselves. But granting the connection, there can still be differences about which of the related terms is the dominant factor. Max Weber's view that the spirit of a particular mode of production like capitalism must precede the development of capitalist institutions is of a piece with the bourgeois idealist thought of the Germany of his time. R.H. Tawney's compromise, that sometimes the ideal, sometimes the material, takes precedence, is characteristic of British empiricism which itself is the way of thought of a class so successful in that period that it feels it can afford to dispense with theory and 'muddle through' pragmatically.

Marx's historical materialism which places the emphasis on economic considerations in the broadest sense, such as the human forces of production and the class relationships determining the distribution of the product, is the ideology of the working class - materialistic because workers cannot doubt the reality of the natural world with which they mix their labour in useful work; historical because the fact of profound social changes in the past validates the working class's mission of bringing about revolutionary change in the future, liberating themselves from wage-labour and all people generally from exploitation; dialectical because the experience of class struggle teaches the working class that on the physical, social and mental levels of existence, all interrelated, reality is not static but a unity of opposites in which process is continuous and change, including mind-directed change, is possible.

The view that only economic considerations in the narrowest sense determine in a unilateral way our philosophical ideas would rule out the possibility that ideas, abstracted from material conditions, by gripping the working masses could react on the circumstances which gave rise to them making thought practical. This kind of deterministic economism is mechanical materialism and must not be confused with dialectical materialism. Isaiah Berlin, in a series of lectures on historical Inevitability in 1953, seemed to think that in demolishing a determinist, mechanical interpretation of history he had finally finished off Marx, to say nothing of Hegel, Condorcet, Spengler and others. As far as Marxism is concerned he never came to grips with the subject at all. F.H. Bradley refutes mechanical materialism by arguing that if a series of mental states are assumed simply to mirror a series of events causally related, each particular mental state may be considered passive in respect to the event of which it is the image but nevertheless, as one element in its total cause, must be admitted to be active in respect to a successive event. This is no criticism of Marxism but support for the dialectical relationship of matter and mind. 'Men make their own history. But they do not make it just as they please; they do not make it under circumstances chosen by themselves, but under circumstances directly encountered, given and transmitted from the past.'[26]

We can only decide which assumption about the relationship between socio-economic ground and human consciousness, between material base and ideological superstructure is more nearly true by considering whether holding one or the other yields the more fruitful consequences - not on the opportunistic, pragmatic grounds that what works is true but on the genuinely practical assurance that what is true works and can be proved workable in social practice. Which assumption, for example, has proved the sounder in respect to the advance of our physical knowledge of the universe - the view that nature is merely the phenomenal aspect of mind and can be deduced in an a priori way from the logical categories of thought, or the view that nature is the objective context in which minds have developed with laws of its own, discoverable precisely because it provides the original ground of the birth of human consciousness?

Similarly, the proof of historical materialism is whether it gives us a better understanding than any alternative hypothesis of human relationships and the conditions of social change and thereby enables us the better to control our future as people working and living together - much as an understanding of physical laws has given us our control over nature. And almost as a by-product of this effort to understand the world in order to change it, historical materialism also explains why those who disagree with it have come to think as they do.

CLASS DIVISION AND ETHICAL RELATIVISM

'The history of all hitherto existing society is the history of class struggle.'[27] We have been considering changes in ethical attitudes as a result of changes in modes of production which are different forms of the relationship between exploiting and exploited classes. These revolutionary changes, which are critical stages in the class conflict characteristic of all class-divided society, revolutionise ethics itself.

These differences in the ethical attitudes of successive modes of production appear at any one particular time as the opposed ethical attitudes in the same society of the exploiting ruling class and the exploited class which is to succeed it. This opposition is fundamental but because only the ethical attitudes of the exploiting ruling class tend to be published and propagated as the attitudes of society as a whole, the real character of the opposition has to be grasped by appreciating the basic nature of classes themselves.

This task is, however, made easier by the simplification of class antagonism under capitalism which makes it possible for the first time in history to define exactly what classes are.

Society as a whole is more and more splitting up into two great hostile camps, into two great classes directly facing each other: bourgeoisie and proletariat. The bourgeoisie has stripped of its halo every occupation hitherto honoured and looked up to with reverent awe. It has converted the physician, the lawyer, the priest, the poet, the man of science, into its paid wage-labourers...has pitilessly torn asunder the motley feudal ties that bound man to his 'natural superiors', and has left remaining no other nexus between man and man than naked self-interest, than callous 'cash-payment'...in one word, for exploitation, veiled by religious and political illusions, it has substituted naked, shameless, direct, brutal exploitation.[28]

Thus, in the oldest capitalist country, Britain, this process has reached a point where it can now be said that there are only two classes: workers and capitalists, those who live by the sale of their labour-power whatever form it takes and those who traffic profitably in the labour-power of others. Sociological apologists for the capitalist system like to think that, because there has been a reduction of the proportion of industrial workers, the working class is shrinking in size; but this is to ignore the enormous accession to working class strength of teachers, office workers, civil servants, journalists, nurses and technical workers of all kinds who are organised on the model of industrial trade unions and have increasingly come to think of themselves as working class.

This polarisation of classes is, of course, the social manifestation of the law of contradiction in things, the law of the unity of opposites which is the basic law of materialist dialectics. 'Dialectics in the proper sense', Lenin writes, 'is the study of contradiction in the very essence of objects.' It is on this conception of the essential contradictoriness at the heart of everything from the atom, which is a unity of negatively and positively charged elements, right up to the most complicated social structure, which is a unity of the class opposition of exploiters and exploited, that the Marxist understanding of development and change is based.

> There is internal contradiction in every single thing, hence its motion and development. Contradictoriness within a thing is the fundamental cause of its development , while its interrelations and interactions with other things are secondary causes...Changes in nature are due chiefly to the development of the internal contradictions in nature. Changes in society are due chiefly to the development of the internal contradictions in society, that is, the contradiction between the productive forces and the relations of production, the contradiction between classes...[29]

Materialist dialectics does not exclude external causes -'external causes are the conditions of change and internal causes are the basis of change, and the external causes become operative through internal causes', which is the dynamic of revolutionary change as opposed to the 'metaphysical' conception of change as mere decrease, increase or repetition of isolates whether idealistically or materialistically conceived.

Because reality is dialectical, valid thinking must be dialectical and the rules of thought reflect the essential contradictoriness in all things. One of Mao Tsetung's contributions to the formulation of the dialectical materialist rules of thought is his emphasising that in the process of development of any complex thing there is necessarily a principal contradiction which reveals the essential quality of the thing, a main contradiction 'whose existence and development determine or influence the existence and development of other contradictions. For instance, in capitalist society the two forces in contradiction, the proletariat and the bourgeoisie, form the principal contradiction' and give us the essential character of such a society.

Also that principal contradiction, depending on its stage of development, has a principal aspect. The contradiction between the proletariat and the bourgeoisie is present in both capitalist and post-revolutionary socialist society; but it is the relative political strength of the two social forces as one is superseded by the other which gives society its capitalist or proletarian aspect. This rule of dialectical thought, look for the major contradiction in any object under study and understand which aspect of that contradiction is presently the principal one, has helped make dialectical materialism a useful tool for peasants and workers in solving production problems and a sharp weapon for the working class in its political struggles. It further frees the materialist dialectic from such idealistic Hegelian expressions as the 'negation of negation' which does not help anyone see how the dialectic is actually to be used rather than merely appreciated intellectually. This is also the difficulty with Althusser's 'over-determination' in which a plurality of contradictions on different levels have to coincide for change to take place. It may be a useful conception of the dialectic for studying history but not for making it.

We have already noted the tendency, though at no time so clearly marked as under capitalism, for the development of the division of labour in society to result in two broad classes -those primarily concerned with the laborious production of goods and those whose interest is centred in the possession and enjoyment of them. The basic moral sensibilities of these two groups are distinguishable because production and consumption with which they are respectively associated became separated under the system of commodity exchange developing out of the division of labour. These broad moral sensibilities with their implications in terms of ideas about what is right are part of the whole conception of value once it has been differentiated according to the respective experience had of value-bearing goods by those who make them and by those who, by and large, possess and enjoy them.

Production is social in the obvious sense that people must enter into close relationships with each other in the creation of useful things, and indeed language itself probably originated in the cries and signals of associated labour. Consumption is private and individualistic since no one else can satisfy our physical needs for us. Production involves workers in a direct causal relationship with the material environment by which satisfactory goods are recognised for what they are, the result of practical human effort. Consumption in itself, as we have so frequently noted, can give rise to the notion that the provision of goods is merely preceded by the desire for them. These goods represent for their producers certain specific amounts of expended energy; but to consumers they appear simply as abstract quantities of money, itself an abstraction. The surplus product which is alienated from those whose labour created it takes the form of a profitable increment to those who acquire it through their control of the means of production.

From these familiar observations can be deduced quite different basic ethical inclinations characteristic of these two broad classes - a practical, down-to-earth, socialistic morality in which there is a strong sense of alienation on the one hand, and a reflective, abstract, acquisitive, individualistic morality in which there is a strong note of self-justification on the other.

> All moral theories have been hitherto the product, in the last analysis, of the economic conditions of society obtaining at the time. And as society has hitherto moved in class antagonisms, morality has always been class morality; it has either justified the domination and interest of the ruling class, or, ever since the oppressed class became powerful enough, it has represented its indignation against this domination and the future interests of the oppressed.[30]

The distinction between manual and mental labour which is one aspect of class differences explains why class relationships in the broadest sense correspond in general with phases of the Marxist theory of knowledge. A class intimately concerned with the physical world in the practical task of growing or making things corresponds with the perceptual stage of understanding. A class at one remove from material reality through not being under the compulsion of manual labour, a class for whom that reality and indeed relationships generally are mediated by money, corresponds with the stage of abstract thought and inferential judgment. Both tend to be arrested at a particular phase of the total act of knowledge by the partiality of their experience and to fall short in different respects of the full understanding which requires all three moments - sensuous contact with the external world, conceptualisation and re-arrangement of sense impressions in drawing logical conclusions and the application and verification of these hypothetical conclusions in social practice.

This class correspondence draws attention, through the Marxist theory of knowledge, to the two kinds of human knowledge there are, which Mao Tsetung describes as follows:

> Ever since class society came into being the world has had only two kinds of knowledge, knowledge of the struggle for production and knowledge of the class struggle. Natural science and social science are the crystallisations of these two kinds of knowledge, and philosophy is the generalisation and summation of the knowledge of nature and the knowledge of society.[31]

We shall have occasion to consider subsequently this knowledge of the forces of production and knowledge of the relations of production because it is when the relations of production become an intolerable check on the growth of the forces of production that revolutionary change is indicated. Now we are simply concerned with pointing out that knowledge of the struggle for production through the development of the physical sciences is the ground of all truth about the world we live in. Knowledge of class struggle through the development of the social sciences, including as its most consistent, comprehensive and compelling expression, Marxism, that is, scientific socialism, is the ground of all truth about our relations with each other in society including the relation of morality.

A social development which has altered the rough correspondence between manual workers and the perceptual stage of knowledge on the one hand and mental workers and the conceptual stage of knowledge on the other is capitalism's requirement, with the advance of technology, for educated workers, industrial workers who are fully equipped to think through the most abstruse problems of production. At the same time the previously mentioned tendency of capitalism to simplify class structure by proletarianising the intelligentsia, teachers, designers, artists, managerial staff and all others who by living on their wages have the same relation to the means of production as industrial workers, has meant a swelling of the ranks of workers with a capacity for both manual and mental tasks and has brought the working class as a whole more nearly into line with all three phases of the Marxist theory of knowledge. Capitalism in creating the working class 'produces its own grave-diggers'. In producing a literate, educated, skilled working class it makes sure that the grave will be nicely squared off and efficiently dug.

Only the moral attitudes of the class with a possession and consumption bias are likely to be expressed in published writings, expounded from platforms and taught in schools. As Marx reminds us: 'The ideas of the ruling class are, in every age, the ruling ideas', since 'the class which has the means of material production at its disposal, has control at the same time over the means of mental production'.[32] Control of the means of production inevitably involves political control: without political oppression or the threat of it there can be no exploitation. Marx goes on to say that:

> The division of labour...manifests itself also in the ruling class...so that within this class one part appears as the thinkers of the class (its active conceptualising ideologists, who make it their chief source of livelihood to develop and perfect the illusions of the class about itself), while the others have a more passive and receptive attitude

to these ideas and illusions, because they are in reality the active members of this class and have less time to make up ideas and illusions about themselves. This cleavage within the ruling class may even develop into a certain opposition and hostility between the two parts, but in the event of a practical collision in which the class itself is endangered, it disappears of its own accord and with it also the illusion that the ruling class ideas were not the ideas of the ruling class and had a power distinct from the power of this class.

It is like, and just as inconsequential as, the apparent conflicts that develop in Britain, say, between the major industrialists and financiers on the one hand and the political ideologists of capitalist government on the other, whether Labour or Conservative, since the state, whoever nominally heads it, is 'an organ of class, an organ for the oppression of one class by another' and can never have any real differences with the ruling capitalist class of which it is the 'executive committee'.

Critics of Marxism often make the charge that identifying certain views with class interests is an attack on the integrity of reason itself and that pointing out the class character of ethical attitudes has the effect of introducing a relativism destructive of true morality. But class bias is not something Marx either invents or advocates: it is a social fact to be recognised if we are serious about wanting to know how society works. Such recognition provides a critique of reason which not only shows what its limitations are in class-divided societies but also what relative degrees of validity it can achieve within those circumstances and how by a change in those circumstances distortions can be progressively eliminated. Knowing why we think as we do is a necessary step in affirming or correcting our ideas. Similarly, we shall have to show that the understanding that ethical standards change with changes in the economic base of society or with changes in class perspective within the same society does not, in fact, turn morality into a mechanical response to a particular social situation nor does it cynically brush aside all ethical considerations to clear the way for the operation of naked self-interest.

Marxism's first contribution to the problem of relativism is to bring some order into the chaos of conflicting moral standards by showing that at all periods since the disruption of primitive communistic tribal units different classes have had their distinctive forms of conduct; and, further, that at any particular period the pattern of socially-recommended behaviour has reflected the mode of production prevailing at that time. Since these modes of production are historically limited in number and fairly determinate in form, general patterns of behaviour derived from them are similarly limited and recognisable. And before the time when one of these modes of production, capitalism, developed to the point at which the obvious polarisation of society into exploiting capitalists and exploited workers made possible the Marxist analysis of thinking and morality themselves as class-influenced, thinking and morality were not freer from class subjectivism: people were simply ignorant of the class nature of ideology, that is all.

But let us look more closely at this question of the class subjectivism of ideology. If the history of all hitherto existing society - or at least, since primitive communism is preliterate, the written history - is the history of class struggles, if at any time we dip into history we find that the whole character of the period is being shaped by class forces contending for economic and political domination, then the only way thinking at any time can intervene effectively is in a class form. Only in its character as class ideology can thinking be practical. As 'objective' in the sense of being above or outside the class contention which is making that historical epoch what it is, thinking would not be somehow 'purer'; it would simply be irrelevant.

Not that for Marxists it is a matter of indifference, from the point of view of relative truth, which class one is identified with. According to the Marxist theory of knowledge truth is a result of the social practice of production. It is not to be found in the minds of certain exceptional individuals. Its source is the productive experience of the broad mass of the working people everywhere, renewing and enriching itself from generation to generation - the source socialism taps in unleashing the energies, skills and knowledge of the whole people. The test of this truth is the enormous expansion down the ages of people's productive forces, limited only by the relations of production which are the particular form class exploitation takes in any given period.

Working class ideology, in so far as it is the democratic expression in terms of knowledge of the vast practical experience of working people everywhere, really is truer than any ideology more partially based. Marxism's identification with and development of this ideology is not the result of some kind of sympathy for the underdog but of a concern for truth in the most complete form it can take in our era. The political expression of this claim made for working class ideology is that 'the proletarian movement is the self-conscious, independent movement of the immense majority, in the interest of the immense majority', while 'all previous historical movements were movements of minorities'.[33] Or as Marx makes the same point in terms of successive forms of class rule:

> Every new class, therefore, achieves its hegemony only on a broader basis than that of the class ruling previously, in return for which the opposition of the non-ruling class against the new ruling class develops all the more sharply and profoundly. Both these things determine the fact that the struggle to be waged against the new ruling class, in its turn, aims at a more decided and radical negation of the previous conditions of society than could all the previous classes which sought to rule.[34]

Furthermore, with the growing contradictions within bourgeois society there is a degeneration in the ruling class's regard for the truth, and bourgeois ideology becomes increasingly a false ideology. Marx writes in 'The German Ideology':

The more the established form of intercourse in society, and thus the conditions of the ruling class, come into conflict with the developed productive forces, and the greater therefore is the dissension within the ruling class itself and between it and the subject class, the less viridical naturally becomes the consciousness which originates from and expresses this form of intercourse; i.e. it ceases to express it. The earlier conceptions of these relations of intercourse, in which the real individual interests were asserted as general interests, decline into mere idealising phrases, conscious illusions and deliberate deceits. But the more they are condemned as falsehoods, and the less they satisfy the understanding, the more dogmatically they are asserted and the more deceitful, moralising and spiritual becomes the language of established society.

The truth of Marxism itself, which both philosophically and politically is the most cogent expression of working class ideology, can only be tested and proved, according to its own theory of knowledge, in social practice. Marxism recognises the class nature of all philosophy in class-divided society and puts the knowledge based on this recognition at the service of the working class. Realising that where class divisions exist there can be no disinterested philosophy, Marxism declares its own interest openly. But at the same time it maintains that this knowledge depends on practice, that social practice is not only the sole criterion of knowledge but an essential step in the very production of knowledge. In other words, having avowed its class subjectivism, Marxism goes on to include the means for proving the objectivity of knowledge.

It might be thought that the question of class subjectivism only affects our social knowledge, knowledge concerned with the relations of production. After all, whatever people's class allegiances, they all share the same natural environment, they all live in the same physical world. But quite apart from the fact already noted that the world can look very different to those constrained to physical contact with it in manual work from the way it does to those who can command the results of the labour of others at the ring of a bell, workers by hand or brain, as a productive force directly involved with the real world, experience it concretely; capitalists see that same world abstractly as an investment possibility for profit.

For Marx science and ideology are not antithetical: they are complementary. Just as science is our knowledge of the physical world in which human production takes place, so ideology is our knowledge of the human relations of that production. The two kinds of knowledge, knowledge of the struggle for production and knowledge of the class struggle, require different forms of expression because while human beings do not make the physical world, they do 'make their own history' - even if 'they do not make it under circumstances chosen by themselves'. What Marx says about not merely interpreting the world in various ways but changing it belongs, of course, to the second kind of knowledge, knowledge of the relations of production. And how does ideology, how does theory change the world? 'Theory also becomes a material force once it has gripped the masses.'

Critics of Marxism like Eugene Kamenka complain that it confuses 'absolute truth' in the sense of total knowledge to which our actual knowledge must be relative with 'absolute truth' in the sense of 'conveying an unambiguous issue, of being either true or false and not both.'[35] This is really a protest at Marxism's no longer subscribing to a view of reality as static and therefore subject to an either-or logic. Only dialectical materialism can cope with the real dynamic world of opposites of which we are an integral part, ever changing and developing and producing novelty at once unpredetermined and explicable. Lenin explains in 'Materialism and Empirio-Criticism':

> the limits of approximation of our knowledge to objective, absolute truth are historically conditional, but the existence of such truth is unconditional, and the fact that we are approaching nearer to it is also unconditional. The contours of the picture are historically conditional, but the fact that the picture depicts an objectively existing model is unconditional.

When and under what circumstances we reach, in our knowledge of the essential nature of things, the discovery of, say, oppositely-charged particles in the atom is historically conditional; but that every such discovery is an advance of 'absolute objective knowledge' is unconditional. Truth in relation to the whole and the truth of a particular aspect of the whole can be distinguished but they cannot be separated. The dialectic of process and change is absolute but statements made about a changing reality are, at any given instant, bound to be indeterminate. The whole itself is not some static hypostatised ideal reality to which truth approaches as a postulant to a shrine. These critics would either dissolve all truth into general relativism or else they still hanker after discrete absolute truths handed down from on high on tablets of stone. For Marxists truth, whether of physical nature or of human relationships, is grounded in social practice. In stressing Marxism's attitude to truth one can do no better than to quote again the Second Thesis on Feuerbach:

> The question whether objective truth can be attributed to human thinking is not a question of theory but a practical question. In practice man must prove the truth, i.e. the reality and power, the 'this-sidedness' of his thinking. The dispute over the reality or non-reality of thinking which is isolated from practice is a purely scholastic question.

The reality of the objective world as the pre-existent context of human thought and action prevents this practical vindication of truth, which is the concluding stage of the dialectic of knowledge, from degenerating into a subjective pragmatism.

Just as the recognition that thinking is inevitably influenced by considerations of class does not represent an attack on reason as such but a critique of reason based on the realisation of how it is anchored in reality, so recognition of class influence on ethical attitudes does not represent an attack on morality as such but an explanation of its real nature and practical limitations. Thinking about ethics and acting in a moral way take place in the context of an existing society with a certain mode of production and a certain relationship of classes; and normative judgments are relatively valid to the extent that they concern themselves with the real purposes implicit in that mode of production and the real effects on different classes. In the same way that there has been a progression in the clarity with which class relationships have revealed themselves, so that with the final commoditisation of labour-power itself in the capitalist mode of production it became possible to define exactly what classes are, there has also been a progression in the openness of declarations of real class interests in contrast to all the mystical, religious or pseudo-political banners under which social movements have marched and fought in the past.

This recognition of the way ethical beliefs and practices cannot but be the expression in terms of class relationships of life in a particular society leads Marx to say: 'Right (in the ethical sense) can never be higher than the economic structure of society and its cultural development conditioned thereby'.[36] It would be quite pointless to expect people to behave in ways that were uncharacteristic of the 'cultural development' of a particular society. As has been noted before Marxists 'do not put to people the moral demand: Love one another, be not egoists, because they know very well that egoism is under certain conditions the necessary form of the individual's struggle for survival.' Marx rejects the kind of abstract, universal morality based on no understanding of the nature of society or the classes that make it up which has always been the form of religious teaching. It is like the 'philosophy' we have seen Marx rejecting when he says:

> Where speculation ends - in real life - there real, positive science begins; the representation of the practical activity, of the practical process of the development of men. Empty talk about consciousness ceases, and real knowledge has to take its place. When reality is depicted, philosophy as an independent branch of activity loses its medium of existence.[37]

Philosophy as a separate branch of study carried out by 'gifted individuals' is what Marx is attacking, not to put an end to philosophy but to free it to play its proper role. As Mao Tsetung puts it: 'Liberate philosophy from the confines of the philosophers' lecture rooms and textbooks and turn it into a sharp weapon in the hands of the masses'.[38] In the same way 'morality' must be freed from the professional moralists who cannot or will not recognise its social character so that its role in terms of the aspirations of oppressed masses can be understood.

It is precisely the revolutionary appeal to end such oppression and establish a classless socialist society in which 'the free development of each is the condition for the free development of all' which gives Marxist morality a claim to precedence over any morality reflecting this or that form of the exploitation of labour in class-divided society. Being involved in the associative labour of producing the goods on which society depends at the same time that they are robbed of surplus-value gives workers a tendency toward 'a practical, down-to-earth, socialistic ethics with a strong sense of unjust alienation' while at the same time they are naturally involved in the same selfish acquisition of goods for individualistic consumption as their employers - but to nothing like the same extent or the same amount! It is the moral effort of ensuring that the socialistic production side of their nature takes precedence over the individualistic consumption side which fits them for the collective moral task of changing capitalist society dominated by property-owning consumers into a socialist society of producers fairly sharing the fruits of their labour. 'Our morality,' Lenin says, 'serves the purpose of helping human society to rise to a higher level and to get rid of the exploitation of labour.'

Many contemporary philosophers treat Marx's rejection of bourgeois morality as a rejection of morality as such, as a denial that normative ideals play any part in the social actions that bring about changes in modes of production. Nothing could be more absurd than to regard Marxism as some form of positivism. In Capital Marx provides as objective an analysis as is possible of the way the capitalist system works by dealing with individuals 'only in so far as they are the personification of economic categories, embodiments of particular class relations and class interests'; but there is never any question but that this analysis is intended to serve the normative ideals of the Communist Manifesto. There is no way that a word like 'exploitation' can be deprived of normative significance and the very concept of 'surplus-value' bears a normative charge. Marx's derivation of 'value' from the practice of production and distribution enables him to make value judgments about how socially-produced means of production ought to be publicly owned, not privately operated for profit. 'From the standpoint of a higher economic form of society, private ownership of the globe by single individuals will appear quite as absurd as private ownership of one man by another.' Such judgments cannot legitimately be made by a 'de-valued' utilitarianism or positivism.

Since the exploitation of one section of society by another is the basis of class divisions and since all thinking in class-divided society inevitably has a class bias, the struggle to eliminate exploitation is also a struggle to free thought from class subjectivism. If the working masses liberate themselves from wage-slavery, the final form exploitation of class by class takes, they also free ideology from its character as special pleading on behalf of some partial interest to become the objective thought of socialist humanity. The ideology of the working class which is already truer than any other by virtue of its more democratic base becomes the even truer and more extensive knowledge of people who no longer exploit each other but only nature in their united co-operative interest. 'This whole semblance, that the rule of a certain class is only the rule of certain ideas, comes to a natural end, of course, as soon as it is no longer necessary to represent a particular interest as a general interest or "the general interest" as ruling.'[39]

The transition from class-divided to classless society requires a change in the economic basis of society from a capitalist to a socialist mode of production. Class relationships, as we have seen, are ultimately determined by the relations of different sections of the community to the means of production and when the means of production belong to society as a whole, that is the beginning of the abolition of classes. This change is only different from other fundamental alterations in the social base which have already occurred in that, while previous changes concerned which class was to exploit workers, the working class itself exploits no one and in emancipating itself it liberates all society from exploitation.

Moral systems in the past, arising within class-divided societies, have 'represented either a dominant class's sanction to rule or an exploited class's consolation in suffering' as two aspects of the same antagonistic social situation. Even so obviously an ethic of consolation for the oppressed and of resistance to the Roman oppressor as primitive Christianity could also be turned into an ideological instrument for the prosecution of the most ruthless class rule of the oppressed, both under feudalism and capitalism. Any attempts of these moral systems to reconcile conflicting class interests have been spurious because no practical programme for changing the basic social conditions out of which class conflict arises were ever proposed. Since society was to go on being divided, any resolution of class antagonism had to wait on the advent of utopias where either there was such an abundance of goods that with no necessity for work no one need go without or where beings with no material bodies to sustain did not need goods anyway. And these earthly or heavenly paradises of the future could be used by those who might be highly sceptical themselves of any such eschatological happy ending to persuade the working masses to moderate their claims for goods here and now, so that the very hope of a classless society of human brotherhood and plenty was turned into a class weapon in the hands of the exploiters.

In a world like ours where class differences not only divide capitalist exploiters from the workers in their own countries whose lives they more or less dominate but also from the toiling masses of the colonial and semi-colonial world where millions upon millions live on the verge of starvation, to talk in terms of vague expressions of general good will and universal brotherhood is meaningless. Nobody loves the people who feel no hatred for their oppressors and exploiters. The principle of humanism cannot bridge such a gulf without becoming stretched so thin that it is without content. Expressions of 'loving one's fellow human beings' in such a situation are not just hypocritical or impractical: they are obscene - like urging the Vietnamese people, when the United States aggressors were raining down on them the most vicious and diabolical weapons ever devised, or the people of Nicaragua or Angola or Cambodia when thugs supplied by the United States with weapons of mass destruction were killing men, women and children, 'to turn the other cheek'! As Mao Tsetung has said:

> as for the so-called love of humanity, there has been no such all-inclusive love since humanity was divided into classes. All the ruling classes of the past were fond of advocating it, and so were many so-called sages and wise men, but nobody has ever really practised it, because it is impossible in class society.[40]

Therefore Marxism preaches no morality of brotherly love in general in material circumstances rendering it impossible. Instead it considers how those circumstances themselves can be changed by studying the means whereby the foundations for a classless social order can be laid. Now in the context of moral systems based on various forms of class division, a theoretical and practical collective effort directed toward altering that very basis of all past morality is not merely relative to those other moral systems: it is absolute in the only sense in which we can ever know absolutes - as a conflict of opposites in which one aspect so completely overcomes the other that the whole situation is completely altered and entirely new considerations come into play.

Marxism is thus a completely radical approach to the question of morality because it envisages a fundamental change in the very conditions under which thinking about morality takes place. In the process of changing those conditions people also change themselves. What Marxism ultimately says in normative terms is simply this: if you are serious about wanting a world in which all people can work together in harmony, helping one another to realise the full human potential in each, then there is a certain kind of social organisation you must struggle to achieve. And, further, it says: since 'mankind only takes up such problems as it can solve because the problem itself arises only when the material conditions for its solution already exist or are at least in the process of formation',[41] this moral challenge to transform society only sounds when the means for its realisation are at hand.

CONSCIENCE AND CLASS CONSCIOUSNESS

Just as the foetus recapitulates various stages through which the human animal has developed in its evolution so there is a subconscious moral and emotional recapitulation of the stages the human animal has passed through on its way to becoming a communicative social human being. Dim fleeting reflections of some of these subconscious stages of inner development may seem like the magical or religious myths which circulated among our human race in its infancy.

Everyone is born in a particular social environment and is subjected from the earliest days to a number of influences which become part of that subconscious emotional development and begin, even before the child is aware of it, to guide conduct and even to give some kind of shape to ideas about how one ought to behave. These conditioned responses are so habitual at first as to seem almost instinctive. They develop into an inner regulator of behaviour called conscience, an internal censor which governs conduct much as any memorised set of rules regulates some specific form of activity. But life is not a game one can choose to play or not and everyone has to live in society so these learned patterns of behaviour which are socially determined acquire a compulsive force.

This guidance from within is practically automatic except when some occasion arises for acting against its dictates, whereupon one becomes acutely aware of it through a sense of uneasiness, a foreboding of impending disaster, a feeling of guilt. Since conscience is the individual's built-in compendium of social rules, to defy its injunctions is to act out in some degree the old tragedy of breaking a taboo and finding oneself ostracised from the tribal group.

Because all who grow up in society acquire a conscience and because all social groupings have certain human relationships more or less in common, it is often assumed that the moral contents of everyone's conscience must be the same. The kind of sanction invoked in a particular society to give social rules a greater force will also be used to explain the origin of the individual conscience: if such rules are taken to be prescriptions handed down from on high by some supernal being, then conscience is described as the god-given faculty enabling the individual to appreciate the relevance of those rules to daily life; if rules of social behaviour are deduced from an eternal and universal reason, then conscience is the individual's innate rationality by which the validity of such ideal principles can be recognised. Whatever the form of these sanctions they all rely for their authority on the assumption that they apply to all people under all circumstances.

But, in fact, conscientious behaviour reveals the same variety as the patterns of social mores which have characterised different societies or different classes within the same society. The exploited and their exploiters, even though they may subscribe to the same religious creed and be subject to the same civil laws, reflect very different social influences in their built-in moral compulsions. Members of the working class, for example, are likely to be most conscientious about collective solidarity with workmates. 'Sending someone to Coventry' for an infringement of that solidarity is the proletarian equivalent of tribal ostracism. The bourgeoisie, on the other hand, are likely to be most conscientious about individual contractual agreements. For non-compliance with such obligations they are likely to pursue each other, even the closest relatives, through the courts in endless litigation. Even in respect to those relationships which all would seem to have in common, like attitudes toward sex and marriage and toward parental and filial obligations, the classes diverge in what they naturally consider right conduct.

Differences in norms of behaviour as rooted in the consciences of people with different social experiences become crucial for the moral philosopher when confronted with the problem that people who it may be widely agreed have perpetrated the vilest acts in history often seem to have been perfectly sincere in believing that they were behaving conscientiously - and, furthermore, have been able to persuade others under the same morbid social conditions that they were doing right. This has even led some writers on ethical questions to enter a plea for a life of personal indulgence as opposed to one of high moral endeavour on the ground that if the former achieves nothing to the benefit of human kind it at least, unlike the latter, avoids the risk of doing any great harm either. But, of course, what is really wanted is a critique of the individual conscience, implying thereby a critique of the social order conscience reflects.

In relatively stable societies, like the village communities of Asian feudalism in which life may have gone on virtually unchanged for centuries, the implanted consciences of individual members may be in such harmony with society's moral requirements that the whole ethical pattern of life is a more or less unconscious, religion-governed repetition of well-established customs. But in a situation of social mobility where individuals may be altering their class position or where classes themselves may be experiencing a change in their relationship to each other, people find that their consciences conservatively refer to a social context which no longer exists for them. This inevitably involves the individual in a moral crisis; and conscience can offer no guidance since its irrelevance to present circumstances is the very source of the trouble. Such a crisis in which the fundamental principles of conduct no longer seem to apply can, in times of rapid social change, afflict whole communities with a general malaise and the various neuroses which psychiatrists attempt to treat in terms of complexes rooted in a personal past are often individual instances of this wide-spread discrepancy between private consciences and altered public conditions.

The therapeutic treatment implied by a Marxist diagnosis of the problem is not unlike the effort to restore a patient to mental health by uncovering deep-seated disturbances and bringing to light unsuspected impulses - except that the cure has to be conceived in social rather than in individualistic terms. The private conscience must be raised to the level of awareness where its moral content can be studied and criticised: it must be seen for what it really is - unconscious group allegiance. Seeing it for what it is transforms the private conscience into class consciousness. Once it is realised that conscience is the uncritical and spontaneous form of one's sense of belonging to a particular class, it is possible to affirm those social ties consciously in purposeful activity or, if they do not seem to be in one's real interest or do not appear to conform to one's real class circumstances, to break them in order to adopt social ties that do.

The problem of a conscience at odds with real class interest is particularly characteristic of an exploited class. The fact we have already noted that 'the ideas of the ruling class are, in every age, the ruling ideas' and therefore the only ideas to circulate freely contributes to the problem. The ruling class has every interest in foisting its own ideology on those it oppresses in order to exploit. The capitalist system produces a working class whether its members realise it or not, a class-in-itself; but when its members are fully conscious of being exploited workers and examine their ideology to make sure that it really is their own and not simply foisted on them, then it becomes a class-for-itself.

In its knowledge of capitalist society, the proletariat was only in the perceptual stage of cognition in the first period of its practice, the period of machine-smashing and spontaneous struggle; it knew only some of the aspects and external relations of the phenomena of capitalism. But when it reached the second period of its practice, the period of conscious and organised economic and political struggles, the proletariat was able to comprehend the essence of capitalist society, the relation of exploitation between social classes and its own historical task; and it was able to do so because of its experience of prolonged struggle, which Marx and Engels scientifically summed up in all its variety to create the theory of Marxism for the education of the proletariat. It was then that the proletariat became a 'class-for-itself'.[42]

Only as a class-for-itself does the working class become a revolutionary force, hence the concern of the bourgeoisie that the working class should not know itself for what it really is, particularly in terms of its historic mission as the liberator of human kind. Full conscious membership in this liberation force, the working class, is an act of deliberate choice over and above the mere fact of having a certain relationship to the means of production - a choice which insofar as it is made on the basis of one's long-term interests is rational and, in so far as it commits one to the ethical standards of a class-for-itself, is moral. The choice, whether it is actually put into words or merely expresses itself in the quality of behaviour, is quite fundamental since it amounts to a decision about what system of ethical principles one intends all future actions to be judged by.

Marxist morality consists of an identification in struggle with the oppressed and the exploited against the oppressors and exploiters. By such a commitment one has chosen not only the class morality which is to be the standard of one's present actions but also the course of social conduct which will eventually resolve conflicting moralities into one embracing ethic reflecting the aspirations of all in an undivided society from which oppression and exploitation have been eliminated - what Lenin describes as 'helping human society to rise to a higher level'.

The whole of working class ethics is implicit in class struggle. In the idea of an exploited 'class' is all fellow feeling, comradeship, sympathy and concern for one's workmates - not a profession of regard in general for oppressors and oppressed alike which in embracing everyone actually clasps no one, nor comes to grips with anyone either; but a real, mutual, practical working relationship with all those sharing the same great historic task of ending that exploitation. In the idea of 'struggle' is the realisation that it is not a question of simply understanding the world but of changing it and of changing oneself in the process. It is the conviction that human nature can be changed - not by private conversion but by social revolution, by overthrowing a system where exploitation and inhumanity pay and establishing a system built on co-operative work and a general sharing of the good things of life.

These are the ideas, drawn from the historical experience of the working people of the world and elaborated in the Marxist theory of revolutionary change, which taken back to the working masses grip them and become 'a material force which changes society and changes the world'. Or as Enver Hoxha has expressed it:

> Marxism-Leninism is not a privilege and monopoly of certain able-minded people who can understand it. It is the scientific ideology of the working class and only when its ideas are mastered by the working class does it cease to be something abstract and become a great material force for the revolutionary transformation of the world.[43]

The working masses recognise these ideas, as concentrated in revolutionary theory, because they came from them to begin with and 'have the mark of the people on them'. This is the meaning of the mass line - from the masses to the masses, taking the ideas of the masses, scattered and unsystematic, concentrating and systematising them and then going to the masses and propagating and explaining these ideas 'until the masses embrace them as their own, hold fast to them and translate them into action, and test the correctness of these ideas in action.'[44] Because, of course, the gripping of the masses by ideas which thus become a material force is simply the third stage of the process of knowledge - the social practice without which the act of knowledge remains incomplete and there is no proper relationship between theory and practice. 'Theory becomes purposeless if it is not connected with revolutionary practice, just as practice gropes in the dark if its path is not illuminated by revolutionary theory.'[45]

Once the examined conscience, as a result of self-realisation in a struggle situation alongside one's comrades, appears as what it really is - class consciousness, then morality can appear as what it really is - the morale of a class force conscious of the justice of its struggle. Marxism lays great stress on the importance of morale which is the ethical aspect of ideas becoming a material force. In people's war, for example, which is the colonial, anti-imperialist form of class struggle, waged by the working masses against the vastly superior and infinitely better-armed professional armies of invaders, morale is the decisive factor. It enables the people of a small or industrially backward country to defeat and repel the aggressive forces of powerful imperialist countries. Mehmet Shehu who was one of the partisan leaders in Albania's war of liberation against Fascist Italy and Nazi Germany describes this advantage of morale:

> In fighting on the plains as well as in the mountains man is the decisive factor that determines the fate of the war regardless of armaments. A small army can defeat a bigger one, superior in numbers and means, if it wages a just war and if it is made up of men who are politically enlightened on the just nature of the war they are waging.[46]

The fighting morale of the Vietnamese people, under the leadership of Ho Chi Minh, sustained them through thirty-five years of continuous war during which they successively and decisively defeated the imperialist forces of Japan, France and the United States. The same point is made by Stalin in writing of the Great Patriotic War against Nazi Germany:

> The strength of the Red Army lies, primarily, in the fact that it is waging, not a predatory war, but a Patriotic War, a war of liberation, a just war...No German soldier can say that he is waging a just war, because he cannot fail to see that he is forced to fight for the plunder and oppression of other peoples. The German soldier has no lofty and noble aim in the war to inspire him and rouse his pride.[47]

For enlightened workers, class conscious workers, morale, in the same way, is their ethical conviction that their class war to end oppression and exploitation is a just war. This keeps the working class in good heart for the great liberation battles they have to wage, reminding them that they have class brothers and sisters in struggle the world over. In Mao Tsetung's inspiring words: 'Countless revolutionary martyrs have laid down their lives in the interests of the people, and our hearts are filled with pain as we the living think of them. Can there be any personal interest, then, t hat we would not sacrifice or any error that we would not discard?'[48]

In the act of commitment to this class struggle one has not only taken a decision about one's own ethical conduct, one has also expressed a concern for the ethical conduct of those yet unborn by fighting for a socialist form of society in which - because it is characterised by shared sufficiency rather than selfishly manipulated scarcities, because it is based on co-operation rather than competition - 'being good' in the fullest human sense will not only be the right thing but also, to a much greater extent than under capitalism, the natural thing to do. This attitude can be contrasted with the moral athleticism of those thinkers who, usually in the comfort of their studies, are prepared to accept social injustice and human suffering as a sort of ethical challenge by which people test and prove themselves. Of such 'moral heroism' one could say with Brecht 'Happy the land which has no need of heroes'. Marxists summon us to action thus: Let us end the infamy of starvation in a world capable of plenty and the waste through unemployment or misemployment of the creative talents of millions and millions of people; let us smash once and for all a system which values things but not the people who make them and rests on the bodies of innumerable babies condemned at birth to death, rejection or misuse; and let the future use its ingenuity to find its own moral causes when all completely unnecessary suffering has been eliminated!

They say this because such a moral response is simply part of what it is to be a class-conscious worker, conscious of one's ties with working people everywhere and a Marxist because Marxism is the ideology of the working class. Confronted with the innumerable victims and the incalculable damage to the environment of capitalist imperialism Marxists 'see the necessity and at the same time the condition of a transformation both of industry and of the social structure'. The Marxist Party which is the political organisation of the working class vanguard, in concentrating and elucidating the political consciousness of the working class, is its moral conscience also.

In making a point of the consciousness of this fundamental moral choice, which is simply an affirmation of working class allegiance in full understanding of all its implications, it is interesting to note that it is a privilege of the historical time we live in to choose with greater awareness than ever before of just what that choice entails. Past transformations of society resulting from the conflicts of classes have either taken place over so long a time scale that individuals at any particular period would hardly have been aware of the change, or else they have assumed obscure ideological forms like religious or dynastic wars so that people could not always recognise the nature of the economic interests at stake. The beginnings of feudal societies are never distinct enough to assign even approximate dates to their origin. The change from feudalism to capitalism was marked by certain precise engagements in this country or that; but these struggles often failed in definitiveness and, because they usually involved the recruitment of class forces not intended to benefit from the change, were fought out under a confusing multiplicity of banners.

There has thus been a progression in history by which each succeeding transformation has been a more distinct event in time and a more consciously-orientated social change than the one preceding. Lenin makes this point when he says that in the bourgeois revolution the new economic organisation 'gradually matured in the womb of feudalism'[49] while the socialist revolution is faced with the problem of transforming all capitalism's institutions in conformity with its abolition of the exploitative relationship. This implies both that revolutionary theory plays a more dynamic role in this most decisive of all social changes and that the real nature of the class interests involved reveal themselves more positively than in any past transition.

So now in the capitalist world we are confronted with the most distinctive, the most sharply-defined change of all history - the change from bourgeois rule to working class rule as the transitional stage of the change of class-divided to classless society. This transition from capitalism to socialism will also involve revolutions and counter-revolutions, victories and defeats, advances and retreats in the eventual transformation of capitalist barbarism into socialist civilisation. This transition will not take so long, however, because it is a much more conscious development. Those involved in the ideological conflict between capitalism and socialism are much clearer about the class interests, private profit or the collective good, which they respectively serve.

There are only the two sides now, the exploiters and the exploited, those who want to keep things as they are and those who want this great revolutionary change. There are no neutrals. Not to choose at all is to opt for the side with every interest in maintaining things as they are. Few can pretend that they do not know what the issues are and can therefore be absolved of the responsibility of choosing what is socially right.

This transition is also much more revolutionary since it involves humanising the very laws of supply and demand. The international market, which has been dominated by capitalists seeking private profit through their monopolies and cartels backed up by imperialist force, will reflect instead the needs of the world's peoples and the scarcity or abundance of various world resources. Stock markets instead of arenas where finance capitalists can profiteer from insider deals, take-overs, asset-stripping and withdrawing financial backing from where it is needed most to plump for the latest money-making gimmick will be organised under international control to show where investment is most needed and ought to be provided for the general good. The competitive 'law of the jungle', which is more the rule of human selfishness and greed than of any natural survival of the fittest, will be transformed into the co-operative order of human beings bringing together their individual talents to be employed in the collective interest of all. Previous changes in the basic mode of production altered the nature of class exploitation. Slave labour, serf labour and wage labour have been the successive forms of ruling class exploitation in the change from primitive mercantilism to feudalism to capitalism. The change from capitalism to socialism ends class exploitation altogether and establishes the only firm foundation for real political democracy.

THE ETHICS OF REVOLUTIONARY CHANGE

The economic base of capitalist society will not be altered because people arbitrarily decide that the cultural and ethical superstructure which might be raised on some other social base would be preferable. Cracks have to appear in that capitalist base, internal contradictions must reach a critical point before the utilitarian amorality in which economic rules usurp the role of moral standards breaks down. As long as the economic system appears to operate automatically and continues to hold out at least some promise of expanding material benefits for the majority, it will not be successfully challenged. A protracted crisis in such a system, however, precipitates morality out of its solution with economic rules to resume its place as a distinguishable, though never unrelated realm of discourse. The basic ordering of society, having failed to achieve what people had a right to expect, becomes once more a subject for normative speculation. An unresolved crisis in the capitalist mode of production must lead in time to its supersession by another, which simply means that the capitalist ruling class in whose interest society was basically organised is no longer able to maintain its rule and is supplanted by another whose very class nature involves an entirely different ordering of the economic base.

During the period of violent transition, since classes do not voluntarily abdicate from supremacy, the ethical implications of these conflicting forms of social organisation confront each other in fierce debate. Then with a new material foundation, the entire immense superstructure is more or less rapidly transformed. In considering such transformations a distinction should always be made between the material transformation of the economic conditions of production, which can be determined with the precision of natural science, and the legal, political, religious, aesthetic or philosophic - in short, ideological forms in which men become conscious of this conflict and fight it out.[50]

Not only must a distinction be made between the material transformation of the base and the ideology of the new class to assume economic and political power, but unless that new ideology is purged of the elements of the ideology of the overthrown class in a moral revolution as sweeping as the economic transformation, the base can be subverted by that unreconstructed ideology. Marx goes on to say in the same quotation:

Just as our opinion of an individual is not based on what he thinks of himself, so can we not judge of such a period of transformation by its own consciousness; on the contrary, this consciousness must be explained from the contradictions of material life, from the existing conflict between the social productive forces and the relations of production.

We have noted some of these religious and philosophical forms of special pleading in which class conflict in past periods of transformation has been fought out, and we are familiar in the present with the attack on Marxism, that is, on working class ideology, as godless, immoral, subversive of eternal truth, scientifically unsound and in every way vicious and reprehensible. But Marxism itself, as shown in the above quotation, is capable not only of characterising the way in which interested participants may fail to do justice to the actual contradictions of material life but also of expressing the working class's own consciousness of the real nature of the conflict between the forces and the relations of production, a conflict which can only be resolved by a revolutionary change in those relations.

Present-day capitalism is in a state of crisis as a result of the exacerbation of its inherent internal contradictions, contradictions which are just so many economic forms of class struggle. This has been so throughout the history of class-divided society. Slave revolts, peasant uprisings, organised working class resistance to exploitation are successive forms of the contradictions in the relations of production which have brought about social change. Fully developed commodity production depends on a free market for ordering the outlay of capital among various kinds of goods to be made; but the falling rate of profit under free competition, which is partly due to organised defence by workers of their standard of living, requires capitalists to try to gain control of the market in respect to the goods they themselves produce. The resulting monopolisation interferes with the free market and upsets the mechanism which preserves the balance between investment in means of production and investment in consumable goods. Attempts to increase profits by rises in productivity while real wages are cut is self-defeating since it increases output at the same time that it restricts effective demand.

Hence the massive investment in the armaments industry which is the one form of production where the capitalist does not have to wait for his commodity to be bought on the open market to collect his profit. The aggressive economic imperialism of capitalist governments will ensure opportunities of putting such arms to use, if not in the hands of its own soldiery then in the hands of thugs hired to murder those who seek to liberate their lands from capitalist imperialist domination.

The attempts by capitalists to evade contradictions at home by concentrating their activities abroad brings them into conflict with capitalists from other industrialised countries seeking the same remedy. This may not lead to another inter-capitalist imperialist war like World War I, but it certainly leads to trade wars and attempts to take over a competitor's industrial citadels. The formation of cartels, like the growth of monopoly in a single country, reproduces on an international scale the domestic effects of tampering with the freedom of the market while not replacing it with a rational scheme of production and exchange. And also the export of capital abroad where labour may be cheaper and profits higher deprives domestic industry of investment and erodes the production of value at home on which an economic empire must ultimately be based. The stock markets which originated as a means of raising investment capital for industry become the arbiters of which industries shall survive and increasingly they control the whole economy like a tail wagging the dog. The phase of finance capitalism, of commodity speculation more and more dissociated from the creation of value in the actual making of things, is like the second purely idealist and sterile speculative phase of the acquisition of knowledge once it is cut off from any base in the real world where nature is transformed for use and theory is vindicated in practice.

What all this means is simply that an anarchic system of production for profit, rather than a rational system of production geared to people's needs, cannot indefinitely survive the class antagonism it engenders. Capitalism will be destroyed by its internal contradictions, the essence of all these contradictions being that between exploiters and exploited, the class struggle. Revolution triumphs in Lenin's words when 'the lower classes do not want the old way, and when the upper classes cannot carry on in the old way'. What is essential for revolution is first, that a majority of the workers (or at least a majority of the class conscious, thinking, politically active workers) should fully understand that revolution is necessary and be ready to sacrifice their lives for it; secondly, that the ruling class should be passing through a governmental crisis, which draws even the most backward masses into politics.[51]

The working class revolution in the relations of production puts an end to production for profit by destroying its base in property rights. Since production is social, ownership of the product cannot equitably be based on the private ownership of property. This is not to suggest that justice would consist in disentangling for the purpose of fair payment the contribution of each separate person to social production. Once capitalist private property in the means of production has been established by divorcing peasants from the land and crafts people from their tools, it is not feasible to return to Locke's simple formula of deducing rights in specific things from the individual labour that produced them. Instead property in means of production itself must be socialised by common collective ownership, whereby a social right in things is fully established on the basis of the co-operative efforts of all who are associated in the productive process.

Under capitalism, particularly in its final and most corrupt phase, neither an individual nor a social relationship properly exists between productive effort and appropriation, and there is thus no ground for an ethical deduction of 'rights' in general, which means that there is no longer any basis for capitalist morality. The tendency of capitalism in Marx's words to 'establish an accumulation of misery' at one pole, 'corresponding with an accumulation of capital' at the other, whether within the metropolitan capitalist country itself or, even more catastrophically, within its economic empire increases to extremes which can only be called grossly immoral on a world scale.

Even if it were possible for the capitalist system to function in such a manner that there was a fairer sharing of the goods among those whose efforts are value-creative, as reformist social democrats never tire of proposing as an alternative to revolution, it would not meet the real objection to the system. It is an example of that consumers' bias which vitiates all such petty bourgeois schemes of pleading with capitalism to behave itself better. Alienation of the product is not the only or even the gravest crime of capitalism against the working class. More serious is the alienation of the workers' creative ability in the act of production, so that the very source of value, that which makes them human beings, is prostituted to profiteering and brings forth an increasing number of articles of questionable long-term value at an ever increasing long-term social cost, a production process in which workers have no say. This is not free labour but wage-slave labour.

In the succession of modes of production there is no gradual advance from lower to higher. Progress depends on shifts in the unity of opposites, which is the basic nature of everything, including societies, until one aspect of the major contradiction determining the character of a thing suppresses the other and a new unity of opposites, that is to say, a new thing is born. This process of change cannot but be discontinuous, revolutionary rather than evolutionary.

Each of the modes of production must find conditions right for its inception, grow to its full extent and exhaust all its possibilities before giving way to a successive mode. But progress may also be discontinuous in the sense that a society which experiences the earliest and fullest development of a particular mode of production, while generating the ideas which will help shape the next stage, may have become so encumbered with a bureaucratic and military apparatus, so encrusted with all the forms and institutions of an outworn ideology that it will not itself be the immediate locus of revolutionary change. Such change will begin on the periphery of the unevenly developed system where its organisation is weakest and where the forms of an even earlier mode of production still exist but are in process of rapidly collapsing - as in the case of Russia, and to an even greater extent as far as the very primitive development of capitalist institutions is concerned, countries like China, Albania and Vietnam.

Critics of Marx have tried to make capital out of his alleged mistake of prophesying that the working class revolution ought to begin in one of the older industrialised countries. At various times in the shifting historical perspective of nineteenth-century Europe Marx thought various countries might be the scene of the first successful proletarian revolution, including Russia which might proceed directly to a successful 'socialist revolution without the intervention of a developed bourgeois stage'.

But this would mean that the first workers state would come into being without the experience and institutions of liberal democracy even in its limited capitalistic form. Lenin was aware of this problem. He says: 'The whole difficulty of the Russian revolution is that it was much easier for the Russian revolutionary working class to start than it is for the West European classes, but it is much more difficult for us to continue.' It was easier for the Russian working class to overthrow a semi-feudal ruling class but it will be much easier for a West European or North American working class, used to defending its democratic rights by trade union organisation, to turn the limited democracy of capitalism into the full democracy of socialism.

Mao Tsetung was also aware of this problem and contributed to its solution with his proposal for a two stage revolution. The first stage would be a bourgeois-democratic revolution to establish the social conditions enabling a more highly developed working class to proceed to the second stage of a full proletarian socialist revolution. The 'proletarian cultural revolution' was intended to facilitate the transition by helping a predominantly peasant population to come to terms with working class ideology.

Lenin's backward step of a 'new economic policy' and Mao's two-stage revolution were both ways of compressing the history of capitalist development into as short a period of time as possible in order to get on with the building of socialism which has to grow out of the rejection of capitalism.

There is a kind of glee with which critics point out that the revolution Marx predicted has not occurred in any of the advanced capitalist countries, even though they would hate it if it had! One of the forms of their criticism of Marx's predictions is to take what he described as tendencies and treat them as mechanical laws disproved by the slightest deviation. Think of all the arguments against the falling rate of profit when the whole impulse of monopolisation at home and massive investment abroad is a tribute to it. Or that other tendency which has aroused such controversy - the pauperisation of the working class. With the uneven development of capitalism it has been possible at particular times and places, during transitory periods of prosperity, for a well-organised working class to wrest some economic and political concessions from the employing class; but never to the point of altering basically the relative positions of a tiny capitalist minority, on the one hand, owning and controlling a huge proportion of the wealth of the country and the vast working majority, on the other, never, at the best of times, more than a year away from penury. And always there is a poverty-stricken 'reserve army' of unemployed available to drive down the market value of labour-power and keep wages from rising above the subsistence level characteristic of that particular society. Britain in the 'eighties has been an example of what happens to welfare schemes won by past struggle when capitalism is in decline.

What has been made most of in this context is the greater degree of oppression and misery of workers in colonial territories compared with workers in metropolitan countries and the effects this is supposed to have had on the revolutionary elan of the latter. Naturally the ruling class in the metropolitan countries would like to associate the working class ideologically, but not of course economically, in their colonial depredations. Certainly the Fabians and other social democrats sometimes based their case for social reforms on the argument that only a well-fed, well-educated working class could help run a world-wide economic empire. But since there is no more material basis for workers in the metropolitan country to think of themselves as sharing in the exploitation of workers in the underdeveloped world than for a skilled worker in a factory to think that his higher rate of pay means he has joined the ranks of management in exploiting his workmates, the illusion of 'sharing in the crumbs' of the imperialist feast could take no firm hold on workers' minds.

Some thinkers of the left have fallen for the line of treating imperialist exploitation as some new kind of conflict, between rich and poor countries or even between whites and other races, which made capitalists and workers in the metropolitan country partners in crime. For them the working class of the older industrialised countries has become so fat and corrupt with good living that emancipation can only be conceived of in terms of a liberative force of poor workers and peasants from the colonial world arriving on the shores of the metropolitan country to free it! Other leftists also divide the working class from the workers and peasants of the colonial world and by mechanically applying a class analysis to liberation movements and pronouncing them non-revolutionary because they are not led by a large urban proletariat argue that they are bound to be frustrated in their political aims on achieving independence by industrial backwardness. If according to the former the older industrialised countries are too rich to have a socialist revolution, according to the latter all other countries are too poor to have one.

But then if working class revolutions are for the present ruled out everywhere 'revolutionary' intellectuals are not called on to do anything about their radical sympathies. Such intellectuals, who like to think of themselves as sacrificing their middle class privileges to put themselves at the head of the working class, are a nuisance anyway.

They should realise that the polarisation of classes in advanced capitalist society has turned them into workers, too, with nothing but their mental labour power to sell. They need to learn about class struggle from fellow workers with a much longer experience of the enemy. They have a tendency to turn every conflict between workers and employers into one between different sections within the working class - as when they attempt to set unskilled against skilled workers, unorganised against organised, rank and file against stewards and officials, ostensibly because the worst off are supposed to be the more revolutionary, actually because they are thought to be easier dupes of these would-be leaders. If there were an automatic relationship between degrees of oppression and degrees of revolutionary fervour, every real revolutionary would have to be primarily concerned with making the working class as miserable as possible!

To these tamperers with working class unity must be added all those agents of the bourgeoisie who try to split up workers academically - sociologists who want to compartmentalise them on the basis of income differentials, status symbols, accent or what not. They all serve the same overriding interest of the ruling capitalist class whose policy toward workers at home or abroad is always 'divide and rule' - just as the policy of the working class must always be 'unite and liberate'.

Workers can only fight where they are and the best service the workers of a metropolitan country can do for their embattled class brothers and sisters overseas is to make revolution in their own land - just as immigrant workers themselves can only be mobilised for revolutionary struggle within the organised ranks of their working class brothers and sisters in the adopted land where they are presently being exploited. At various times the class struggle may be more intense within the major capitalist countries or between imperialists and the working masses of the semi-colonial territories; but these struggles are always complementary since they are being waged against the same class enemy.

Another critic of Marx, Ralf Dahrendorf, sees a greater diversification of the working class as having the effect of weakening it as an anti-capitalist force; but as we have already noted, so-called 'white collar' workers in Britain including the professions, clerks, sales people, nurses and health workers and employees in local and national government not only belong to unions and adopt the same means of struggle as industrial workers but increasingly recognise themselves as belonging to the working class. Dahrendorf also makes much of the diversification within the ruling class itself between owners and controllers of the means of production as though this distinction invalidated somehow the revolutionary prescription of expropriating the owners. But Marx had made the same distinction himself in his discussion of joint-stock companies and had realised that it was a distinction without a class difference and certainly did not, as some of his critics maintain, turn capitalism into some different mode of production.

Most of these apologists for capitalism are victims of their own propaganda. They adduce as reasons for rejecting the Marxist analysis 'changes' in the nature of capitalism which are often capitalism's superficial attempts to pretend to be something else in order to avoid the consequences of that very Marxist analysis. If they really did think that re-definition of classes or changing capitalism's name had made revolution impossible, they would probably not go on making it their life's work to show why revolutions cannot happen. Perhaps they are only trying to reassure their employers or, perhaps, they are 'moles' serving the workers' cause by disarming their employers to the end of a less violent transition!

The moral crisis of capitalism is a reflection of the economic crisis - not just a periodic depression but the chronic under-employment or misuse of human skills and productive capacity. Just as a particular ordering of the material basis of society and its characteristic relations of production give rise to a productive potential on which those relations begin to act as a limitation, so it also gives rise to moral ideas which cannot be realised within its confines. Implicit in the development of capitalism was the promise to free people from subservience to others and abolish the relationship of subjection. What it actually did, as we have seen, was to conceal the fact of exploitation behind a commodity deal - and in its external relations with technologically less developed regions it dispensed with any mask at all. 'The colonies secured a market for the budding manufacturers, and, through the monopoly of the market, an increased accumulation. The treasures captured outside Europe by undisguised looting, enslavement, and murder, floated back to the mother-country and were there turned into capital.'[52]

From the law of value, as the fundamental principle of commodity exchange, was deduced by way of the equalisation of human labour the idea of the equality of human beings; and this same principle both recalls the primitive formula that what people have mixed their labour with ought to belong to them and points ahead to a rational and moral order in which the values produced socially will belong to the whole society. But the fact of surplus-value, as a levy the class controlling the means of production exacts from the class possessing only its own labour-power, negates these ethical ideas of past and future. Colonialism is only the most blatant and brutal form of the scramble for surplus-value. Marx describes it as 'the strange god' who perched himself on the altar cheek by jowl with the old Gods of Europe, and one fine day with a shove and a kick chucked them all of a heap. It proclaimed surplus-value making as the sole end and aim of all humanity.'[53]

> The direct aim of capitalist production is not the production of goods, but the production of surplus-value, or of profit in its developed form; not the product but the surplus product. From this standpoint, labour itself is productive only in so far as it creates profit or surplus product for capital. In so far as the worker does not create it, his labour is unproductive. Consequently, the sum total of

> applied productive labour is of interest to capital only to the extent that through it the sum total of surplus labour increases. Only to that extent is what is called necessary labour time necessary. To the extent that it does not produce this result, it is superfluous and has to be discontinued.

Marx goes on to say:

> It is the constant aim of capitalist production to produce the maximum surplus value or surplus product with the minimum of capital advanced; in so far as this result is not attained by overworking the labourer, it is a tendency of capital to seek to produce a given product with the least expenditure - economising labour-power and costs. The labourers themselves figure in this conception as what they actually are in capitalist production - only means of production; not an aim in themselves and not the aim of production.'[54]

And yet in spite of profits being the sole aim of capitalist production, the rate of profit in Britain, the oldest capitalist country, has fallen catastrophically. The capitalists' rate of profit is determined by the amount of unpaid labour, or surplus-value, he extracts from workers divided by the amount he spends on means of production - rent, machinery, raw materials and so forth - together with the amount he spends on wages. It is a simple arithmetical fact that if he spends more on new and improved machines to secure a competitive advantage while the amount of surplus-value remains the same, then the rate of profit will fall. In fact, in Britain the rate of profit has been estimated to have fallen from about 16 or 17 per cent at the time of Marx's death in 1883 to 14 per cent just before the First World War; to an average of around 11 percent in the inter-war period; and is now, in many branches of manufacturing, no more than 1 or 2 per cent.

At the same time the share of wages in production has changed very little: 38.6 per cent in 1870, 36.6 in 1913, 38.3 in 1939 and 41.8 in 1950. This means that the class struggle waged by organised workers over this period has kept the amount of surplus-value relatively constant. Therefore, with the increase of investment in means of production, what Marx calls a rise in the organic composition of capital, there has been a steady decline in the rate of profit - now so low as to threaten the future of British industry, unless the working class can be cajoled or bullied into accepting a drastic reduction in their standard of living.

To the very extent that capitalism fails to justify the economic and ethical hopes which were the ideological motive force of its conquest of feudalism it is preparing the way for its own supersession. The same process which perverts and exploits human labour in setting up profits for a small capitalist class as the sole aim toward which the entire energy of society is directed also produces the agents of its own transformation - an organised working class with no share in the ownership and control of the means of production, no voice in the direction of the economic system of the country and, therefore, every reason for wishing to see it replaced by a democratic system.

Not that it is simply the induced misery of a labouring class which leads to the overthrow of a particular form of exploitation: people have lived at a bare subsistence level for long periods without revolting against their conditions. There must also be the awareness that some other form of social organisation is possible; and this depends in part on the productive forces having attained such a level that further expansion is seen to be thwarted not by the limits of people's ability but by arbitrary restrictions imposed in the interest of profit. Workers who know that products which are the fruits of their labour could be made to last by using better materials or that good materials, the fruits of other workers' efforts, should not be wasted on gimcrack products; inventors who see their ideas bought up simply to be suppressed; social scientists who are employed to use their understanding of human motivation to intensify exploitation; research workers whose facilities for experiment depend on a government's military aggressiveness in policing overseas investments - all of these may be brought to a realisation that there ought to be some social system which would free their talents and skills for the unhampered creation of values that all people could share in peace. This 'ought' crystallises the moral impulse which cannot find its proper expression in the existing system. It can only be realised in a revolutionary transformation in the material conditions of life by which the commodity form of articles disappears and production is directly related to human needs.

Let us see how Marx treats the change in the normative concept of 'right' in the transition from capitalist to socialist society. To begin with we are dealing with 'a communist society not as it has developed on its own foundations, but, on the contrary, just as it emerges from capitalist society; which is thus in every respect, economically, morally and intellectually, still stamped with the birth marks of the old society from whose womb it emerges.' In this society which we would call socialist:

> The individual producer receives back from society - after the deductions have been made (cost of government administration, of education, health, funds for those unable to work etc) - exactly what he gives to it. What he has given to it is his individual quantum of labour...He receives a certificate from society that he has furnished such and such an amount of labour, and with this certificate he draws from the social stock of means of consumption as much as the same amount of labour costs...The same principle prevails as in the exchange of commodity equivalents: a given amount of labour in one form is exchanged for an equal amount of labour in another form. Hence equal right here is still bourgeois right, although principle and practice are no longer at loggerheads (bourgeois right freed from bourgeois exploitation)...This equal right is an unequal right for unequal labour. It recognises no class differences, because everyone is only a worker like everyone else; but it tacitly recognises unequal individual endowment and thus productive capacity of the worker as natural privileges...Further, one worker is married, another not; one has more children than another, and so on. Thus, with an equal performance of labour,

> one will in fact receive more than another, one will be richer than another.[55]

Marx goes on to say:

> These defects are inevitable in the first phase of communist society as it is when it has just emerged from capitalist society. Right can never be higher than the economic structure of society and its cultural development conditioned thereby.

In the classless society of the future, once all exploitation has been eliminated and all the habits, customs and ways of thought characteristic of an acquisitive society have been purged, people will be engaged in a co-operative social effort giving everyone full scope for self-expression in creative work and at the same time providing the fund of goods from which everyone draws at need. The whole process of production and consumption will have become united once more, as in the case of a peasant family or a primitive communist tribe - but with the difference that it will represent, through the enormous increase in the knowledge of productive technique during the commodity period, a direct sharing of wealth instead of poverty. 'In place of the old bourgeois society, with its classes and class antagonisms, we shall have an association, in which the free development of each is the condition for the free development of all.'[56]

A social change of this order will take a very long time indeed. There will be successful revolutions and liberation wars to end exploitation in this place or that followed by more or less successful attempts to establish socialist relations of production in which human beings do not exploit each other. There will also be counter-revolutions and re-conquests, retreats as well as advances. But the goal of a genuinely free society from which exploitation has been eliminated will have been set up so that these successes and failures can be measured. The working people of the world will come to know the kind of society they are struggling for, one in which 'the vivid creativeness of the masses' is directed toward producing the goods to satisfy their needs, not to make profits for the few.

In such a society the law of value, relieved of the task of relating the disparate acts of people working blindly in an atomised society, will vanish; and goods themselves will no longer pass through a phase in which their relative pricing marks them as abstract values in contradistinction to their usefulness. Labour and satisfaction will cease to be separated from each other, healing the breach between duty and pleasure, reason and feeling. The distinguishable elements of value and utility which we found within the very meaning of a word like 'good' will coalesce; and anything whatever which is conducive to the realisation of the human potential in all of us, by way of creation or recreation, will be designated as good in a completely integrated sense. The conception of labour as 'disutility', something painful and unpleasant by its very nature, partly because of the actual conditions of work where labour is exploited and partly because of attitudes toward physical effort by a detached intelligentsia, will disappear. As Marx describes it:

> In a higher phase of communist society, after the enslaving subordination of the individual to the division of labour, and with it also the antithesis between mental and physical labour, has vanished; after labour has become not only a means of life but itself life's prime want; after the productive forces have also increased with the all-round development of the individual, and all the springs of co-operative wealth flow more abundantly - only then can the narrow horizon of bourgeois right be crossed in its entirety and society inscribe on its banners: From each according to his ability, to each according to his needs![57]

CHAPTER II RIGHTS

1 *Marx, 'The German Ideology', p14*
2 *John Locke, 'Second Treatise of Civil Government', p15*
3 *Marx, 'The German Ideology', p22*

4 *Marx, 'Capital', vol, I, p79*
5 *Marx, 'Capital', vol, I, p13*
6 *Marx, 'The German Ideolgy' p22*
7 *Marx, 'The german Ideology'*
8 *Marx, 'Grundrisse'*
9 *Plato, 'The Republic', p293*
10 *Ibid., p287*
11 *Ibid., p316*
12 *Aristotle, 'The Nicomachean Ethics', pp222-3*
13 *Aristotle, 'Politics', p15*
14 *'Studies in Ancient Greek, The Prehistoric Aegean.*
15 *Aristotle, 'The Nicomachean Ethics', p36*
16 *Aristotle, 'Politics', p37*
17 *George Thomson, The Prehistoric Aegean, 'Studies in Ancient Greek Society', pp357-8*
18 *Aristotle, 'Politics', p19*
19 *R.H. Tawney, 'Religion and the Rise of Capitalism', p53*
20 *Marx, 'Critique of Hegel's Philosophy of Right'*
21 *Engels, Preface to 'Poverty of Philosophy', p13*
22 *Marx, 'The German Ideology'*
23 *Marx, 'Capital', vol, III,*
24 *Marx, 'The Poverty of Philosophy'*
25 *Marx, 'The Civil War in France'*
26 *Marx, 'The Eighteenth Brumaire of Louis Bonaparte' Selected Works vol, I, p225*
27 *Marx and Engels, 'The Communist Manifesto' Selected Works, vol I p33*
28 *Ibid., p35*
29 *Mao Tsetung, 'On Contradiction' Selected Works, vol, I, p313*
30 *Engels, 'Herr Eugen Duhring's Revolution in Science' p109*
31 *Mao Tsetung, 'Rectify the Party's Style of Work' Selected Works vol, III, p39*
32 *Marx, 'The German Ideology' p39*

33 *Marx and Engels, 'The Communist Manifesto' Selected Works vol, I, p42*
34 *Marx, 'The German Ideology' p41*
35 *Eugene Kamenka, 'The Ethical Foundations of Marxism' p129*
36 *Marx, 'Critique of the Gotha Programme' Selected Works vol, II, p23*
37 *Marx, 'The German Ideology' p15*
38 *Mao Tsetung, as quoted in 'Philosophy no Mystery'*
39 *Marx, 'The German Ideology' p41*
40 *Mao Tsetung, 'Talks at the Yenan Forum on Literature and Art' Selected Works vol, III, p91*
41 *Marx, 'Preface to the Critique of Political Economy' Selected Works vol, I, p329*
42 *Mao Tsetung, 'On Practice' Selected Works vol, I, p301*
43 *Enver Hoxha, 'Report to the Vth Party Congress' p177*
44 *Mao Tsetung, 'Concerning Methods of Leadership' Selected Works vol, III, p119*
45 *Stalin, 'The Foundations of Leninism'*
46 *Mehmet Shehu, 'On the Experience of the National Liberation War'*
47 *Stalin, 'The Great Patriotic War'*
48 *Mao Tsetung, 'Unite and Fight to Accomplish the Party's Tasks' Selected Works vol, III, p31*
49 *Lenin, 'Report on War and Peace' Selected Works vol, II, p293*
50 *Marx, 'Preface to the Critique of Political Economy' Selected Works vol, I, p329*
51 *Lenin, 'Left-wng Communism, an Infantile Disorder' Selected Works vol, II, p621*
52 *Marx, 'Capital' vol I p753*
53 *Ibid., p754*
54 *Marx, 'Theories of Surplus Value' part 2 chapter 18*
55 *Marx, 'Critique of the Gotha Programme' Selected Works vol, II, p23*
56 *Marx and Engels, 'The Communist Manifesto'*
57 *Marx, 'Critique of the Gotha Programme' Selected Works vol, II, p23*

Chapter 3
Obligations – The meaning of Moral Imperatives

INTRODUCTION

In the previous section we saw how normative judgments expressing the idea of 'rights' or 'the right' are grounded in certain specific claims and their recognition inherent in a particular mode of production and in the exploitative class relationships characteristic of that mode. When one is confronted with alternative modes of production in periods of social transformation, the need arises to judge normatively between two different systems of normative judgment. Which of two contrasting moralities is closer to the realities of social production, thus providing a sounder basis for the exercise of human purpose, or which of them seems to guarantee a fuller, richer life for the vast majority of people, thus broadening the base of human creativity for the general good? These are considerations which transcend the conditions of ethical thinking identified with a class concerned with preserving its own interests by defending an existing exploitative situation.

Having stated the circumstances under which judgments of this 'transcendent' type become incumbent and having indicated the ethical superiority of socialism over capitalism as an ordering of human affairs, we ended the last section with the obligation of commitment in the social struggle to bring the superior system into being. This is the moral aspect of Marx's famous dictum: 'The philosophers have only interpreted the world, in various ways; the point, however, is to change it'.[1] This statement, by postulating the unity of theory and practice, draws attention to the link which, we have argued, must be found between the descriptive and prescriptive aspects distinguishable within our ethical concepts. We have dealt with the question of how the same philosophical language can accommodate both facts and value and also explained the relationship between them. Now we shall be concerned with what is basically the same problem but now taking the form of how there can be scientific socialism, or knowledge of the laws of social development making collective action to change society effective and how, at the same time, there can be the freedom of individual action which makes it sensible to urge people to change society and, since social existence determines consciousness, to change themselves in the process.

Of course, as we have seen already, such a choice of action is not made in a vacuum. Marx has said of human activity in general: 'Men make their own history. But they do not make it just as they please; they do not make it under circumstances chosen by themselves, but under circumstances directly encountered, given and transmitted from the past'.[2] People make their own choices, but they do not at the same time choose the conditions under which such choices are made, nor even, generally speaking, do they choose the class influence through which, for them, historical conditions are filtered, profoundly colouring the moral attitudes which are the basis of choice. The question of the extent to which people acting under the compulsion of class interests can reasonably be applauded or condemned for their actions according to standards of conduct based on more comprehensive human interests is a bit like the question of the moral culpability of soldiers carrying out orders in time of war. What we have to consider is whether these historical and social qualifications of individual choice leave any freedom of action at all; and if so just what is meant by it.

We have dealt with the whole question of value by analysing the concept of 'good'; we have dealt with the question of claims on people and things by analysing the concept of 'right'; and now the question of the limits and scope of freedom of choice and action requires us to analyse the concept of 'ought'. When we say that a person ought to do a certain thing, we normally mean both that he has some kind of obligation to do it and that he can do it. We would not say that a person ought to do something he could not conceivably accomplish.

Nor would we be likely to say that he ought to do something he cannot possibly help doing. This ordinary usage indicates some element of freedom in the very meaning of 'ought'. Many philosophers have elaborated accounts of human action in which there was no such element; but the very logical absurdity of urging, on the basis of such accounts, that people ought not to use sentences with 'ought' in them draws attention to some of the problems about this aspect of morality. We must try to discover what this element of freedom is and how Marxism with its own account of the springs of human action accommodates it, thus allowing Marxists their legitimate expression of political urgency implying moral imperatives which can only be advanced in 'ought' sentences.

MOTIVES AND EFFECTS

In the first section it was pointed out that one use of the word 'good' is for the purpose of commendation. A thing can be designated as good because it is something which ought to be approved. This use of 'good' as the ought-to-be-approved cannot be a mere description of what the thing actually is, for commending it implies that it need not have been what it is, that it could have been something else of an inferior nature. Descriptive statements about a thing's utilisable qualities are limited to the present; but the prescriptive meaning of 'goodness', as expressed in the injunction that it ought to be liked or approved, refers us back in time to the purpose for which the thing was originally made and the constructive efforts of the maker to serve that purpose. In other words, value judgments, by linking an object's observable properties which satisfy a human need here and now with the purposive effort which went into its fabrication at some time in the past, give us the history of that object in human terms. Such judgments thus combine, in making appraisal possible, the presently existing object with a reminder of its non-existence in a previous period when it was as yet only an unrealised intention.

This combination of existent thing with the idea of its non-existence in order to appreciate it properly is the practical application of the purely idealistic synthesis between Being and Non-Being which sets the Hegelian dialectic in motion.

Similarly, any moral judgment that an action is what ought to have been done and therefore one of which we ought to approve, includes not only a description of that act in terms of its immediate consequences but also a reference back to the motives of the actor before it was ever performed and to the moral exertion its performance required. According to whether the present results of an act or the past decision to perform it is emphasised, we get quite different theories of morality. If the descriptive aspect of an act is stressed, our moral judgments can be translated into factual propositions about the objective changes which the act has effected. If, however, more importance is given to the original choice of performing that particular act rather than some other, then we must concern ourselves with such subjective considerations as the nature of the impulse which led to its performance, whether, on the information available, the most reasonable means to a proposed end was selected and also, going more deeply into the matter, just how free that original choice was and, even, what such 'freedom' means.

To say that a particular effect of some action is good or bad irrespective of how or why it was brought about, thereby divorcing the idea of morality from the motive for producing that effect, would make all action a complete ethical gamble with no possibility of knowing until after a thing was done and its results observed whether it had been right or not. In placing the onus of moral judgment on the act as objectively described we are saying that the act itself has the character of ought-to-be-doneness, which makes obligation a function of the act's performance. We have already noted that part of the meaning of 'ought', the very part we are interested in as the source of some degree of freedom, is bound up with the possibility of an enjoined act not being done; and this possibility can characterise the one who acts or does not act but not the act itself. Assertions containing the terms 'ought' or 'ought not' attribute a certain urgency not to a certain activity but to a certain person. In any attempt to explain the morality of actions in terms of their objective results alone, we are either denying ourselves the use of a moral language altogether and cannot therefore say that a particular result of an action is good or bad in any ethical sense, or else we are committing the naturalistic fallacy of employing moral terms which cannot be legitimately deduced from the mechanical materialist theory of human action we have adopted.

But if we attempt to attach moral significance solely to the motives from which an act is performed, the difficulties are just as serious. For one thing, motives are seldom simple and, taken on their own, we can hardly ever say even in the case of actions we perform ourselves to what extent they are to be accounted for in terms of doing our duty, serving the interests of others, wishing to be thought well of or any number of other considerations, some admirable, some not. And, of course, in the case of actions performed by others the problem of judging motives is still more complicated. Furthermore, while at any particular moment we can decide to do a certain thing, we cannot decide then and there to have certain motives for doing it. Our motives seem to be part of the given situation in which the decision to act occurs; and if 'ought' sentences are only about them, this idealist approach has brought us no closer to finding the element of freedom which is part of the meaning of 'ought'.

Objections to either the view that we are obliged to produce certain results or that we are obliged to act from certain motives have led some philosophers, as W. David Ross notes, to argue that morality consists in the setting of ourselves to produce certain results.[3] It is thus the intention in an act, including to some extent both motive and result, which makes it right or wrong. By partially relating motive and result this view meets some of the objections raised before. If the setting of ourselves to achieve a particular result is what we are obliged to do, we would not have to know in advance all the effects of our act nor even if it is going to prove possible to carry out our intention. And it may be that, within limits, we can set ourselves to act from one motive rather than another. However, if it is psychologically possible for our intentions at the moment of choice to be distinguished from our motives to the extent of being able to select among them for the right one, such intentions, divorced from any very compelling force to act, are likely to remain idle; and if it is not possible, then we have not really avoided the difficulties of a purely subjective account of obligation.

Now these two aspects of any action subjected to moral analysis, the objective results it brings about and the subjective motives which led to its performance, cannot be explained nor can the relationship between them be found by fixing our eyes steadily on the individual action itself - any more than we could account earlier for the two aspects of a commodity, its utility and its value, simply by staring hard at any particular commodity. 'Turn and examine a single commodity, by itself, as we will, yet in so far as it remains an object of value, it seems impossible to grasp it.'[4] Study an isolated act as we may, we do not discover what it is about the act or its performance that gives it moral significance. We only succeeded in accounting for the value of commodities by considering their history as extended in time and by understanding the social relationships encapsulated in them. It is only by looking at actions in the same manner that we can hope to explain the nature of their morality and understand the extent of our freedom to perform them. Looked at in this way we can see that motive and effect are inseparably related aspects of human action in the world. As Mao Tsetung expresses this:

> How can we tell the good from the bad - by the motive (the subjective intention) or by the effect (social practice)? Idealists stress motive and ignore effect, while mechanical materialists stress effect and ignore motive. In contradistinction, we dialectical materialists insist on the unity of motive and effect...The criterion

for judging subjective intention or motive is social practice and its effect.[5]

So the test for the moral nature of an action is the same as the test for the validity of an act of knowledge - social practice, without which we are like 'a doctor who merely writes prescriptions but does not care how many patients die of them'.

OURSELVES AND OTHERS

Once we have put actions back into the social context in which they actually occur, the distinction between objective results and subjective motivation can appear to us as a distinction between the actions of others and our own acts. In the case of our own acts we are primarily aware of what we intended to do; but as far as other people's actions are concerned, we tend to describe them solely in terms of their observable effects. Since ought-to-be-doneness cannot be characteristic of actions themselves and since the moral conduct of others has to be inferred from the actions we observe them performing, we seem to be in the curious position of only being able, with any certitude, to apply 'ought' sentences to ourselves. In fact, when we judge the behaviour of others, we do often make such remarks as: 'With such a background what could you have expected?' or 'Could a man with his habits have acted otherwise?' We are much less likely to exonerate ourselves in this manner; and, indeed, it sounds odd to say: 'I know I did wrong, but with my past history how could I have done anything else?' It sounds odd because we are in a position to know whether we could have avoided a certain action or not and if we could not, we would not characterise it as morally wrong. While we take our intentions and our limitations into account in any self-appraisal, others judge us as we judge them - strictly in terms of the objective results of our acts; and what seems to us a relatively free expression of some intention appears to others as but one act in a completely determined series of actions and consequences.

There is thus room for considerable difference between what we think of ourselves and what others think of us. Since our amour propre is constantly threatened by the opinions others have of us based on our naked acts, existentialist writers have even gone so far as to call other people our personal hell. But this conclusion may well be derived as much from the conditions of life in capitalist society where all people tend to be in competition with each other as from the analytical problem of moral judgment associated with such conditions.

This discrepancy which complicates the question of morality is precisely like the problem of other minds which has so absorbed the attention of analytical philosophers. The same sort of distinction between ourselves and others in respect to an analysis of moral actions also appears in an analysis of mental facts. If we say that we are in pain, we are referring more to our awareness of suffering than to any overt signs of it; but if we say that others are in pain, all the statement can mean literally is that they display certain expressions or that their bodies are in a certain physical state. Propositions about personal feelings thus have a different meaning for those who make them and for those to whom they are addressed. Just as we found that we only seemed able to make moral judgments about ourselves, so by the same sort of analytical approach we can only assume the existence of our own minds.

This analogy helps us to see where we have gone wrong. The view that people are shut up incommunicado within the confines of their own private experience is flatly contradicted every time any philosopher who holds it tries to express it in any way whatsoever. It is not possible to develop a solipsistic theory with consistency because it is false for a person to claim the exclusive experience of mental states if that person claiming it is anyone but ourselves. Since we know that we do experience mental states ourselves, we merely have to be able to imagine anyone else's holding the view of exclusively experiencing them to realise that the view is wrong.

Our mistake on the ethical plane, as on the epistemological, consists of starting from an unreal basis -ourselves as isolated individuals arrived at by a Cartesian abstraction. This mistake is compounded by thinking of reality, all that out there, as something mechanical, like a watch, which can be dismantled and re-assembled while we stand apart from it and deal with all the bits and pieces by means of a disjunctive, classificatory logic. It is this way of looking at moral questions which fails to see how the social whole is present in both the motive and effect of any action, in both the individuality and sociality of any actor, so that they are all linked together in a network of internal relations.

This inability to grasp the ways in which the social whole is present in any particular entity, so that it is seen as independent of the whole, as a mere abstraction, is itself characteristic of capitalist ideology. As we have seen before, the split between production and consumption reaching its greatest degree of separation under capitalist commodity exchange results in ideologists of the system being more involved with prices, money, ideas which are all abstractions than with concrete reality which is the raw material workers co-operatively shape into useful objects with particular qualities. Furthermore, capitalism's promise to 'free' the human individual from any master but money by replacing collective social ties with individualistic economic ones has had the effect of 'atomising' society as far as any fellow feeling is concerned and this is reflected in these extreme forms of analytical thinking. Once such thinking has isolated an entity as an abstraction, its uniqueness, that is, all the particular ways it is linked to other things within the whole, disappears and what is left is its superficial resemblance to other abstractions which can be arbitrarily lumped together. Intelligence degenerates into mere classification - almost as an ideological counterpart of the pigeon-holing of order forms and the assorting of items for dispatch in connection with the distribution of exchange values.

The technologically superior forces of production under capitalism involve the working class in working together co-operatively in large collectives; but capitalist relations of production involving the alienation from workers of surplus-value by the owners of these greater means of production have an alienating effect on workers themselves which tends to isolate them. Just because wage-slavery is not so obvious a form of exploitation as slavery or serfdom its effects of inhibiting valid modes of thought by separating individual workers out of their natural communal association with other workers may be more subtle. These alienated workers 'are separated from their work because they play no part in deciding what is to be produced and how, which represents a break between individuals and their life activity; they are separated from their own products appropriated and disposed of by others, which represents a break between individuals and the material world; they are made to compete with one another for goods and for the right to work at all, which represents a break between individual and individual.[6] All these divisions can be reflected in seeing things in as fragmented and disconnected a way as the capitalist system's own ideologists.

But in so far as resistance is generated by capitalist relations of production, the working class realises that its unity is its only strength and that it must reverse all attempts to divide and atomise it. The natural co-operation of working together in the creation of value expresses itself in the formation of trade unions effectively organising their common interests. There is thus for the working class the beginnings of a communal ethics of its own opposed to the individualistic ethics of capitalism, a start toward replacing what is for it the false ideology of the class enemy with its own Marxist working class ideology.

Putting actions back into their social context is not enough to get at their moral significance: we must also put ourselves firmly back into the society in which we developed in order to understand the conditions of moral conduct. As Marx puts it: 'What is to be avoided above all is the re-establishing of "society" as an abstraction vis-a-vis the individual. The individual is the social being'.[7] People's very senses only become human to the extent that their objects have become social, human objects - objects emanating from one human being for another. The senses and enjoyments of other men have become my own appropriation. Besides these direct organs, therefore, social organs develop in the form of society; thus, for instance, activity in direct association with others has become an organ for expressing my own life, and mode of appropriating human life.[8]

It is only through our relationships with others that we have obligations at all and, therefore, only in society that we can hope to find the meaning of 'ought' sentences and that element of freedom they presuppose. 'Only in association with others has each individual the means of cultivating his talents in all directions. Only in a community therefore is personal freedom possible.'[9] To 'construct' other moral beings like ourselves out of the obligations we happen to feel or on the basis of particular actions we merely observe, like the idealistic 'construction' of the universe out of private sense data, is a perverted sophistication which reverses the real order of our developing awareness within an objective social context.

Marx, in his notes to James Mill's 'Elements of Political Economy' indicates how things would mediate social relationships in circumstances of unalienated labour under socialism:

> Suppose we had produced things as human beings; in his production each of us would have twice affirmed himself and the other. In my production I would have objectified my individuality and its particularity, and in the course of the activity I would have enjoyed an individual life...In your satisfaction and your use of my product I would have had the direct and conscious satisfaction that my work satisfied a human need, that it objectified human nature, and that it created an object appropriate to the need of another human being...In my individual life I would have directly created your life; in my individual activity I would have immediately confirmed and realised my true human and social nature. Our

productions would be so many mirrors reflecting our natures.[10]

Once we realise that it is ourselves and others as moral agents within society, and not this or that individual act, which must be the starting point for an investigation of ethical concepts, we can begin to understand the relation between motive and results. As long as attention was concentrated on the isolated act, the impulse to perform it and the effect actually achieved appeared quite distinct. But when the object of study becomes the moral agent acting over a period of time within a social context, this distinction between motive and effect turns into a relationship between what can only be separated at the cost of the meaning of each. Their separation is a result of the split we have come to recognise as that between people as makers or doers and people as enjoyers or appraisers which is a characteristic of people in commodity-exchanging society in its extreme capitalistic form - the origin of the breach between the subjective and objective or between theory and practice which can take the ideological form of a breach between idealism and mechanical materialism.

In the case of specific acts the motive for them seems to be 'given', almost as part of the situation with which we are confronted; and the intention to produce certain results has no scope within which to operate. But over a longer period of time we can intend to be animated by different motives and may even succeed, within limits, in changing the nature of the impulses which move us. The injunctions that prompt isolated acts are addressed solely to the will, urging the choice of this or that alternative almost as an end in itself; but over a longer period of time, there is room for reason to review and criticise these discrete decisions in the light of an overall direction or purpose. While any particular act may be more or less typical of our general moral attitude, the sum of our actions over a lifetime cannot but express that attitude faithfully, together with all its modifications in the course of our development. In fact, the total consequences of everything we have done simply is our morality in a final resolution of intentions and results. It is not by this or that specific action that we expect our fellow human beings to judge us, nor even by this or that thing we say about ourselves at any particular period, but by a way of life revealed in the totality of the difference our being alive has made to others. 'The criterion for judging subjective intention or motive is social practice and its effect.'

But the question of just how free we are actually to change the nature of the impulses that move us and to modify our conduct in the light of an overall direction or purpose is not a question we can pursue in respect to individuals alone. Robinson Crusoe on his island was only free in respect to one choice - to survive or perish, a freedom shared with every living thing. There are clear statements of the Marxist view of the capacity of people to change themselves, which is the greatest freedom possible, but always in a social context, as when Mao Tsetung says: 'The epoch of world communism will be reached when all mankind voluntarily and consciously changes itself and the world'.[11]

FREEDOM AND CLASS INTEREST

For people in class-divided society reality is inevitably mediated by class. We must see how this affects the question of moral freedom.

It is not possible to arrive at any proper conception of morality by starting from a particular act performed by a certain person at a precise moment in time. But once the nature of morality has been understood in its social and temporal aspects, then individual acts can be considered in moral terms. We have seen how an appreciation of productive relationships interacting through time gave us the meaning of 'value' as a measure of the effort to create useful goods; and we were thus able to understand what was involved in making a value judgment about any particular object. An appreciation of socially-determined human relationships imposing obligations on individuals throughout their lifetime gives us the meaning of morality as the measure of the effort to act in accord with these obligations; and this standard, once formulated, can be applied to individual actions. People enter into associative production to make things which sustain life and thus create value. People at the same time, through these same productive relationships, make society and in making society they make themselves and thus create morality.

Because production for use is mediated in capitalist society by production for the profit of the capitalist class, the relationship between usefulness in the broadest sense and value simply in terms of the amount of labour constructively employed becomes complicated and even distorted. As much value is incorporated in the shoddy, frivolous and harmful things it may pay the capitalist to palm off on people as in the things society really needs. To describe as 'goods', we said, cheaply-made articles which quickly wear out or break in use, or insufficiently-tested drugs and medicines with dreadful side-effects, or the proliferation of private motor cars which clog our streets and poison the atmosphere, or all the pornographic rubbish in whose production whole forests are destroyed - to call these things 'goods' seems to do violence to our language. When this kind of distortion occurs, we can see how a proper relationship between utility and value could be restored by a moral consideration of the kind of society we are making through the sorts of things we are producing and the way they are being distributed. The social obligations which are our evidence for freedom of choice and our occasion for acting morally are not just so many opportunities for kindly, polite or considerate behaviour in our personal relationships, but, ultimately, our responsibility for creating a society with a certain quality of human life and, in the process, for creating not only ourselves but generations yet to come. The real proof of some degree of freedom is goal-setting; and beyond the aim of mere communal sustenance there is, as evidence of our freedom to judge and act, the overall end of the sort of society we want for all human beings.

Just as labour can be misdirected in the interests of a selfish minority into the creation of disvalues instead of values, so moral effort, the mere amount of spiritual energy exercised in the attainment of some goal, can operate partially on behalf of a selfish minority to the detriment of the quality of life in human society in general. Like the ingenuity and physical effort that may go into the making and distribution of useless, wasteful or harmful objects are the devotion and courage of, for example, missionaries who pave the way for the conquest and exploitation of primitive peoples, of officials and police who bravely support an unpopular and oppressive regime, of teachers untiring in their efforts to inculcate imperialist ideas of racial supremacy. Even though these actions will have the 'moral' approval of the selfish exploitative minority in whose interests they are performed, they are as far from being 'right' as are addictive drugs furtively sold from being 'goods'. Only a moral critique of the class relationships within a particular contemporary society or within the capitalist system generally can enable us to judge what the moral language in use really means.

But to talk about the quality of life of human beings in general is to beg the question. As was pointed out before, humanitarianism cannot stretch across the gulf between exploiters and exploited without losing most of its real content. The social circumstances in which humanitarianism could be meaningful have to be created. The only form of moral commitment that does not degenerate into some vague utopian dream of a better world is embracing the interests of the exploited in the struggle to end exploitation. Marx specifically denounces any prescription of the socialist ideal of 'an association in which the free development of each is the condition of the free development of all' which neglects or ignores the struggle of one class with the other and concerns itself not with 'the interests of the proletariat, but the interests of human nature, of man in general, who belongs to no class, has no reality, who exists only in the misty realm of philosophical fantasy'.[12] And Mao Tsetung makes the same point:

> Is there such a thing as human nature? Of course there is. But there is only human nature in the concrete, no human nature in

the abstract. In class society there is only human nature of a class character; there is no human nature above classes.[13]

If the evidence for some degree of freedom is the capacity to set ourselves goals, either immediate ones concerned with our own well-being or the ultimate one of improving the quality of life in society and, of course, of improving ourselves in the process, then anything which makes such a goal realisable, like class involvement in the struggle which is necessary if society is to be changed for the better, cannot be considered a denial of freedom but rather a condition of its practical exercise. But we must look a little deeper still into this question of how the freedom of choice implicit in the concept of 'ought' can be reconciled with the social determination of our moral obligations. How, in other words, can we, by following the discovered laws of our own social activity, help to bring about a freer society?

One sense such freedom might have has already been suggested by the analysis of what is meant by commending an object as 'good'. Just as some human-made article can be better than it need have been because of the extra labour and craft bestowed on it, so an action performed in accord with a particular standard of morality may go beyond what is strictly required, a free exercise of extra moral effort on the part of the actor. Even if this extra effort can be factually accounted for, still the difference between it and a more conventional response can only be described in moral terms as a free exercise of will over and above the norms required. Socialism has its moral heroes who are an inspiration to others in the worldwide class struggle against exploitation - those countless revolutionary martyrs who have laid down their lives in the interest of the working class.

But something more extraordinary than this may be meant by freedom of choice - the possibility of acting in completely spontaneous ways. If it is assumed that conduct dictated by personal interest is rational but neither moral nor free, then freedom would consist in acting with wild abandon regardless of how it affected one's own interests.

But 'interest' itself is a term which can have a very different significance in different social contexts. In primitive tribal groups the distinction between individual and communal interests hardly exists. As we have seen, the idea of private as contrasted with public interest is largely bound up with the projection of the ego in the development of private property; and extreme individualism is closely associated with the rise of capitalism which substitutes for human relationships a cash nexus, which dichotomises society more neatly than ever before into exploiters and exploited and which, particularly among the exploiters, turns each person's hand against all others. Only in such a highly competitive society does 'interest' come so exclusively to mean rights asserted against everyone else.

And yet even in an atomised society like ours the morality of family and clan still survives. A mother frequently risks her life to save her child. A person foregoes commercial advantage at the expense of a friend. People lay down their lives for their country. This does not mean that they act against their own interest but that their interests include the well-being of child or friend or even nation. In socialist countries people voluntarily accept limitations on the production of consumer goods to increase the output of production goods which will raise the standard of living of the next generation; and they do this not by way of acting against their own interests but by way of extending their own interests to include the interests of those as yet unborn. This can be contrasted with capitalism's way of using up the world's resources as though there were no tomorrow. The socialist use in the general interest of a surplus by the government when the government is in the hands of the whole people who own the means of production in no way resembles the appropriation of surplus-value by a tiny capitalist class whose very decision to invest any of it at all in expanding production depends on the expectation of further profits accruing to them alone.

Acting on behalf of class interest may mean supporting the 'right' of a minority to exploit the vast majority or it may mean identifying oneself with the class of those who in emancipating themselves from exploitation help to put an end to exploitation itself. The former 'interest' involves a check on freedom, not just because it is grounded in considerations of class, but because it is grounded in considerations of an exploitative class which to keep in bondage the vast majority of the people must impose restrictions on society which even limit the liberty of the very minority in whose interest the bondage is maintained.'Those who enslave others cannot themselves be free.'

'Interest', then, has an indefinite extension ranging from the self-assertive egoism of a single individual to a concern for fellow workers everywhere, and in classless society, for humanity itself. It refers to whatever commands our sympathies as practically expressed in purposeful action. The idea that freedom involves acting without thought of one's interests would really mean that only completely pointless actions could be free. But a deliberately purposeless act is inconceivable since even its performance simply to prove the possibility of such acts would give it point enough to keep it from qualifying.

Indeed, the development of class consciousness, which for the working class under capitalism can only be revolutionary consciousness, does not arise spontaneously out of the conditions of capitalist society. For this development there must not only be the sense of the unjust and illegitimate character of the existing social order but also the recognition of the possibility of a social order on an entirely different basis. This development cannot be generated automatically within the material and intellectual confines of the very system to be superseded.

It comes about from the conception of a new organisation of human experience suggested by the critical analysis of the capitalist system exposing its explotative character which, once presented to the working class, is assented to as belonging to it in a way that the false consciousness acquired within a system coloured through and through by the interests of a capitalist class never could. In this recognition of and acceptance of its own revolutionary ideology and its social implications the working class demonstrates an element of rational and moral choice at the deepest level. As Lenin says: 'Class political consciousness can be brought to the workers only from without, that is, only from outside of the economic struggle, from outside the sphere of relations between workers and employers'.[14] The economic struggle can be conducted by trade unionists but this is not yet revolutionary struggle which depends on being able to generalise all manifestations of tyranny, oppression and injustice into a single functional picture of an exploitative society, which Marxism first did for the working class and which the communist party of a new type continues to do, keeping ever before workers 'the world historic significance of the proletariat's struggle for emancipation'.

We have already seen how the peculiar notion of individual freedom as spontaneous, unconditional and utterly irrelevant arises. The division of labour which leads, through the development of classes, to those mainly involved in mental tasks being primarily concerned with the consumption side of the productive process, tends to arrest their thinking at the idealistic phase of the process of knowledge, the phase in which concepts become detached from their roots in material reality. These 'free' ideas which can be juggled with, transposed and re-combined suggest the possibility of actions which would be 'free' in the same sense. The equivalent of ideas completely abstracted from the objective world would be actions without effects; but actions can only be performed in the objective world and can never have that sort of detached inconsequentiality. They can never be anything but the final phase of the process of knowledge, bringing all ideas down to earth again and subjecting them to the rigorous critique of reality.

The same idealistic attitude is responsible for another distorted view of individual freedom which ends in a similar kind of frustration. Subjective states such as happiness or equanimity are seen, like abstract ideas, as somehow separate from the objective conditions which they normally reflect. Thus detached, they can be set up as goals to be achieved on their own without attempting to do anything about material circumstances. We are free, it is argued, to attain peace of mind or contentment with our lot whatever those circumstances may be.

Within limits this may be true, but it is one thing to rise superior to petty vexations afflicting us and quite another to be calmly detached about other people starving to death. In any case the striving for purely subjective goals usually proves psychologically self-defeating in the end. Those who pursue happiness with the greatest persistence may be the least likely to find it: the wish simply to have a clear conscience can carry with it a sense of guilt. The unhappiness of hedonists and the moral doubts of monks who must realise that the slightest assurance of their own salvation may cost them that hope are each in their way suffering the penalty of chasing shadows. Marxism, just as it does not merely attempt to change moral ideas themselves but also the social conditions from which those ideas arise, gives no warrant for seeking solace in subjective states. It counsels instead of any such utopianism the active effort to achieve objective ends; and such states as satisfaction, contentment or happiness are realised as the by-products of the concerted struggle alongside one's fellow human beings for a fairer society.

There is a form of idealism to which many contemporary writers calling themselves Marxists are prone. They treat Marx's metaphors to explain the dialectical relationship between social existence and the consciousness of people as if they were rigid objective structures. Base and superstructure, economic foundation and ideological reflection, material conditions of life and theoretic formulations, forces of production and relations of production, these are all ways of suggesting the dialectical materialist relationship between people's social existence and their consciousness. They are not static representations of that relationship.

These writers treat ideology, all ideology, as a screen between people, all people, and reality, so that the real becomes unknowable, like Kant's thing-in-itself, and there is no distinction between the ideology of an exploited working class seeking the practical means of ending their exploitation and the capitalist exploiters who have every reason to conceal the fact that workers are exploited at all. This interposing of an ideological screen between people and reality is like neo-empiricists who prove themselves actually to be subjective idealists by inserting a screen of sense impressions between themselves and reality. Hypostatising ideas, treating concepts as things is rank idealism, even if the concepts happen to be Marxist. One suspects that the motive for this brand of 'Marxism' devised by intellectuals is to keep ordinary workers from getting their hands on social reality in order to change it.

Although the obligations we feel are conditioned by the type of society we live in and by our class allegiance in that society, this could only be considered a fatal limitation on our freedom of action if it could be reasonably argued that we should be able to make up our own sense of obligation just as we please and without reference to what anyone else might expect of us. The very word 'obligation' indicates a link or tie with something outside of ourselves and not, therefore, subject to our private whims. Marxism does not forge our links with the class to which we belong by our role in the productive process, but in revealing the nature of that link it helps to make us conscious of the social springs of our actions and the social ends those actions serve; and only conscious actions can be free.

Freedom to live according to the particular ethical standard apposite to our circumstances is the bare minimum for our acts to be considered moral at all. In showing how that standard came to apply through an understanding of the social conditions which gave rise to it, in providing the material criteria by which it can be judged in terms of the quality of social life it implies, and in calling on us, in the fellowship of our class relations with all who are exploited, to change those very social conditions, Marxism opens up a whole new vista of freedom in which we recognise obligations quite distinct from those acquired simply by the accident of being born into and of growing up in particular surroundings.

This potential freedom is inseparable from the social force whose mission it is to bring about the classless society of communism because only when there is no exploitation of human beings by human beings can people be truly free. Indeed, the very idea of freedom, of the free person, only arose when its opposite, the enslaved person, the earliest form of exploitation, became a feature of primitive society. Then also was born the new idea of emancipation

The proletariat carries out the sentence which private property, by creating the proletariat, passes upon itself, just as it carries out the sentence which wage labour, by creating wealth for others and poverty for itself, passes upon itself. If the proletariat triumphs, this does not mean that it becomes the absolute form of society, for it is only victorious by abolishing itself as well as its opposite. Thus the proletariat disappears along with the opposite which conditions it, private property.[15] That is to say exploitative class rule disappears because it is based on the ruling class's proprietorial grip on the means of production.

> Only in communist society, when the resistance of the capitalists has been completely crushed, when the capitalists have disappeared, when there are no classes (i.e. when there is no difference between members of society as regards their relation to the means of production), only then 'the state ...ceases to exist' and it 'becomes possible to speak of freedom'.[16]

FREEDOM AND PREDICTION

Critics of Marxism contend that freedom is incompatible with historical materialism. If, they argue, Marxism claims to be a science of society capable of making necessary predictions such as the supersession of class-divided society by a co-operative society without classes, it cannot at the same time issue a valid call to ethical action in pursuance of such a goal. If the capitalist system of exploitation is inevitably doomed, then it cannot be anybody's duty to bring about its end.

These critics, either intentionally or inadvertently, have mistaken historical materialism for some form of mechanical determinism which prescribes the lines of human development as ineluctably as metal rails determine the route of a train. In assuming that Marxism relegates consciousness to a mirror-like role of merely reflecting what would be happening whether or not consciousness existed they suppose that there is no room for human voluntarism. But Marxism is nothing like that. The determining agency is a specifically human reality. The material base of a society, which is the preponderant influence in shaping the ideas and attitudes of people in that society and guiding their future actions, is simply a system of human productive relationships. 'History itself is nothing but the activity of men in pursuit of their ends.'[17] 'Freedom is won by the people through struggle...' and 'the people, and the people alone, are the motive force in the making of world history.'[18] To say, therefore, that if a particular system of exploitation is doomed, no one can have the duty of bringing about its end is like saying that, because a cure for cancer will one day be found, research workers need not bother to go on looking for it. One is not in either case, speaking of something which will happen in spite of people's actions but of something which will be brought about through that very agency.

Marxist predictions are not about an inescapable fate that is to overtake mankind - though the end of exploitation may well seem to capitalists like the cooling off of the sun; nor, on the other hand, are they mere pious hopes for the future in the form of imagining ideal utopias or of encouraging people to behave differently without in any way changing the circumstances that incline them to behave as they do. Marxist predictions are about what people will do, based on a knowledge of what they are, and what they are depends on productive relationships they have entered into in order to sustain and enrich human life. It also includes what it is possible for them to become on the basis of understanding those relationships well enough to be able to change them - and thus change themselves. Prognostications about the revolutionary founding of societies from which the exploitation of labour has been eliminated are no different in kind, though more radical in effect, from past predictions that working people at a particular stage of development suffering a certain form of exploitative relationship like slavery or serfdom would rebel and emancipate themselves. Accurate forecasts about what people will certainly do in time, based on an understanding of their collective reaction to oppression, far from representing any restraint on their freedom of action explain how that freedom will operate in practice.

Such predictions about vast social movements, depending on an understanding of the complex productive relationships of an entire society, can only be made at a stage in those productive relationships when the possibility of profoundly altering them already exists. Indeed, a proper appreciation of historical development in general is a result of the extent to which people are able to enter into those developments and take an active class-conscious part in shaping their own destiny, of the extent to which, history having made people, people begin to make history.

This connection between understanding historical developments and being able to enter into and control them explains one form the criticism of Marxist prediction takes. History itself appears quite different to a class which has enjoyed power and feels itself threatened than to a class which is gathering its strength to assert itself positively on the world stage. A class which is losing its control of historical processes is bound to view those processes as inimical, as something imposed on them in spite of their own will. The apologists of such a class would like to deny that any pattern can be found in history because any pattern they can discern is working against the interests they represent. And, since they are no longer identified with a class making history, they really do find it more and more difficult to understand history's course. It has become alien and malign to them. The same class apologists, who in the period of capitalism's ascendancy saw history as a steady progressive advance, now dismiss the very idea of progress and describe history as just 'one emergency following on another'.

At the peak of bourgeois power their historians could praise the revolutions which laid the basis for it; but at a time when social change could take that power away, all change becomes suspect - even that change in the past from feudalism to capitalism. 'You can't change human nature!' is not so much, with them, a statement of fact as a despairing plea. If it was previously possible for a dominant class to be overthrown, it might happen again; and in order to deny that such a change will ever occur in the future, it becomes necessary to deny that real change has ever occurred at any time, the world having always been, if we could but realise it, frozen in a timeless, changeless Platonic state. According to scholars like Wittfogel the West has always been 'free', while from the time of ancient hydraulic societies like Egypt or China down to the present the East has always been totalitarian: no change of any significance has ever taken place in either hemisphere and the Cold War ought to have been dated from the last Ice Age![19]

Even if change were conceivable, it could only, from the point of view of the capitalist class and its hirelings, be for the worse. Tinkering with things as they are to effect a few minor adjustments is as much as they dare contemplate. 'Piecemeal technology' or 'social engineering', superficial tampering which leaves everything basically as it is, are the terms used by Karl Popper in the course of his attempts to make social democracy philosophically respectable.[20] Since history is assumed to have no discoverable pattern and all change is blind, its consequences quite unforeseeable, only the utterly irresponsible could ever embark on a course of radical alteration. One of the reasons advanced in support of this petty reformism is that any prediction of major change is bound to have its prior influence on society, thus destroying the objectivity of the prediction. An example given of the futility of forecasting future events is that if a fall in the price of shares in three days' time were predicted, everyone connected with the market would sell before that time causing an earlier decline and thus falsifying the prediction. Anyone relying on the accuracy of the forecast would have been badly caught out. While this may be one of the trivial truths of the reformist world of 'piecemeal technology', there are countries where, on the basis of Marxist predictions of real social change, it has been shown that such gambling in commodities can be done away with altogether.

Marxists would certainly not deny that predicting the overthrow of an exploiting class is bound to have its prior influence of provoking that class into frantic efforts to falsify the prediction, whether by disproving it on paper or in fact. A great deal of economic and sociological writing since Marx's time has been devoted to demonstrating just how wrong he was, and the constant succession of books which 'finally demolish' his work is a fine tribute to Marxism's creative growth as the ideology of the working class. There have also been those whose reaction to Marxism, as in the case of Keynes for example, was to try to eliminate some of the more vulnerable aspects of capitalism while preserving its basic exploitative character. What can be categorically denied is that any amount of subtle argument or improvised tinkering can save a system whose demise has been predicted on the grounds of a critical internal contradiction - the conflict between capitalist class and working class which can only be resolved by the ascendancy of that class which can do without the other and, in dispensing with the other, ends the exploitative relationship between people in society. The only way the capitalist ruling class can finally meet the challenge of such a prediction is by removing that crucial contradiction - which would mean, since it cannot do without the working class who are the creators of wealth on which human life depends, eliminating itself, thus anticipating not falsifying the prediction. Most capitalists, apart from those who jump off skyscrapers when there is a stock market crash or when they are caught out in their fraudulent actions, prefer to take refuge in an attitude of 'it'll last out my time'.

Criticisms of Marxist prediction which take the form of trying to prove that in tipping its hand Marxism allows itself to be circumvented are based on the belief that ideas determine material conditions and therefore that combatting the idea of material change, through being forewarned of it, is tantamount to preventing change itself. Such idealism, as we have so often noted, is the characteristic attitude of a class no longer in the ascendant - and particularly of the apologists for that class who by the very nature of the clerical tasks they are paid to perform tend to be cut off from reality. These ideologues may not call themselves idealists, but the empiricism they avow is as different from the practical Baconian philosophy of trial and error of a more hopeful period of bourgeois history as is their attitude of deploring real change from an earlier belief in progress.

An empiricism of observation alone, divorced from experimental social practice, which is all mere reformism can claim by way of philosophical justification, can prove nothing about the future of anything and ascribes its own short-sightedness to history's inscrutability. Far from being what it pretends, a method for securing tentative social advance, this sort of neo-empiricism realises its main purpose in putting a check on any real social change at all; and it betrays its non-materialist character not only in reducing reality to ideal elements like sense-data or language but also in the utterly sterile and scholastic nature of its formulations generally which it often makes up for by tipping over into a jejune mysticism. The argument that no prediction can be absolutely correct in every detail and therefore no real social change can ever be envisaged no matter how bad things get shows up this so-called empiricism to be, in effect, as static an idealism as the philosophical foundations of Plato's arrested Republic.

If one prong of the critical attack on historical materialism takes the form of denying the possibility of valid prediction in the name of random, irrational and unplanned 'freedom', the other maintains that if prediction is possible there must be laws of social development, and if there are such laws, if Marxism is a science, then it can have nothing to do with morality and has no right to urgent expressions of the 'ought' type. Social conduct, explained in terms of class interests rooted in the material conditions of life, is thus no more moral than obeying the law of gravity.

This argument ignores the distinction Marxism makes between history which is the account of people's actions in pursuit of their aims and the physical sciences which describe the pre-existent stage on which these actions take place. This, as we have seen, is the distinction between the two kinds of knowledge, knowledge of the struggle for production which grows out of the contradiction between human beings and nature and knowledge of class struggle which grows out of contradictions within society, a distinction which itself represents a contradiction between the forces of production and the relations of production.

Both knowledge of the struggle for production, the physical sciences, and knowledge of class struggle, the social sciences, have their laws; but while the laws of physics operate with a regularity independent of whether anyone is aware of them or not, the laws of social development, which are simply the pattern of changing human relationships, while independent of what any individual person or ruling class would like them to be, are nonetheless affected by people's consciousness of them and, sufficiently understood, are the means by which people realise their aspirations for a better life for all. Where subject and subject matter are the same, a more thorough knowledge of the subject matter cannot but be accompanied by and interlinked with changes in the subject. Consciousness develops in the context of a pre-existent natural world; human consciousness develops in the context of social being; individual human consciousness develops in the context of class consciousness; but while logical and temporal priority belong to the context, the relationship between context and development, between ground and emergent is dialectical, not mechanically deterministic. Once consciousness develops in some material context, it belongs to a larger whole including both, both being internally related within that whole. There is no warrant in dialectical materialism for dealing with causality in unilinear terms of single effects following single sufficient causes, like stations on a railway line with a stop called 'consciousness' coming after a stop called 'economic materiality' and therefore unable to react back on it.

Consciousness is not mechanically determined by any single thing in the social context in which it develops nor is it part of any one-way causal chain; but the entire social situation gives rise to it, conditions it, shapes and influences it and, in short, determines that the range of its reactions back on that social situation will be limited to what is meaningful within the larger whole including both situation and awareness of it. The idea of changing society, therefore, does not arise until the material conditions of that society as described by the laws of social development are ripe for it. That is why Marx limits the scale of conscious action in a society which has discovered the law of its own movement to 'shortening and lessening the birth-pangs' of a new order.[21] Such a new order does not originate in an ideal conception but is generated out of contradictions both within the social organisation it replaces and between that social organisation and the world-wide productive experience of the working masses. These contradictions which are in the process of weakening that older form of society and strengthening the forces which are to change it can be set down with all the rigour displayed in the classics of Marxism-Leninism-Maoism, those classics themselves being simply the theoretical formulation of the historical experience of the working masses in struggle. Once people understand this process of change involving them in their class character, once they appreciate the possibilities it holds of a better society, they then become agents for actualising those possibilities which the old society is pregnant with in the quickest and most painless way, even setting aside immediate and personal interests attaching them to the old order to act in the name of their class interest in realising the new. Though the idea of the new society originated in the contradictions of the old, it cannot be born without the conceptualisation of it by the working class which, changing and being changed by revolutionary action, is both midwife and new born child. 'Without a revolutionary theory there can be no revolutionary movement'.[22] This is the not inconsiderable area of moral action staked out by the Marxist conception of predictable social change.

Of course it cannot be denied that a social change which is to free the working class from the yoke of capital is at the same time a curtailment of the liberty of capitalists. 'Free enterprise' is nothing but the liberty to exploit the labour of others. Just as 'freedom of the press' is the freedom to buy up newspapers and journalists in the interest of creating a public opinion hostile to change; or just as prohibitions against workers enforcing union discipline are called 'freedom of work'. To the ideologists of capitalism any change which diminishes the prerogatives of those for whom they speak is bound to seem totalitarian; but a struggle to free the working masses of the world, even at the expense of those who exploit them, obviously deserves to be described as liberative. Lenin explains how the freedom of the vast majority can only be won at the cost of the freedom of their oppressors. Simultaneously with an immense expansion of democracy, which for the first time becomes democracy for the poor, democracy for the people, and not democracy for the money bags, the dictatorship of the proletariat (that is, the assumption of state power by the working people) imposes a series of restrictions on the freedom of the oppressors, the exploiters, the capitalists. We must suppress them in order to free humanity from wage slavery...[23]

Dialectical materialism is the dynamic pattern of change and growth in the objective world and, since minds developed in that world, it is also the form of the relationship between subject and object, between thought and action, between consciousness and the material conditions in which it arose and on which it in turn reacts. Dialectical materialism, in short, takes its character from the nature of changing reality as extended in time and may be contrasted with any conceptualisation involving, as the method of investigation, an attempt to stop the whole process in order to have a closer look, obtaining thereby a view of reality as static and dead on which it would be impossible to act.

FREEDOM AND TIME

We have already touched on the importance of extension in time for an understanding of individual morality. An analysis of specific acts at a particular moment did not yield any element we could designate as moral, and only when we considered the agent in a given social context over a long enough time span to embrace major life purposes as manifest in action were we in a position to appreciate the nature of moral choice. Value gives us the history of a commodity in its social context. Morality gives us the history of an act in that same social context.

Kant has described people as living in two worlds, the phenomenal and the noumenal. In the former they are subjected to the necessity of natural law and, since every event is inevitably linked to its cause, there is no scope for human freedom and hence no possibility of moral action. But through the mind they belong also to the transcendental realm of pure reason which exists behind the mere sensuous appearance of the phenomenal world; and in this realm they are free because they are capable of responding to the dictates of universal reason which legislates for things as they really are. Every action can be explained deterministically insofar as its results occur in the physical world of strict causation; but it may also be free if it is motivated by purely rational considerations which do not originate in that physical world. In other words, for Kant as for all idealists, freedom only exists in the second idealistic phase of the process of knowledge and cannot survive translation into social practice.

What must have suggested this Kantian solution to the problem of necessity is the experience we seem to have of past and future - the encountered and unalterable past where necessity reigns absolute, and the free and undetermined future which is the realm of moral choice. The present seems to stand as an instant without duration between what has already been irrevocably done for all time and what is still a matter of free election. Once we dichotomise time in this way, even if we try to extend experience of the past into the future by planning to bring about a certain effect, the very intention of setting up an end to be realised in the free future becomes itself a part of the determinate past the moment it has been willed and thus subject to an unbreakable causal chain, as is also the case with each means toward the attainment of that end as it comes to be employed and, eventually, with the end itself. By this account freedom takes on the illusory character of a distant mirage which always disappears as soon as we get to it. Indeed, all time necessarily becomes an illusion if it is simply the infinite repetition of an instantaneous present dot without extension instead of an enduring arrow indicating the direction of continuous change and development in the world of which human time is a small portion of that universal continuum with a tiny arrow pointing, of course, in the same direction.

We have learned to recognise an anomaly like this temporal one as an indication that things which are dialectically related within a more comprehensive whole are being treated as separate entities. We also know that this analytical tendency is connected with the separation of production and consumption which class division, particularly in the final capitalist phase of commodity exchange, turns into an almost unbridgeable ideological gulf - a gulf appearing in our present instance as the bifurcation between past and future. The exploiting class, whose very title to the property holding on which its rule is based lies in the past, becomes completely identified with a conservative effort to keep that past from ever changing; and the exploited class, whose liberation lies in the future, sees its mission as the destruction of the past in order to achieve its freedom in a new society. Any urge for people to go back to a glorious past almost always turns out to be an invitation to a fascist future.

This same account of the realm of necessity and the realm of freedom as the difference between past and future is also related to the distinction between the world of nature as described by the physical sciences and the world of human beings described by the social sciences. Necessary regularities in the natural order tend to make the past dominate the future, while the possibility of transforming social organisation enables the future to dominate the past. But this is also, as we have so frequently noted, the distinction between the two kinds of knowledge, knowledge of the struggle for production and knowledge of class struggle, which can be expressed as the distinction between the forces of production and the relations of production which, in turn, takes us back again to that original split between production and consumption. All these distinctions within a given whole link as well as divide, identify as well as distinguish, universalise as well as particularise. But in the false ideology which underwrites separatism in the drive to perpetuate class differences, which exalts individual interests against social interests and which knows only the tactic of divide and rule, these distinctions become absolute and generate such familiar philosophical problems as the irreconcilable split between mind and body or between human beings and nature or between freedom and necessity, which are also reflections of the class conflict between rulers and ruled, exploiters and exploited, capitalists and workers.

The consciousness on which some degree of freedom depends cannot be tied to an instantaneous present, helplessly watching the endless transformation of the undetermined into the determinate. Its field is rather an effective present which is simply the measure of the time between ideal objective and actual accomplishment it is possible to grasp. The extent of its reach is precisely what distinguishes human beings from other animals; and this distinction is grounded in the material fact that human beings 'produce their means of subsistence'.[24] Consciousness thus originates as the mental correlate of the productive process of drawing on past experience to create goods to meet future needs by postponing present satisfactions. Self-consciousness identifies the co-operative self who joins with others to produce their social sustenance with the individual self who in time personally consumes a life-sustaining share of the goods produced.

In terms of discrete instants consciousness is quite inconceivable. As an effective present consciousness implies that the spurious isolates of thoroughly necessitated past and completely free future must be seen in their dialectical relationship as qualifying each other in the course of purposive action to achieve some end. Necessity qualifies freedom, 'men do not make their history as they please'; but necessity does not devour freedom, men do 'make their own history'. Normative judgments relating to actions which ought to be performed are logically possible as well as factual propositions referring to what is already the case; and their relationship is maintained through this effective present which consciously combines elements of past and future.

The content of this human consciousness is the total experience of producible effects in the minds of the working people of the world, the mass knowledge which is liberated for limitless creativity by class emancipation and which is appealed to in the mass line, 'from the masses to the masses'. Beyond the productive effects achieved in this or that kind of society is the effect of altering society itself which consciousness can only bring about when it is class consciousness, when to the general content of consciousness is added the specific ideological form peculiar to the class position of exploited workers in a particular society, turning them from mere receptacles of productive experience into a dynamic social force. That is the function of Marxism - the revolutionary combination for a class exploited by capitalism of the two kinds of knowledge, knowledge of the struggle for production and knowledge of class struggle, at a time when the capitalist relations of production have obviously become a crippling limitation on the social force of production.

Though firmly rooted in the material conditions of life Marxist morality demonstrates that it is more than the passive response to a given social situation precisely to the extent that it includes the notion of changing that very situation. This notion can only signify that consciousness in its class form, which is the only way it can be effective in class-divided society, is a dynamic moment in the process of history, that consciousness in this socially effective role is itself an alteration in being, an enormous broadening of the scope for purposive action represented by a yet more expansive consciousness. This is not to suggest for a moment that ideas in themselves effect any changes but only that in revealing the objective nature of a situation which is not itself static they also show something more - what it is possible through social practice for that situation to become; and it is in taking up an active attitude in their class identity toward this progressive possibility, still lying outside a present social context though realisable through a conscious extrapolation of its current laws of development, that workers exercise collectively what we are calling Marxist morality.

Few philosophers would wish to deny the pattern of necessity and freedom in our individual lives appearing to us as an extended present within which a planned course of action has meaning. Without predictable regularities based on experience of the past, planning would be pointless; without an element of freedom offered by the future, choice would be impossible. And yet, as we noticed before, critics of Marxism often seem to agree that when we turn from individual to social action no such pattern is discernible. No regularities in history, nor any trends of development in the organisation of societies are there for us to study and learn from. Either there is no change at all and the appearance of it is illusory or change is completely 'free' in the random sense that any social formation can arbitrarily succeed any other. This would be a meaningless freedom since we could not hope to bring about a better state of affairs by a course of rational action. Indeed it would be pointless on this reading of the matter so much as to pass any opinion at all on the existing state of things; and it is unlikely, in that case, that we would ever have acquired so otiose a faculty as a capacity for judgment.

But these critics are quite prepared to accept the conclusion that history is meaningless - such is their dislike of what a meaningful history might hold in store for the exploitative class they serve. They will allow us to study the past as long as we are careful not to draw any lessons from it, for that would be to court the error of historicism. We must not, in other words, try to make sense of the life of a society by applying to it the concept of an effective present which enables us to make sense of our own individual lives. And yet 'history is nothing but the activity of men in pursuit of their aims'; and if history is essentially meaningless, so are the lives of all of us who make it. It is rather a heavy price to ask us to pay for their fear of social change.

THE DIALECTICS OF FREEDOM

Some degree of freedom is presupposed in making normative judgments and acting on them. Ultimately the possibility of this freedom must be found in the essential nature of reality and the manner in which growth, development, change take place. Obviously if there is no change at all or if change is illusory, then there is no possibility of freedom; and morality, in the sense of anything incumbent on people to do which they need not necessarily do, is also an illusion. The Marxist dialectic of knowledge is the consciousness of the dialectical nature of reality itself. 'The law of contradiction in things, that is, the law of the unity of opposites, is the fundamental law of nature and society and therefore also the fundamental law of thought'.[25] It is because there is internal contradiction in every single thing that there is motion and development. 'Contradictoriness within a thing is the fundamental cause of its development, while its interrelations and interactions with other things are secondary causes.'[26] This motion, development, change is not simply things being pushed around by external forces like billiard balls being knocked about on a table but is generated internally by the contradictions inside things. 'External causes are the conditions of change and internal causes are the basis of change and external causes become operative through internal causes.'[27]

This dialectical materialist world is quite different from the static 'metaphysical' world we have inherited from Aristotle and has its own logic. A classificatory, either-or logic is very useful for dealing with problems of particularising, identifying and sorting the myriad things we are presented with over a short enough period of time for them to be relatively stable; but when it comes to growth, change and development it is a logic which produces anomalies, and poor Achilles never catches the tortoise. A 'metaphysical' reality consisting of separate and independent parts - one body moving when another bumps into it - requires an outside agitator, an 'unmoved mover' who intervenes to set things in motion to begin with, and perhaps to destroy them in time. It gets things backwards by invoking the human consciousness which has developed somewhere along the course of universal development as the original initiator, in some godlike form, of that very development. Dialectical materialist reality, developing out of inner contradictions, generating its own dynamism from within is relatively open-ended. We who developed in the course of it are ever more consciously and co-operatively intervening in that development and developing ourselves in the process - a process only a dialectical materialist logic can describe.

> In its negative aspect, then, freedom is simply a things not being acted upon by outside forces to which it responds inertly. In its positive aspect freedom is the novelty that is created by qualitative changes resulting from alterations in the balance of opposites within a thing. In each thing there is contradiction between its new and its old aspects, and this gives rise to a series of struggles with many twists and turns. As a result of these struggles, the new aspect changes from being minor to being major and rises to predominance, while the old aspect changes from being major to being minor and gradually dies out. And the moment the new aspect gains dominance over the old, the old thing changes qualitatively into a new thing. It can thus be seen that the nature of a thing is mainly determined by the principal aspect of the contradiction, the aspect which has gained predominance. When the principal aspect which has gained predominance changes, the nature of a thing changes accordingly.[28]

This struggle of opposites which with 'many twists and turns' brings forth the new in revolutionary change is found throughout nature and society and is reflected in our very thinking, thinking itself being just such a novelty arising from qualitative changes in the productive struggle between human beings and nature. The combination of thinking or consciousness with the degree of freedom generated by revolutionary change from within makes morality possible.

Contradiction is universal, therefore the possibility of freedom in the sense of the new coming into being through a self-generated resolution of opposites acting within a particular context is all pervasive. Mao Tsetung gives examples of this revolutionary character of social change.

> The contradiction between the proletariat and the bourgeoisie is resolved by the method of socialist revolution; the contradiction between the great masses of the people and the feudal system is resolved by the method of democratic revolution; the contradiction between the colonies and imperialism is resolved by the method

of national revolutionary war; the contradiction between the working class and the peasant class in socialist society is resolved by the method of collectivisation and mechanisation in agriculture; contradiction within the Communist Party is resolved by the method of criticism and self-criticism; the contradiction between society and nature is resolved by the method of developing the productive forces.[29]

Where contradictions are antagonistic, as in the case of the conflict between proletariat and bourgeoisie whose very definition as classes is that the one exploits the other, the only resolution is the elimination of the one, as a class, by the other. Where the contradiction is not necessarily antagonistic, because not expressing a fundamental opposition of class interests, as between workers and peasants, the resolution is found in changing the conditions in which the opposition was rooted. Being able to distinguish between antagonistic and non-antagonistic contradictions is one of the most important aspects of dialectical thinking in the political sphere.

Freedom has been described by Hegel as the appreciation of necessity; but Marxists can no more accept this formula as the last word on human freedom than they could take over without standing it on its materialist feet the Hegelian dialectic. If consciousness is simply the passive privilege of being aware of the inevitable categorical unfolding of self-evolving thought, then freedom may indeed be no more than the consciousness of necessity; but is it still freedom? Not in any Marxist sense. As Mao Tsetung says: 'Freedom is the understanding of necessity and the transformation of necessity - one has some work to do,too'.[30] And Marx denies the Hegelian principle that 'what is real is rational' with stating instead that 'what is rational is destined to become real', through enlightened human activity. Indeed, it could be said in terms of the dialectical materialist theory of knowledge that just as Hegelianism absorbs empiricism as one moment in the dialectic of mind, Marxism absorbs the dialectic of mind as one moment in the thinking process of self-conscious matter, ourselves. Engels describes how, under socialism, with the replacement of anarchy in social production by systematic definite organisation,

> 'the struggle for individual existence disappears and, for the first time, man is finally marked off from the rest of the animal kingdom, and emerges from mere animal conditions of existence into really human ones...because he has now become master of his own social organisation.

The laws of his own social activity, which have hitherto confronted him as external, dominating laws of Nature, will then be applied by man with complete understanding and hence will be dominated by man...it is only from this point that men, with full consciousness, will fashion their own history; it is only from this point that the social causes set in motion by men will have, predominantly and in constantly increasing measure, the effects willed by men. It is humanity's leap from the realm of necessity to the realm of freedom.[31]

Freedom as the consciousness of necessity does apply in the struggle for production against the forces of nature as, for example, when consciousness of the law of gravity and the fixed properties of an air stream enables people to construct aeroplanes and soar above the earth, not in defiance of but in intelligent compliance with natural law. The freedom of flight has been won by the consciousness of physical necessity; but it is not a moral victory.

But there is not the same applicability when it is a question of class struggle waged with the consciousness of the laws of social development. If, for example, some people, conscious that a revolutionary change from capitalism to socialism is imminent, hastily set about acquiring the kind of qualifications they hope will assure them success and influence in the new social situation, they are not intelligently complying with social law to rise above circumstances. They are condemning themselves to the unfreedom of having no part to play in a revolutionary change which only occurs because there are others who choose, in an exercise of freedom, to reject the extreme self-interest of bourgeois morality by anticipating the new morality of socialism in which individuals no longer seek nor enjoy that kind of egotistical success and influence. While a freedom acting through a knowledge of natural laws, whose necessity operates in spite of people, is sufficient for the production of value, morality presupposes a freedom acting through a knowledge of social laws whose exigency operates through people, which actually brings about a new situation where new laws apply. 'Morality serves the purpose of helping human society to rise to a higher level and to get rid of the exploitation of labour.'[32]

Knowledge and morality, while closely connected in their derivation from the material conditions of people's social existence, are not identical. As we have often remarked, the productive process is also the process of knowledge. If we prove in social practice the correctness of our conception of some natural phenomenon by reproducing it ourselves and making it serve our own purposes, we have knowledge that is certain beyond anything we could ever know in terms of some 'copy' theory of the relationship between idea and reality. What we can actually make we thoroughly understand and in the productive process of making, object and subject interpenetrate each other in a mutually transformative way that does not leave over, as inexplicable isolates, the dichotomies of mind and matter or human beings and nature. The Kantian ungraspable thing-in-itself becomes, once we are able to produce it, a thing-for-us.[33]

Similarly, if we can apply our knowledge of the laws of society's development to hasten the advent of a better system of productive relationships with a fairer and more efficient ordering of social effort, we have acted morally in a sense that goes beyond any mere compliance with customary ethical rules. For in the activity of changing the conditions of social existence we change ourselves: changing ourselves is the greatest freedom we can know and where freedom is greatest there the highest form of morality is possible. But if knowledge and morality are distinguishable, they are also closely related. What, morally speaking, ought to be the case in terms of human companionship and co-operation also makes up the ideal productive relations for the greatest possible application of people's productive force - and that, of course, is reflected in turn in an increase in knowledge.

Since morality depends on freedom and since freedom depends on consciousness, we must decide as a moral issue whether consciousness is merely the awareness of dialectical changes which would have worked themselves out along the same lines anyway or whether it is itself a moment in that dialectic which must be taken into account in the course of subsequent developments. Marxism, dialectical materialism, as we have seen, subscribes to the second of these alternatives; consciousness does react on the material conditions that gave rise to it, and the sort of freedom which morality presupposes is an emergent aspect of matter having, at a particular stage of development, become conscious.

This historical development is recapitulated in each specific example of the dialectical unity of theory and practice. We start with a concrete situation which is like the objective material condition prior to the origin of consciousness; that situation is reflected in abstract thought, like the appearance of consciousness on the natural scene and those thoughts take the form of an ideal theory about the initial situation; that theory is then validated or refuted by application through social practice to the situation with which the process began, and this final stage represents consciousness reacting on material reality.

We have seen how at various stages of this process different philosophical attitudes, representing the partial experience of this or that social class, provide an adequate account of only one particular moment, and now we can see how freedom is accommodated by these attitudes. The concrete situation as passively reflected in ideas can be described in terms of mechanical materialism and freedom does not appear at this level at all. The subsequent phase of active thought shaping abstract ideas into a theory about the situation can be seen as idealism, and freedom, in the sense of a release from the bare 'givenness' of the original circumstances, comes into the picture at this point; but so far it is the freedom of a purely conceptual movement without any actual consequences.

In the act of applying this theory to the posited situation, the freedom of conception is subjected to the stern criticism of objective conditions and only such elements of novelty are retained as can be incorporated into whatever new situation develops out of the first. If these objective conditions are physical, the result of this process is the transformation of things in conformity with natural law which is production at the level of action and scientific knowledge at the level of consciousness. If the conditions are social, the result is the transformation of society in conformity with the laws of people's productive relationships which at the level of action is political change and at the level of consciousness is the understanding of society which makes that political change possible. But the freedom of conceptualisation which in the first type of tranformation is the consciousness of natural law, of necessity, in the second is the consciousness of the social law that people make their own history and, even if they do not make it just as they want to, they can involve themselves in the struggle to bring about a social change for the better which can only occur through human intervention of a profoundly moral character.

We have also seen how these various phases of the theory of knowledge are expressed in different languages. The language of the first phase is purely descriptive - empirical propositions about objective conditions as merely reflected in consciousness. The language of the second phase is either logical, drawing deductive conclusions from abstract formulations, or imaginative, spinning out ideal fantasies about what might be. Only in the final phase do we get prescriptive sentences in the form of value or normative judgments with their implicit imperatives that some object ought to be approved as worthy of choice or that some action ought to be performed as productive of good results. This moral 'ought' has been prepared for by the appearance of an ideal freedom in the preceding phase. It is because Marxism stresses the interconnectedness of the whole process and does not take the various phases as separate alternatives that it can be at once a science of society, a logic of social consciousness and a call to action.

All these languages can be found in Marxism. 'Capital' is predominantly an abstract analysis of the capitalist system making it possible to describe precisely how the system really functions. In 'Capital' and the other classics, by applying different levels of abstraction, Marx works out the logic of a science of society and shows how various modes of production with their internal class conflicts are related to each other in the history of human development. In the 'Communist Manifesto' capitalist society is judged in ethical terms and the moral appeal for revolutionary action on the part of the working class to change it is trumpeted forth.

In the preface to 'Capital' Marx explains that he is primarily concerned in this account with describing how people function economically in capitalist society:

> Here individuals are dealt with only in so far as they are personifications of economic categories, embodiments of particular class relations and class interests. My standpoint, from which the evolution of the economic formation of society is viewed as a process of natural history, can less than any other make the individual responsible for relations whose creature he socially remains, however much he may subjectively raise himself above them.[34]

But in the same passage he does judge the capitalist class morally when he speaks of the individualistic entrepreneurial ambitions of which they boast as 'the most violent, mean and malignant passions of the human breast, the furies of private interest'.[35] He contemptuously refers to the transformation, by the exploitation of the working class, of 'vulgar and half-educated upstarts' into 'eminent cotton spinners', 'extensive sausage makers' and 'influential blacking dealers'.

Indeed, Kautsky chides Marx for letting 'the influence of the moral ideal break through his scientific research' since 'science stands above ethics and its results are just as little moral or immoral as necessity is moral or immoral'.[36] For Kautsky the only part ethics has to play is in providing the proletariat with the morale for carrying out economic changes on the basis of a purely scientific analysis.

This absolute distinction between scientific and ethical human beings was the sign of Kautsky's conversion to the revisionist creed of supposing that social change would come about automatically without the need for revolutionary struggle. All we have to do is wait for social trends which are going the way we want to go anyway to sweep us to victory - a programme of sheer opportunism. Kautsky also shows his contempt for the working class in treating the moral ideal as a kind of fairy tale to make them behave as they are supposed to according to economic theory.

Revisionism began with Bernstein who not surprisingly spent some time in Britain where he became familiar with the social democratic ideas of the Fabians. 'Revisionism' is, really, a misnomer, suggesting that it is merely a distortion or reworking of Marxism. In fact, it is nothing but the ideology of capitalism disguised under a pseudo-revolutionary rather than a pseudo-liberal democratic mask. If social democracy is bourgeois morals and politics wearing a cloth cap, revisionism is bourgeois morals and politics decked out in odds and ends of Marxist terminology. Bourgeois morality exemplifies the naturalistic fallacy of assuming that members of a society in each pursuing his or her own individual self-interest will somehow bring about the moral result of the general good. Revisionist morality commits the same fallacy in assuming that contradictions working themselves out automatically will bring about all the moral consequences of a socialist revolution without anyone being put to the inconvenience of actually revolting.

Just as bourgeois morality cannot conceive of anyone's acting other than on the basis of immediate selfish interests so revisionism sees the working class as capable only of responding to material incentives - so that socialism will be built by capitalist motives. It is manipulative rather than liberative and its typical political form is a bureaucracy acting on behalf of the working class because it knows better what is good for them - never the capture and consolidation of state power by the workers themselves. The clearest statement of revisionism in Britain, the CPGB's 'British Road to Socialism', by which was meant the parliamentary road, turned out to be the 'British Road to Thatcherism'.

It is true that in explaining scientifically the way the capitalist system works Marx may sometimes use expressions which look like an economic deterministic approach to social existence and which would be incompatible with expressions of moral indignation at crimes against the working class or any summons to that class to liberate itself. Sometimes, in rejecting all the claptrap of bourgeois morality, Marx may seem to be throwing out the moral baby with the bourgeois bath water. But these are only individual remarks taken out of context - as for example the statement in the 'Communist Manifesto', that communism 'abolishes eternal truth and all morality'. But Marx goes on to show that what is being abolished with the total disappearance of class antagonisms is class truth and morality passing themselves off as eternal, which is the ideological form of all past ages characterised by 'the exploitation of one part of society by another'. The overall import of Marx's work is unmistakably that dialectical materialism allows full scope for a call to action that is at once practical and ethical, a call not just to interpret the world but to change it.

Many critics have charged Marx with economism, with making economic interests in a narrow sense the mechanical determinant of our actions which would provide no scope for morality. But as Engels has said on this point:

According to the materialist conception of history, the ultimately determining element in history is the production and reproduction of real life. More than this neither Marx nor I have ever asserted. Hence if someone twists this into saying that the economic element is the only determining one, he transforms that proposition into a meaningless, abstract, senseless phrase. The economic situation is the basis, but the various elements of the superstructure: political forms of the class struggle...constitutions established by the victorious class...judicial forms, and even the reflexes of all these actual struggles in the brains of the participants...also exercise their influence upon the course of the historical struggles and in many cases preponderate in determining their form.[37]

Some calling themselves Marxists incorrectly hypostatise these concepts 'material base' and 'ideological superstructure' into permanent fixtures of society with base always determining ideology which remains reflective and inactive; but such a society would be unchangeable. Marx uses the terms 'base' and 'superstructure' metaphorically to describe the fundamental materialist principle that 'It is not the consciousness of men that determines their being, but, on the contrary, their social being that determines their consciousness.' But the relationship between social being and consciousness is dialectical not mechanical as is clear from Marx's description of the nature of revolutionary change.

At a certain stage of their development, the material productive forces of society come in conflict with the existing relations of production, or - what is but a legal expression for the same thing - with the property relations within which they have been at work hitherto. From forms of development of the productive forces these relations turn into their fetters. Then begins an epoch of social revolution.'[38]

But the revolution is not going to be made simply by the existence of a conflict of productive forces and relations of production which can then be reflected in human consciousness. It will be made by a large group of people who, conscious of that conflict and the way it affects them, adopt a different ideology from the prevailing one and try to put it into practice while a smaller group of people resist a change which will reflect adversely on them by insisting that the old ideology is correct even if it means great sacrifices in the living standards of the revolting group. The relationship between 'base' and 'superstructure' can thus be seen as that between people's 'struggle with nature for sustenance' and 'the reflexes of class struggles in the brains of the participants'. When translated into human terms the conflict between forces and relations of production as played out freely in human consciousness reacts on social being in ways that can only be described as moral.

But conceptions of morality do not stay the same after a revolutionary change in the economic foundation of society. The entire immense superstructure which is human consciousness's ideological forms of the conflict - legal, political, religious, aesthetic or philosophical - is more or less rapidly transformed. As has been said the action of commitment to revolutionary change is moral in the double sense of not only loyally supporting an exploited class in liberating itself but also in helping to change the very moral standards the liberated society is to be judged by.

Marx suggests that the ideological forms are 'more or less rapidly transformed' and that may be true in the perspective of human history; but the transition between capitalist and communist society is going to be a very lengthy one in terms of the life span of individuals and during much of that period the transformation of the economic base of society will be reflected in a long drawn out ideological class conflict. Based on the experience of the Paris Commune Marx wrote:

> Between capitalist and communist society lies the period of the revolutionary transformation of the one into the other. There corresponds to this also a political transition period in which the state can be nothing but the revolutionary dictatorship of the proletariat.[39]

This dictatorship of the working class, of the enormous majority of the people who live by the sale of their labour-power, replaces the dictatorship of the bourgeoisie, the relatively small minority of those whose ownership and control of the means of production enables them to profit from their traffic in the labour-power of others. The dictatorship of the working class, as long as it is not merely the dictatorship of the party and bureacracy on behalf of the working class, represents a democratic advance. It is a move toward the ultimate in democracy when the working people being all there is cease to exist as a class. But the dictatorship of the working class remains a necessity even after revolutionary victory because class struggle does not suddenly cease with the capture of state power.

The abolition of classes requires a long, difficult and stubborn class struggle, which, after the overthrow of capitalist rule, after the destruction of the bourgeois state, after the establishment of the dictatorship of the proletariat, does not disappear, but merely changes its forms and in many respects becomes fiercer.[40]

The revisionist line on this transitional period, as developed by such deviants from Marxism as Khrushchev, is that class struggle ends with the revolution and there is no need for a dictatorship of the proletariat. Furthermore, since the superstructure is regarded as the passive and mechanical reflection of the material base, once the material base has been technically altered from capitalist to socialist by the expropriation of the private owners of the means of production, socialist human beings will be automatically produced like products coming off an assembly line, with the speed of this production being regulated by material rewards distributed to workers, while, of course, considerably higher material rewards are reserved for the members of party, state and bureaucracy. It has led to counter-revolution.

The Great Proletarian Cultural Revolution in China was instituted as a check to revisionism. It was the ideological change in thinking which reflected the socialist movement of turning individual liberties which had been the prerogative of the upper classes into the collective liberties of workers and peasants generally. Attitudes to the Cultural Revolution were determined by whether one belonged to one of the privileged classes of the past and found it restrictive or to the ranks of workers and peasants and found it liberative.

Marxism recognises that during the transitional period of socialism there must be ideological change complementing the political revolution which has destroyed the economic base of exploitative society, that if the thinking of the people is not also revolutionised so that it is thoroughly socialist and in accord with the socialist economic base, then it will react on that base in a corrosive and destructive way. Objectively revisionism, which refuses to make a revolution on the grounds that socialism can come about automatically, sets out, once revolution has been made, to destroy its achievements on the grounds that a socialist society can best be built by bourgeois incentives. As Lenin goes on to say in the above quotation:

> It requires a fairly long period of transition from capitalism to socialism, because the reorganisation of production is a difficult matter, because radical changes in all spheres of life need time, and because the enormous force of habit of petty-bourgeois and bourgeois property relations can be overcome only by a long and stubborn struggle.

The working class having made the revolution must remain in firm democratic control of socialist development at all levels of society - cultural as well as economic. 'The proletariat must exercise all-round dictatorship over the bourgeoisie in the realm of the superstructure, including the various spheres of culture.'[41] It is precisely in such spheres as education, publication, administration and propaganda work that the bourgeoisie, using its cultural privileges in the previous regime to gain a foothold in the new socialist regime, regroup for the purpose of subverting it. Hence the moral summons to the working class during the Cultural Revolution in China for the defence of socialism: 'Fight self-interest! Criticise revisionism!' In other words, the working class must fight selfish bourgeois habits and customs within themselves at the same time that they expose revisionism as bourgeois counter-revolution and smash it. Emancipation of the working class means not only overthrowing the exploitative system of capitalism but also eradicating within themselves the many vestiges of the bourgeois egoistic ethos.

This ideological revolution by no means involves the suppression by party or state of anti-socialist ideas. Rather it takes advantage of the ending of the private monopolistic control of the media in the interest of capitalist profit for the fullest and most open discussion of democratic ideals and responsibilities. The period of socialist transition should be much more a time of the free adaptation by the majority of the new ideology of the liberated working class than as the punitive imposition on the expropriated minority of an ideology which is alien to them. Socialism is nothing if not democratic, 'the self-conscious independent movement of the immense majority in the interest of the immense majority'. It does not have to worry about the consequences of free expression, only about the suppression or distortion of that expression by apologists of the old order.

Neither does 'the dictatorship of the proletariat over the bourgeoisie in various spheres of culture' mean the censorship of works of art or literature inherited from pre-socialist periods. Just as many products or means of production go on being useful after the mode of production during which they were devised has been changed, so do many works of art and literature transcend the particular class-divided society in which they were created and come to have a more permanent and universal value. Indeed they have the important function of serving as moving reminders of our common humanity which survives the successive periods of inhumane exploitation. Socialism itself, the progressive ideology of the working class, was born and matured in the womb of bourgeois culture. What the dictatorship of the working class in the sphere of culture means is ending any bourgeois monopoly of the arts and literature and throwing them open for both the enjoyment and the creative practice of the whole working class who are to become eventually the entire population.

Marxism, which repudiates any religious idea of our 'creating' the universe by backdating some extrapolated version of ourselves to the timeless moment before the Big Bang and which accounts for morality by analysing the human activity of co-operatively producing and equitably sharing the means of sustenance instead of by adducing some code of conduct handed down from on high, does not, however, countenance the persecution of religious believers. Religion, Marx says, is like flowers entwined in the chains of the oppressed and exploited. The task is not to snatch away the flowers but to break the chains.

The enemies of Marxism like to think that communism or what we call the transition to it, socialism, involves a curtailment or even the abolition of individual human rights. How could this be the case when Marx has made it plain that it is the very essence of socialism 'that the free development of all depends on the free development of each'? What else can the liberation of the working class mean but that a much greater proportion of the people of a society enjoy much greater individual liberty? Unlike the bourgeoisie which is limited to those who own or control the means of production, the working class is open to all: anyone can belong to it who participates in the creation of value in exchange for an equitable portion of the goods produced. But the dictatorship of the working class does not represent for the majority of the people the sort of individual licence and privileges the bourgeois minority exercised over the working class. And in their relations with one another, unlike the competitiveness of the bourgeoisie, Marx has said:

> The proletariat should vindicate the simple laws of morals and justice which ought to govern the relations between individuals.

Since Marxism bases these 'simple laws of morals and justice' on relating the satisfaction by consumption of individual needs and desires to the collective obligations of the co-operative fellowship of the production of the goods required by all, the individual worker can understand the nature of these simple laws that should govern personal relationships and why they ought to be observed. But as Marx says, capitalism establishes an 'accumulation of wealth' at one pole of society and at the same time 'an accumulation of poverty, unemployment, brutality, mental degradation at the other'.

The rich and powerful, through their control of the labour-power of others, are not involved in the productive process. They are merely concerned with consumption and subscribe to the individualistic ethic of utilitarianism. Since they consider it a right to exploit those who live by the sale of their labour-power, no question of morality arises in their treatment of the working class and even in their financial dealings with each other it is difficult to say what is legitimate and what is illegitimate profiteering.

The poor, miserable and homeless at the other end of the scale are also uninvolved in the productive process having fallen through the bottom as a result of the massive unemployment required to keep organised workers under control. They also are obsessed with consumption, wondering where their next meal is coming from. It is natural that they should be driven to crime against the property laws established by the very agents of their misery. They will even find it difficult to abide by the 'simple laws that ought to govern individual relationships'. Marxist morality condemns capitalism for the immorality of the exploitation of the working class and also for the creation of an under class for whom a decent social existence in which those simple laws apply is next to impossible.

The point Marx makes over and over again is that in an exploitative society the individual rights of all become the privileges of the propertied and moneyed few. To explain to unemployed youth sleeping under a bridge or to the inhabitants of a black ghetto or to the millions upon millions of starving people in capitalism's semicolonial territories that, after all, they do enjoy full individual rights to life, liberty and the pursuit of happiness would hardly convince them of the advantages of living in a so-called 'free society'. Socialism is by no means opposed to the Rights of Man: it is the prescription for their practical realisation by the vast majority. The socialist revolution has to be seen as complementary to the French Revolution which established the idea of individual rights. Creating the society in which that idea can be realised on the widest scale involves the change from an egoistic to a socialistic ethic.

One of the lessons Marxists have had to learn from the practical experience of consolidating working class revolutions is that the transitional period will last a good deal longer than was previously anticipated, as much because a new socialist country is surrounded by hostile capitalist countries desperate to intervene and restore capitalism as because the conquest of bourgeois customs and attitudes internally, as Lenin said, is a protracted struggle. But even Lenin did not appreciate just how long it was going to take. In addressing the Youth Leagues in 1920 he supposed that many of his audience would actually, in their lifetimes, be living in communist society. Mao Tsetung, speaking in terms of ten generations, comes much closer to the idea of the transition from capitalism to socialism extending, like the transition from feudalism to capitalism, over many decades. As he says:

> Socialist society covers a considerably long historical period. In the historical period of socialism, there are still classes, class contradictions and class struggle, there is the struggle between the socialist road and the capitalist road, and there is the danger of the capitalist restoration. We must recognise the protracted and complex nature of this struggle. We must heighten our vigilance. We must conduct socialist education, We must correctly understand and handle class contradictions and class struggle, distinguish the contradictions between ourselves and the enemy from those among the people and handle them correctly. Otherwise a socialist country like ours will turn into its opposite and degenerate...From now on we must remind ourselves of this every year, every month and every day so that we can retain a rather sober understanding

of this problem and have a Marxist-Leninist line.[42]

What is involved in this whole question of a cultural revolution is an understanding of the relationship between material base and ideological superstructure and an appreciation of the dialectical character of this relationship. Unless it is possible for people's consciousness, having comprehended the laws governing their social being, to play at certain times a decisive role in social development, then there is no possibility of the kind of freedom of action presupposed by moral imperatives and no morality. There would not then be any legitimate grounds for urging workers in capitalist countries to mobilise their forces to emancipate themselves and the world from exploitation nor for urging the working people of a country where a proletarian revolution has occurred to 'fight self-interest and bourgeois revisionism' in order to safeguard it.

Mao Tsetung explains this dialectical relationship between base and superstructure and also demonstrates the circumstances in which one or other predominates as the decisive factor.

> True, the productive forces, practice and the economic base generally play the principal and decisive role; whoever denies this is not a materialist. But it must also be admitted that in certain conditions, such aspects as the relations of production, theory and the superstructure in turn manifest themselves in the principal and decisive role. When it is impossible for the productive forces to develop without a change in the relations of production, then the change in the relations of production plays the principal and decisive role. The creation and advocacy of revolutionary theory plays the principal and decisive role in those times of which Lenin said, 'without a revolutionary theory there can be no revolutionary movement'. When a task, no matter which, has to be performed, but there is as yet no guiding line, method, plan or policy, the principal and decisive thing is to decide on a guiding line, method, plan or policy. When the superstructure (politics, culture etc.) obstructs the development of economic base, political and cultural changes

> become principal and decisive. Are we going against materialism when we say this? No. The reason is that while we recognise that in the general development of history the material determines the mental and social being determines social consciousness, we also - and indeed must - recognise the reaction of mental on material things, of social consciousness on social being and of the superstructure on the economic base. This does not go against materialism; on the contrary, it avoids mechanical materialism and firmly upholds dialectical materialism.[43]

In other words, it is precisely in revolutionary situations that this reaction of relations of production on forces of production, of consciousness on being, of superstructure on base occurs as part of the dynamic of change and releases in the process that degree of freedom necessary for the highest moral endeavour of those making the revolution. This dialectical relationship can be compared with the mechanical accounts of Bukharin and most bourgeois writers who find the main motive of social change simply in the development of forces of production, like a rise in the level of technology, without appreciating the tremendous liberating effect on the forces of production of a revolutionary change in the relations of production.

There are other examples of how the relationship of dialectical pairs fluctuates in respect to which is the principal factor. In the overall relationship of form and content, content is usually the principal aspect. But form is not always secondary. In limited spheres and temporarily, form can be primary, as in the search for and discernment of new forms of struggle. Attention to changes in form ordinarily lags behind awareness of changes in content. 'It is the old story,' Engels says: 'form is always neglected at first for content.' And, of course, this same relationship obtains between quantitative change, which is evolutionary, and qualitative change, which is revolutionary. Beyond a certain point quantitative alteration becomes qualitative.

The Proletarian Cultural Revolution was complementary to Mao Tsetung's strategy of a two-stage revolution for countries like

China with little industrialisation, a small urban proletariat and a large peasantry. It was an attempt to proletarianise the ideology of the working masses for the advance from the stage of the people's democratic dictatorship to a dictatorship of the proletariat as the condition for the full development of socialist society. It was an attempt to inculcate working class morality as the basic impulse of socialist construction. Mao thought that many cultural revolutions might be necessary to guarantee China against socialist degeneration.

TOWARD A FREE SOCIETY

If Marx had one compelling motive for identifying himself completely with the working class in order to devote his life to leading them out of the bondage of wage slavery, it was his feeling about freedom as the supreme good. This is why he was never interested in petty bourgeois schemes for some redistribution of wealth or some amelioration of the conditions of the poor. The issue was always that of establishing the social foundation on which the major task of human beings, social production, could be carried out in conditions of human dignity, which could only mean that people must enter voluntarily into relations of co-operative production with others, thus changing labour 'from merely a means of life to life's principal need'. Such a free realm in which there was no exploitation of human beings by human beings could only come into existence when not only the material basis of exploitation had been transformed but also the ideas and habits of centuries of class-divided, exploitative society had been replaced with the socialist ideas and habits of freedom. Moreover, while justice may be something that is rendered to people, freedom is something they can only win for themselves. It is not something that can be achieved on their behalf by any elitist grouping. Every form of acting on behalf of people will always turn into another form of their exploitation.

A decision of the Central Committee of the Chinese Communist Party concerning the Proletarian Cultural Revolution puts the point clearly:

> The only method is for the masses to liberate themselves, and any method of doing things on their behalf must not be used. Trust the masses, rely on them and respect their initiative. Cast out fear. Don't be afraid of disorder...Let the masses educate themselves in this great revolutionary movement and learn to distinguish between right and wrong and between correct and incorrect ways of doing things.

There is no way except through mass involvement in revolutionary practice for the working people to learn to make these distinctions. 'What is correct always develops in the course of struggle with what is wrong. The true, the good and the beautiful always exist in comparison with the false, the evil and the ugly and grow in struggle with the latter.'[44]

Marx was always concerned with the dialectic of necessity and freedom, the relation between the physical compulsion of people's basic needs and the liberative energy that people as socially productive beings could display in meeting them and going beyond them to a richer fulfilment.

> Just as the savage must wrestle with nature to satisfy his wants, to maintain and reproduce life, so must civilised man, and he must do so in all social formations and under all possible modes of production. With his development this realm of physical necessity expands as a result of his wants; but, at the same time, the forces of production which satisfy these wants also increase. Freedom in this field can only consist in socialised man, the associated producers, rationally regulating their interchange with nature; and achieving this with the least expenditure of energy and under conditions most favourable to, and worthy of, their human nature. But it nonetheless still remains a realm of necessity. Beyond it begins that development of human energy which is an end in itself, the

true realm of freedom, which, however, can blossom forth only with this realm of necessity as its base.[45]

Here Marx is talking about the change from socialism to full communism when the rule 'from each according to his ability, to each according to his work' has changed to 'from each according to his ability, to each according to his need'. Even communist society must not, of course, be thought of as a final stage of human development in which all contradictions are resolved and from which, therefore, no further advance is possible. There would still be contradictions as, for example, between the new and the old, the known and the not yet known, present and future demands and so on; but since such contradictions would no longer break out along class lines in an exploitative situation they would no longer be antagonistic. Marx does not describe communist society as the end but the beginning of history, true history made by people freely and consciously in co-operative pursuit of their aims both material and spiritual; and everything leading up to it, the various forms of class-divided society with their strife and blindness and inhumanity, must be regarded from this perspective as a prehistoric period.

The mass line, 'from the masses, to the masses', democratic centralism, is the pattern of political freedom in socialist society. From the widely-extended party membership all over the country the ideas, opinions and aspirations of those involved in the struggle for production and in class struggle flow to the centre in the most democratic way. These ideas, opinions and hopes are concentrated in the party line. This line is then given back to the membership for general implementation as the ideology of the working class. This is not a once-for-all process but continuous, like the blood flowing from extremities to the heart and then, purified and revitalised, being pumped back all over the body again, over and over and over. And as with the party and its line so with every other form of organisation - the people's state in relation to the electors who vote on the policies and personnel of the government that rules them for a limited time and can always be replaced, the state planners in relation to factory workers and co-operative and state farmers all over the country who submit estimates of what they need in tools and equipment and what they can contribute to the economy which become the five year plan to be carried out by all and so on down through local government, the various front organisations to the committee and residents of a single housing unit. Power is in the hands of the working class. It flows inwardly, democratically, to a central authority and outwardly as an agreed line of action for the people to follow. They follow it because they recognise it as a line which they have contributed to formulating: it has 'the mark of the people' on it. A line of action for the working people takes the form of a prohibitive line for any whose interests are opposed to those of the working people. The dictatorship of the proletariat is simply the mass line as it appears to enemies of the working class. The mass line, which at the level of organisation is democratic centralism, at the level of understanding is simply the Marxist theory of knowledge based on the conviction of where correct ideas come from.

> Take the ideas of the masses (scattered and unsystematic ideas) and concentrate them (through study turn them into concentrated and systematic ideas), then go to the masses and propagate and explain these ideas until the masses embrace them as their own, hold fast to them and translate them into action. Then once again concentrate ideas from the masses and once again go to the masses so that the ideas are persevered in and carried through. And so on, over and over again in an endless spiral, with the ideas becoming more correct, more vital and richer each time.[46]

The Marxist conception of truth is inseparable from the mass line because the only source of correct ideas is social practice, the practical experience of the people down the ages in the struggle for production and in class struggle. Only those who learn from the masses have anything to teach the masses. Just as value judgments are the tribute we pay to the labour of fellow human beings, so our regard for right thinking is the respect we pay to their hard-won knowledge. 'It has to be understood that the masses are the real heroes, while we ourselves are often childlike and ignorant, and without this understanding it is impossible to acquire even the most rudimentary knowledge.'[47] These correct ideas from social practice, once they are 'concentrated and systematised', are then 'grasped by the masses' and 'turned into a material force'. 'Communists must be ready at all times to stand for the truth, because truth is in the interests of the people; communists must be ready at all times to correct their mistakes because mistakes are against the interests of the people...'[48] A regard for the masses is a regard for truth and a regard for truth is a regard for the masses.

The Proletarian Cultural Revolution in China was a moral struggle for the soul of human beings under socialism at a particular time and place; but something like it has to be going on all the time in socialist countries if they are to honour their revolutionary commitments. In the organisational form of the involvement of the working people, democratic centralism, criticism is the democratic aspect, the right of all to speak their minds freely. Self-criticism represents the centralist aspect, the discipline of the individual in accepting the mass line once democratically established. This principle was expressed in the new constitution of the People's Republic of China adopted in 1975 after the Cultural Revolution:

> Speaking out freely, airing views fully, holding great debates and writing big character posters are new forms of carrying on socialist revolution created by the masses of the people. The state shall ensure to the masses the right to use these forms to create a political situation in which there are both centrism and democracy, both discipline and freedom, both unity of will and personal ease of mind and liveliness, and so help consolidate the dictatorship of the proletariat.[49]

The unity of theory and practice also takes this same form of the mass line.

Start from perceptual knowledge and actively develop it into

> rational knowledge; then start from rational knowledge and actively guide revolutionary practice to change both the subjective and objective world. Practice, knowledge, again practice, and again knowledge. This form repeats itself in endless cycles, and with each cycle the content of practice and knowledge rises to a higher level. Such is the whole of the dialectical-materialist theory of the unity of knowing and doing.[50]

The only solution to the problem of whether theory corresponds to objective reality is to re-direct rational knowledge to social practice and see whether it can achieve the objective one has in mind... idealism and mechanical materialism, opportunism and adventurism are all characterised by the break between the subjective and the objective, by the separation of theory from practice.[51]

This is the pattern of socialist society: everywhere this pulsating motion from extremities to centre and from centre back to extremities again in a never ending dialectic of revolutionary development. Capitalist society under bourgeois rule, in spite of its democratic pretensions, disenfranchises the working people on the one issue they are most concerned about - whether they are to go on being exploited or not. The capitalist ruling class has no real regard for the mass of people - in their work they are commodities; in their needs, consumers; in their existence, statistics and when it comes to defending national capitalist interests, cannon fodder. The general bourgeois pattern is exploitative metropole dominating exploited hinterland, factory management dominating workers, city dominating countryside, capitalist government and bureaucracy dominating wage earners, metropolitan country dominating colonies. Everything in the way of culture, knowledge or programmes of action are presumed to flow out from the centre; nothing is supposed to flow back again but loot, surplus-value. The centre in this capitalist pattern Is like a more and more detached brain with no good red blood flowing to it - and, progressively, no rational orders issuing out from it either.

CHAPTER III OBLIGATIONS

1 Marx, 'Theses on Feuerbach' Selected Works vol, II, p367
2 Marx, 'Eighteenth Brumaire of Louis Bonaparte', Selected Works, vol, I, p225
3 W. David Ross, 'Foundations of Ethics' pp159-60
4 Marx, 'Capital', vol, I, p47
5 Mao Tsetung, 'Talks at the Yenan Forum on Literature and the Art' Selected Works vol, III, p88
6 Bertell Ollman, 'Alienation' p134
7 Marx, 'Economic and Philosophic Manuscripts of 1844' p104
8 Ibid., p107
9 Marx, 'The German Ideology'
10 Marx, 'Notes to James Mill's Elements of Political Economy'
11 Mao Tsetung, 'On Practice' Selected Works, vol, I p308
12 Marx and Engels, 'The Communist Manifesto' Selected Works, vol, I, p55
13 Mao Tsetung, 'Talks at the Yenan Forum on Literature and the Art' vol, III, p90
14 Lenin, 'What Is To Be Done?' Selected Works, vol, I, p201
15 Marx, 'The Holy Family' p52
16 Lenin, 'The State and Revolution' Selected Works vol, I, p201
17 Marx, 'The Holy Family' p125
18 Mao Tsetung, 'On Coalition Government' Selected Works, vol, III, p 207
19 Karl A. Wittfogel, 'Oriental Despotism'
20 Karl Popper, 'The Poverty of Historicism'
21 Marx, Preface to the First German Edition of 'Capital', Selected Works, vol, I, p409
22 Lenin, 'What Is To Be Done?' Selected Works, vol, I, p163
23 Lenin, 'The State and Revolution', Selected Works vol, II, p201
24 Marx, 'The German Ideology' p7
25 Mao Tsetung, 'On Contradiction', Selected Works, vol, I, p345

26 *Ibid., p313*
27 *Ibid., p314*
28 *Ibid., p333*
29 *Ibid., pp321-2*
30 *Mao Tsetung, 'Talk on Questions of Philosophy'*
31 *Engels, 'Herr Eugen Duhring's Revolution in Science' p130*
32 *Lenin, 'Tasks of the Youth Leagues', Selected Works vol, II, p670*
33 *Engels, 'Feuerbach and the End of Classical German Philosophy', Selected Works, vol, II, p336*
34 *Marx, Preface to the First German Edition of 'Capital', Selected Works vol, I, p10*
35 *Ibid.*
36 *Karl Kautsky, 'Ethics and the Materialist Conception of History'*
37 *Engels, 'Letter to J. Bloch', Selected Works vol, II, p443*
38 *Marx, 'Preface to the Critique of Political Economy' Selected Works, vol, I, p329*
39 *Marx, 'Critique of the Gotha Programme', Selected Works, vol, II, p30*
40 *Lenin, 'Greetings to Hungarian Workers', Selected Works, vol, II, p481*
41 *Mao Tsetung, quoted in 'Peking Review', no.7, 14 Feb. 1975*
42 *Mao Tsetung, 'Address to the 10th Plenary Session, VIIIth Party Congress'*
43 *Mao Tsetung, 'On Contradiction', Selected Works, vol, I, p336*
44 *Mao Tsetung, 'On the Correct Handling of Contradictions among the People', 'Four Essays on Philosophy' p115*
45 *Marx, 'Capital' vol, III, pp799-800*
46 *Mao Tsetung, 'Concerning Methods of Leadership', Selected Works, vol, III, p119*
47 *Mao Tsetung, 'Preface on Rural Surveys' Selected Works,vol, III, p12*
48 *Mao Tsetung, 'Unite and Fight to Accomplish the Party's Tasks', Selected Works vol, III, p315*
49 *'The Constitution of the People's Republic of China'Article 13 p20*
50 *Mao Tsetung, 'On Practice', Selected Works, vol, I, p308*
51 *Ibid., p307*

Chapter 4
Alienation and Political Change.

INTRODUCTION

The fact that the social existence of people, particularised in the form of their involvement in the productive process, largely shapes without mechanically determining their ethical attitudes, means that Marxism cannot expect any qualitative change in society based solely on the moral efforts of individuals acting within the range of their own personal relationships. Their very conceptions of what is 'right' in regard to those personal relationships will have been profoundly influenced by the specific form of exploitation in their society and by their own position as belonging to the class of exploiters or exploited. In a situation of intensifying contradictions in the basic mode of production, which are always, ultimately, class contradictions, people's reactions in the moral crisis which is part of the general economic and political crisis are inevitably coloured through and through by which side of the class contradiction they are on.

The moral crisis in the capitalist world is a reflection of the economic and political crisis which results from the fact that capitalism, fuelled by profit-seeking greed, is not capable of ordered, sustained growth like socialism. It is either in a state of rapid expansion in terms of commoditising all labour, manual and mental, at home to provide ever more surplus-value or it is reaching out abroad to grab sources of cheap unorganised labour and raw materials and to dominate foreign markets. The moment capitalism stops or is stopped from expanding it begins to decline. The tendency of the rate of profit to fall overtakes the profitable growth which expansion made possible and the system runs out of fuel. Like Napoleon's bayonet which one could do everything with but sit on, capitalism is capable of doing many things but not, rent as it is with internal contradictions, remaining in a state of peaceful equilibrium.

Once capitalism is in a state of decline there are only two eventual alternatives, however far off people may like to think they are - working class revolution to change it into socialism or fascism to enable it to go on exploiting a rebellious working class.

Fascism is simply capitalism in extremis - a final morbid state in which class struggle is ended by force. The ruling class no more wants fascism which is a flagrant denial of all its ideological pretensions than it wants massive unemployment which yields no surplus-value but, ultimately, it can maintain its political domination in no other way.

Ideologically fascism means replacing the dangerous social fact of class struggle with some phoney principle of unification which cuts across class lines, like national, racial or religious chauvinism. Instead of getting rid of classes of exploiters and exploited, fascism pretends that they are not there - while setting about smashing the trade unions. There may be considerable variations, according to national history, of the form of chauvinism chosen to throw dust in people's eyes but the destruction of trade unions is a common feature of all fascism. Capitalism in decline, as could be seen in Britain in the '80s, does not become more conciliatory: it becomes much more vicious, not only attacking trade unions but frantically clawing back concessions made to the working people in better times. Mass unemployment is intended not only to weaken the trade unions but also to produce a chauvinistic lumpen proletariat from whose ranks can be recruited the force of savage louts which may be needed to keep fascist order.

One of the dangers of the situation is that it comes about gradually enough that those liberal-minded people who might be counted on to protest effectively at the way the rich get richer and the poor get poorer while the whole country goes deeper in debt never experience any particular point at which they realise just how far degeneration has gone and decide that a halt must now be called. There is no firm line between capitalism that still has some liberal pretensions and fascism. We need only imagine what the people who at the end of the War hopefully elected a government committed to full employment, housing for all, expanded public services and a flourishing industry to pay for it would make of today's Britain if it were plonked down on them as the fifty-years-on reality they were then dreaming about!

Naturally such economic and political degeneration is reflected in a moral crisis as grave. Even members of the ruling class may have their doubts about some of the measures employed. There is a time lag between the corruption of personal relations and the deterioration in the ethical standards of the whole ruling class and its hangers on during a period of severe capitalist decline; but this differential in the rate of demoralisation does not provide any real check on the decadence of political action. Policies depriving poor families of child benefits and other forms of relief, of doubling the number of the homeless and of forcing a third of the population to live on or below the poverty line with dire consequences for millions of children are no less immoral simply because they are enacted by those who may well be themselves reasonably good husbands and wives and caring parents.

Marxism is by no means unconcerned with the morality of such individual relationships as those between husband and wife, parents and children, fellow workmates and close friends. Indeed it is the poisoning of those relationships which is part of its indictment of capitalism. But the understanding that these relationships are inevitably stunted or fostered, weakened or strengthened by the prevailing social climate means that real concern about their quality has to take the form of helping to create the atmosphere in which they can flourish. That is to say, it calls for a material foundation of society which can support wholesome, happy, mutually beneficent personal relationships - not just in this country or that, not just among this class or that, but among all people without distinction.

The small, isolated, ingrown bourgeois family of male breadwinner and female house-keeper cum child-minder with its complex-ridden relationships is not the inevitable and eternal context of human development. Just as Marxism sees a progression in social organisation through various forms of class-divided society to a consciously planned communism at a higher level, so it envisages with different types of exploitation corresponding changes in the family - from its natural integration in the tribal community, through the risk of the destruction of the family under slavery, on to the extended joint-family of feudalism, down to the increasingly isolated small family unit of bourgeois society exiling its old and disabled. With the end of exploitation would come finally the re-integration of the family in the collective and co-operative life of the community.

It is, of course, just as absurd to hold the Teutonic-Christian form of the family to be absolute and final as it would be to apply that character to the ancient Roman, the ancient Greek, or the eastern forms which, moreover, taken together form a series in historic development. Moreover it is obvious that the fact of the collective working group being composed of individuals of both sexes and all ages, must necessarily, under suitable conditions, become a source of humane development; although in its spontaneously developed, brutal, capitalistic form, where the labourer exists for the process of production and not the process of production for the labourer, that fact is a pestiferous source of corruption and slavery.[1]

The equality of human labour which led to the idea that all men are equal now takes the more humane form that all people of whatever sex are equal. Marx points out that:

> Modern industry, by assigning as it does an important part in the socially organised process of production, outside the domestic sphere, to women...creates a new economic foundation for a higher form of the family and of the relations between the sexes.

If women are increasingly doing all the kinds of work that men do, why should there be women's work, like looking after babies, bringing up children, cooking meals, mending clothes, cleaning the house which men do not share in?

It is only necessary to think of the effect on personal relationships of the capitalist 'free' market in labour-power and goods to realise how influential in moral terms the mode of production is. The employer, backed up by anti-trade union legislation, is bent on changing the relationship between management and a workers collective united in mutual interest into a contractual relationship between management and each individual worker so that these individual workers can all be made to compete with each other as to who can supply the most surplus-value to management.

The economics of the mass market, greater wealth being gathered into fewer hands while more and more face bankruptcy, spreads to other fields as well. Publishing, for example, ceases to be a number of houses competing with each other in the discovery and distribution of a variety of literature to as wide a market as possible for profit and becomes a few huge conglomerates only concerned with profit, with bigger and bigger rewards for fewer and fewer writers and with questions of quality no longer worth considering - hardly the ideal basis for a good professional relationship between those who live by the pen! And in other fields too, like the arts generally, entertainment and athletics, big money for the few transforms friendly competition and good sportsmanship into bitter rivalry.

A critique of personal relations in bourgeois society can only take the practical form of a call for, in Lenin's words, 'a morality which serves the purpose of helping human society to rise to a higher level and to get rid of the exploitation of labour'. It is a call for a new society in which personal relationships based on feelings of love, companionship and common interests will not be at odds with relations of production based on private ownership, selfishness and competition but will complement, deepen and personalise relations of production based on common ownership, regard for the needs of others and co-operation.

The old society was based on the principle: rob or be robbed, work

> for others or make others work for you, be a slave owner or a slave. Naturally, people brought up in such a society imbibe with their mother's milk, so to speak, the psychology, the habit, the concept: you are either a slave owner or a slave or else, a small employee, a small official, an intellectual - in short, a man who thinks only of himself, and doesn't give a hang for anybody else.[2]

This call for the establishment of the very conditions in which higher ethical standards can be realised is itself supremely moral; but it can only be answered in terms of political activity. Such a social change cannot be brought about by individual changes in personal relationships, though political activity devoted to transforming society has its moral implications for personal relationships. Intimate associations in the family or among friends are not unaffected by the concerted political struggle to achieve a better ordering of social life. Indeed, it is to the extent that people dedicated to changing the very foundations of society are capable here and now of beginning to act on the moral principle of a lively concern for others which will be characteristic of that new society and of having all their relationships profoundly influenced by that principle that such a better ordering of society begins to be realised.

But this call for changing society cannot, effectively, take the form of a vague summons to people to show more regard for each other and observe a more humanitarian attitude in their conduct. It cannot take the form of charity which makes the giver feel good but does nothing to change the circumstances of the receiver. As we have seen, the gulf between exploiters and exploited is so great that no general humanitarian principles can stretch across it meaningfully. There is no morality which can unite in a common pattern of social behaviour people born to live out their pitifully short lives on the verge of starvation and those whom privilege insulates from every natural discomfort, between those whose lives depend on selling their capacity to labour as dearly as possible and those who are in a position to traffic profitably in the labour of others. The acceptance of such differences by subscribing to any system of belief which ignores them, explains them away or justifies them is the negation of morality. Genuine humanitarianism has to start with the demand for an end to the exploitation of one human being by another, which immediately turns it into the morality of a class.

All morality is ultimately class morality. One is either for an existing exploitative social organisation or against it. There is no third possibility. Any attempt to retreat into personal relationships and let the rest of the world go hang, any attempt to opt out of existing society and establish some small communal enclave merely commits one to tacit support of the status quo, a hanger-on of the exploiting class. Setting up such 'cop-out' communes is like trying to organise 'workers' control' in a particular factory while leaving the overwhelming capitalist context all around it intact: it is only a device for deluding any workers not clever enough to see through it into thinking there's some easy road to socialism. Try 'cultivating your own garden', if you are so privileged as to be able to do so, and you are likely to find that the plants are all dying from the pollution it profits somebody to create and nobody to remedy, or defoliated because some wild defenders of the existing system think an urban guerrilla may be hiding there. As a system like capitalism is more and more in conflict with the objective progressive laws of human development, actions in its name inevitably become increasingly immoral.

Marx describes the differences between exploitative societies and a society from which exploitation has been eliminated in terms of the class relationships of individuals. Whereas in all exploitative societies the individual could only participate in the life of the community as a member of some class, 'in the community of revolutionary proletarians, who establish their control over the conditions of existence of themselves and of the other members of society, the individuals participate as individuals.'[3] Since the state is simply the governmental form of the domination of the exploiting class, the ending of class-divided society with the elimination of exploitation means the 'withering away of the state' as class exploitation's strong arm.

If the state is the product of irreconcilable class antagonisms, if it is a power standing above society and increasingly alienating itself from it, it is clear that the liberation of the oppressed class is impossible not only without a violent revolution, but also without the destruction of the apparatus of state power which was created by the ruling class and which is the embodiment of this alienation.[4]

What this means in ethical terms is that in all class-divided society effective morality can only take a political form. In communist society, when classes no longer exist because the very ways of thinking and the habitual actions of an exploitative society will have been eliminated, then politics will take the form of morality.

This revolutionary change in the relations of production with its moral consequences has already been considered in terms of Marx's analysis of the capitalist system. The division of labour results in a distinction between production and consumption which under conditions of fully-developed capitalism becomes an actual separation in the way production and consumption are experienced by the working class and the capitalist class - largely concealed by the commoditisation of labour-power itself.

Marx always says if you want to understand capitalism always start with production, not consumption. Production is collective and co-operative. Consumption is individualistic and competitive. It is only to the extent that the working class is actively involved in production that they can be consumers at all. For them production is primary, not only in the general sense that humanity depends on the production of its own sustenance but also in the personal sense that, basically possessing nothing but their labour power, workers who do not work do not eat. Production is the collective effort of joining with others to mix labour with nature in order to produce the goods on which human life depends. The ideological reflection of this activity is a down-to-earth realism and a social sense of the comradeship in-labour of all those who work together in the production of goods. Consumption is individual and competitive but workers cannot really forget that they can only buy the commodities they need for themselves and their families to the extent that they have jointly sold with fellow workers the labour power which establishes a joint claim on commodities needed for individual consumption. All of this makes quite unconsciously for a kind of primitive socialism.

Through their ownership of the means of production capitalists command the labour-power of others. They are not involved in the physical process of production, only in the profit to be made from it by the appropriation of surplus-value which is unpaid labour. While from the workers' point of view it is production which makes consumption possible, from the capitalists' point of view it is profit or capital which represents a command over a certain proportion of commodities including labour-power which makes production possible. Just as work with nature to produce goods yields a fundamentally realistic ontology, the use of money, an abstraction, to call into being a workforce to produce goods tends to make for a basically idealistic outlook on the nature of things. The relationship of capitalists with other capitalists is not co-operative but competitive. One of the main reasons for amassing profit is to be able individually to consume more than others. All this makes quite unconsciously for a kind of primitive utilitarianism.

The only way that workers can defend themselves .from the capitalist's attempts to increase his profit at their expense is collectively. Individually no worker under capitalism can hope to match the power of the capitalist but workers together considerably outnumber him. Collective bargaining and the formation of trade unions are the forms their struggle takes. In order to increase their collective strength it is necessary to see to it that the individualistic competitiveness of personal consumption which all are subject to is not allowed to get out of hand and damage the unity achieved as co-operative producers which is their guarantee of a share of the commodities produced. The individual rights derived from the equality of human labour in the creation of value, like liberty, various freedoms and the pursuit of happiness can only be preserved by translating them into collective rights like the right to work, the right to organise, the right to strike, that is, the right to withdraw their labour which is all they have to bargain with. The working class requires the collective right to defend their individual rights which otherwise cease to exist.

Society is divided into producer collectives and individual consumers but the division runs through each worker too. The individual worker, therefore, is involved in the moral effort of subjecting his or her individual wants and desires to the collective obligations owed to other workers so that all can enjoy their individual rights together. In a strike to protect themselves from excessive exploitation or, even more, in a revolution to end the exploitation of their class, this need to subject individual wants to collective responsibilities can demand great sacrifices and becomes the moral injunction to fight self-interest for the common good.

The ending of all restraints on the development of trade and industry which marked the transition from feudalism to capitalism was taken by the bourgeoisie to have established the right of individuals to pursue their own self-interest in setting up capitalist enterprises for their profitable aggrandisement. This was justified by the creed of utilitarianism which held that for individuals to act in their own selfish interest in a free market could not but benefit society as a whole. Utilitarianism, like the bourgeois philosophy which first formulated it, is more closely associated with marketing and consumption than with production. It is the self justification of the shopkeeper. There is no morality in pursuing one's own self interest and then finding that, incidentally, one has contributed something to society's benefit - even if the utilitarian contention were true! The isolated individual who is the agent in the setting in motion of the utilitarian social machinery, motivated entirely by the self interest connected with consumption and not at all by the social interest of co-operative production, cannot be a moral agent.

Among the individual rights the bourgeoisie took advantage of in their rise to power were property rights. The right to own property is legitimate as long as it is personal property. But the right to own the means of other people's livelihood is, in a sense, the right to own them and a denial of their individual rights. If they try to defend those rights collectively, this is considered to be a limitation on the free market which is an essential condition for the enjoyment of individual rights and liberties. Capitalists increasingly turn the individual right to make a profit from supplying the needs of others into supplying the needs of others in such a way as to make a profit. They turn the individual rights of all into their individual right to all.

The human activity of co-operating in the production of the goods that, fairly distributed, sustain human life is the basis of human morality. But the division of labour to increase production separates production from consumption which allows the intervention of the exploiter who, through the ownership of the person, of the land or of the means of production, is able to take a large greedy share of consumption. The association of immorality with consumption detached from production can be seen in the moral state of late capitalist society. As Marx has said:

> Capitalism establishes an accumulation of misery, corresponding with accumulation of capital. Accumulation of wealth at one pole is, therefore, at the same time accumulation of misery, agony of toil, slavery, ignorance, brutality, mental degradation at the opposite pole.[5]

The capitalists at one pole of society and the millions of long-term unemployed living on a pittance, of homeless down-and-outs sleeping rough, of mentally-disabled turned loose on the community at the other pole have something in common: they are neither actively involved in production and they are both obsessed with consumption, whether consumption in the sense of buying and possessing all the things that give one pleasure and status or consumption in the sense of just getting enough to eat to go on living at all. Those who drop out of the bottom of production into poverty and those whose possession of the means of production enables them to rise above it are extremely individualistic and competitive in outlook with little sense of the future other than the immediate prospect of making it big, whether that means fame and fortune or the next meal. We are fully aware of the way poverty and degradation drive people to crime against their fellow human beings. We are only just becoming aware of the way ambition and greed drive capitalists and the members of the government that support them to crime against their fellow human beings - because amoral utilitarianism does not indict successful self-interest. The difference between the two lots of criminals is that the miserable and dispossessed did not choose the conditions out of which their criminality grows which greatly diminishes the immorality of their crimes.

Marx's remedy for this situation is the revolutionary expropriation of the owners of the means of production which then become the property of the people who are the creators of value. This makes possible a proper socialist connection between production and consumption - 'from each according to his or her ability, to each according to his or her work'. Under this mode of production a socialised labour force, 'the associated producers, rationally regulate their interchange with nature; and achieve this with the least expenditure of energy and under conditions most favourable to, and worthy of, their human nature.' This revolution is not an attack on individual rights. It is the realisation of the dialectical relationship between individual rights and collective morality with the latter taking precedence - which is the essential basis of human society.

But socialism still remains for Marx a realm of necessity. 'Beyond It begins that development of human energy which is an end in itself, the true realm of freedom, which, however, can blossom forth only with this realm of necessity as its base.'[6] This means that under socialism production will reach a point where it is no longer necessary to tie human labour directly to human consumption. There will be a sufficient abundance for people to work in creative ways with the assurance that their necessities will be supplied. 'From each according to his or her ability, to each according to his or her need.'

ALIENATION AND SURPLUS VALUE

The moral crisis of the capitalist world, reflecting the deepening economic crisis and exacerbating it, is as widely attested as it is superficially accounted for. That something pretty fundamental is wrong is generally agreed, but the care with which pundits in various fields overlook the obvious causes to pick out and elaborate on what are not causes at all but further symptoms of the malaise proves that most of them are afraid that the only cure is, from their point of view, worse than the disease. It is like those international conferences on, say, pollution where all sorts of statistics on the world-wide extent of deterioration are discussed and the under-industrialised countries are warned by the industrialised countries which exploit them of the dangers of rapid industrialisation; but not one word is said about the simple fact that social cost can never be a major consideration under capitalism and that there are no quick profits to be made out of cleaning up after imperialistic capitalism's dirty, money-making raids on the world's resources.

There is a good deal in the writings of contemporary social scientists about the alienation of modern human beings, their sense of estrangement and frustration, their inability as they become more and more isolated to communicate with others at all. Different theories are proposed to account for this feeling of 'homelessness' which turn out to be just a list of additional consequences: life has become too complex for the individuals to do more than resignedly fill in the forms which fix their place in an increasingly corporatised state; the conventional morality of a stagnant social system has made people 'other-directed' instead of 'inner-directed' as they are supposed to have been in more adventurous times; science has outstripped wisdom and looms threateningly as a monster out of control; contractual relationships which engage people in limited capacities have replaced those natural groupings to which they once belonged as whole persons.

Philosophical movements like existentialism reflect this same sense of alienation and the absurdity of life, usually concluding that it is just the way life is and we must learn to make the best of it - by writing innumerable profit-making books and plays about it, for instance. This is all part of that pessimistic strand in philosophy, as the exuberance of bourgeois individualism gave way to despair, which leads from Schopenhauer through Nietzsche, who thought that the death of God who had defended the weak from the strong made way for the superman, to Heidegger who thought that he might have found the superman in Adolf Hitler. This same sense of despair is to be found in a lot of high-brow literature, writers whining about their essential loneliness in an over-populated world and trying to communicate to us the basic incommunicability of human experience!

Marx's use of the term 'alienation', his uncovering of its roots in social existence and his tracing of its relations with other aspects of the material conditions of specific people in their actual productive relationships to a theory of social change which can be acted on, shows his own development from a petty bourgeois intellectual with compassion for oppressed people to a spokesman for, because through active involvement in their class struggle, a member of the working class. Socialism, the ideology of the working class, does not arise spontaneously among workers. It is the application to their own experience in class struggle of the theoretical formulations of the world-wide experience of the social relations of production down the ages. It is in this sense that Lenin speaks of class political consciousness, what makes the proletariat a class-for-itself, as coming to workers from without, that is, from outside of the sphere of relations between workers and employers.[7] The theory of socialism grew out of the philosophic, historical and economic theories that were elaborated by the educated representatives of the propertied classes, the intellectuals. According to their social status, the founders of modern scientific socialism, Marx and Engels, themselves belonged to the bourgeois intelligentsia.[8]

But only as 'proletarianised' by sharing in the struggles of the working class, by taking the lead in founding the first Workers Internationale, was Marx able to apply 'philosophic, historical and economic theories' to the experience of the working class in the first capitalist country and give to workers a revolutionary theory which they could recognise as their own on the basis of the mass line. Today the labour movement of Britain, thanks to Marx, has no need of intellectuals - only intelligent workers.

Hegel uses the word 'alienation' in connection with the ideal process of creativity. The act of creation is to some extent a self-diminution on the part of pure Mind or Spirit, a derogation from its own unity and perfection in order to project a natural world which has a quality of 'otherness' about it as alienated from its maker. In much the same way, people exteriorise their own powers in institutions and objects which are similarly 'other' to their essential nature as pure consciousness. Moreover, although as generalised humans they are responsible for this extension of their being in forms of social life and objects of production, in their individual capacity they cannot recognise them as their own creations and seem to move in a foreign world in which they are bewildered aliens.

Marx recognised the validity of 'alienation' as a description of the state of people in western society; but in his earliest writings he criticises and rejects Hegel's derivation of the term. People are not mere consciousness: they are objective beings whose consciousness reflects their existence.

> A being who is objective acts objectively, and he would not act objectively if the objective did not reside in the very nature of

> his being. He creates or establishes only objects, because he is established by objects - because at bottom he is nature. In the act of establishing, therefore, this objective being he does not fall from his state of 'pure activity' into a creating of the object; on the contrary, his objective product only confirms his objective activity, establishing his activity as the activity of an objective natural being.[9]

If people were alienated, it was not because of some ideal consequence of the act of creation as such: it was because of the specific conditions of production at some historic period of social development. In not realising that people naturally express themselves in productive social effort and in not appreciating that other forms of society are possible than the one developing in the Germany of his day, Hegel extrapolated from the alienation of human labour under capitalist exploitation to the eternal character of creativity in general. Alienation was thus identified with all objectivising activity whatsoever and must remain people's fate as long as they are involved in the necessity of production.

The problem of alienation conceived simply as a state of mind requires only an ideal solution. Hegel argues that the idea of private property is transcended by the idea of morality; but as Marx points out, this dialectic of thought leaves objective reality precisely where it was before. 'In order to abolish the idea of private property, the idea of communism is completely sufficient. It takes actual communist action to abolish actual private property.'[10] The Hegelian concept of annulling what is estranged from people once they have appropriated it for themselves can only become positive when this appropriation is seen, not as an ideal process in which consciousness annihilates the 'otherness' of the objective world, but as an actual appropriation of the products of people's labour through a communistic suppression of private property. 'Private property' is Marx's expression for the objects produced by alienated labour which reaches its culmination in capitalist society. It explains his statement that the 'division of labour and private property are...identical expressions: in the one the same thing is affirmed with reference to activity as is affirmed in the other with reference to the product of the activity.'

It need hardly be said that what is being referred to is not personal possessions but the kind of property whose ownership establishes class dominance. All the empty talk about 'managerial revolutions', 'property owning democracies' and the like is just so much dust-raising to obscure the palpably unjust fact that in all capitalist countries something on the order of two thirds of the wealth in property is in the hands of less than five per cent of the population. It might have been thought that the gulf between property owners and the propertyless was being diminished by the nationalisation of unprofitable but necessary industries or those huge engineering projects too large for private enterprise to handle; but it has now been demonstrated in Britain that this was simply capitalism's cunning way of securing a gigantic sum from taxpayers to invest in run down or too large industries until they became profitable enterprises, whereupon they were handed over to private owners at a fraction of their real value. Indeed, the same class that had been compensated fully for the enterprises when they were temporarily taken over by the state got them back again, restored to profitability by an enormous injection of taxpayer's money, by paying only a small proportion of their new value - and this money was then used by the Government to finance tax reductions for the same class! So much for the idea that the governing state of the ruling capitalist class can be used to bring about any major shift in property ownership as between capitalist and working classes.

What is necessary for real change, as Marx says, 'is actual communist action to abolish actual private property'. But the communism following on the suppression of private property as the objective sign of alienation cannot be based on general envy. That would merely be a case of avarice re-establishing itself in another form constituting the essence of competition, a kind of levelling down which Marx calls 'crude communism'. It must be based on the common need of people in their productive relationships to reclaim themselves through the things they have made.

This appropriation is necessary because people's sense of alienation is rooted in the fact that 'the object which labour produces - labour's product - confronts it as something alien, as a power independent of the producer...The worker is related to the product of his labour as to an alien object';[11] and 'the more the worker spends himself, the more powerful the alien objective world becomes which he creates over against himself and the poorer he himself - his inner world - becomes.'[12] And it is not only the produced object that is alienated from the worker but his very activity of production itself.

Finally the division of labour offers us the first example of how, as long as man remains in natural society, that is as long as cleavage exists between the particular and the common interest, as long therefore as activity is not voluntarily but naturally divided, man's own deed becomes an alien power opposed to him which enslaves him instead of being controlled by him.[13]

In the early 1840s Marx developed his ideas on people's alienation in respect to the objects of their labour as an analogy with the estrangement in the realm of consciousness which takes a religious form.

> In religion the spontaneous activity of the human imagination, of the human brain and the human heart, operates independently - that is, operates on him as an alien, divine or diabolical activity - in the same way the worker's activity ceases to be his spontaneous activity. It belongs to another; it is the loss of his self.[14]

This other under whose 'service, domination, coercion and yoke' the activity of workers is performed becomes progressively in history as well as in Marx's writings the capitalist who determines the form, conditions and intensity of labour, the nature, quality and quantity of its products and even whether or not it will take place at all. And, of course, workers, the products of whose labour confront them as something alien, are not simply manual workers producing physical objects: the mental products of writers, teachers or, for that matter, philosophers are also commoditised and alienated from them, so that they, too, experience the sense of their own power having become something independent of them.

The gods by this religious analogy of Marx's are the effects of people's intellectual estrangement, as private property is the effect of their alienated labour. 'The more man puts into God, the less he retains in himself. The worker puts his life into the objects; but now his life no longer belongs to him but to the object.' And because the object of labour becomes alienated labour in the selling of labour-power to another, 'the greater the product, the less he is himself'.[15] There is thus for Marx at this stage a connection between atheism and communism: in the one case what is involved is people's re-appropriation of the products of their own consciousness; in the other, it is the re-appropriation of the fruits of their own objective labours. 'Just as atheism, being the annulment of God, is the advent of theoretic humanism so communism, as the annulment of private property, is the justification of real human life as man's possession and thus the advent of practical humanism.'[16] But the negative idea of 'annulment' only applies to the stage of transition from alienated to socialist life. Once the real existence of man and nature has been re-asserted in practical, sensuous and perceptible terms, when man has become for man the being of nature, and nature for man as the being of man, the question of an alien being above man and nature has become impossible. Atheism has no longer any meaning, for atheism is a negation of God, and postulates the existence of man through this negation; but socialism as socialism no longer stands in need of such a mediation...Socialism is man's positive self-consciousness, no longer mediated through the annulment of religion, just as real life is man's positive reality, no longer mediated through the annulment of private property.[17]

If people's labour is alienated because its products through commoditisation do not belong to them in any sense, and if those products are turned into money, then money is the universal form assumed by the alienated ability of human beings. In this role of representing people's productive capacity money arrogates to itself the right of pronouncing which of their actual needs can be realised and which cannot. Since a demand on the part of one without money is a mere flight of the imagination, ineffectual and objectless, money thus becomes the arbiter between the real and the unreal. 'The difference between effective demand based on money and ineffective demand based on my need...is the difference between the imagined which exists merely within me and the imagined as it is outside me as a real object.'[18] - the difference between Kant's real and imagined hundred thalers. Money is the common medium which turns an image into reality and reality into a mere image. As the outward form of value by which all things are exchangeable, it is also, in itself, the general confounding of all things, including natural and human qualities. As the effective link between people it is the determinant of all human relationships.

> Money is the pimp between man's need and the object, between his life and his means of life. But that which mediates my life for me, also mediates the existence of other people for me. For me it is the other person.'[19]
>
> Every product is a bait with which to seduce away the other's very being, his money; every real and possible need is a weakness which will lead the fly to the glue pot -general exploitation of communal human nature. Just as every imperfection in man is a bond with heaven, an avenue giving the priest access to the heart, every need is an opportunity to approach one's neighbour in the guise of the utmost amiability and say to him: Dear friend, I give you what you need; but you know the 'conditio sine qua non'; you know the ink in which you have to sign yourself over to me; in providing your pleasure, I fleece you.[20]

And if every need exposes people to having their very substance taken away from them, we have the basis for that morality of extreme asceticism and miserliness which actually characterises the period of primitive accumulation. Self-denial, the denial of life and of all human needs is its cardinal doctrine. The less you eat, drink and read books; the less you go to the theatre, the dance hall, the public house; the less you think, love, theorise, sing, paint, fence etc., the more you save - the greater becomes your treasure which neither moths nor dust will devour -your capital. The less you are, the more you have; the less you express your own life, the greater is your alienated life - the greater is the store of your estranged being.

And even in periods of conspicuous consumption the nature of money can blight the very pleasure it makes possible and end in a kind of pecuniary Oblomovism.

> All the things which you cannot do, your money can do. It can eat and drink, go to the dance hall and the theatre; it can travel, it can appropriate art, learning, the treasures of the past, political power - all this it can appropriate for you...yet being all this, it is inclined to do nothing but create itself; for everything else is after all its servant. And when I have the master...I feel no need of the servant.[21]

There is not much asceticism about these days, except that enforced by poverty, but man, that is, 'affluent man' is as alienated in his pleasures as he once was in his hoarding. Even among those who have very little of it, money can create its illusions by screening, as it were, the relationship between master and worker, between exploiter and exploited. 'In imagination individuals seem freer under the dominance of the bourgeoisie than before, because their conditions of life seem accidental. In reality of course they are less free, because they are more subjected to the violence of things.'[22]

Alienated labour is the source of estrangement among the exploited classes of society; but the alienated ability of human beings in general, which takes a monetary form, gives all people a sense of estrangement. 'The worker is alienated in his life; but the non-worker, the bourgeois intellectual, is alienated in his thought.'[23] They, too, are victims in a world of alienation which strikes at each person or group of persons through precisely what is dearest to them, so that the transcendence of estrangement appears to each in a different guise. Comparing various countries at the time he was setting down these early reflections, Marx comments on how their citizens tend to view the overcoming of alienation in terms of the respective form of estrangement which is dominant in each: in Germany through a philosophical extension of self-consciousness; in France through a political realisation of equality; in Britain through a practical application of economic theory. And these of course - German philosophy, French socialism and British political economy - are the three strands woven into the texture of Marx's own views at this period. But in so far as he already finds the real roots of alienation in commodity production, which dehumanises workers in turning them also into commodities, and brutalises the capitalist in making him a dealer in people, Marx has isolated the common source of estrangement in all exploitative societies where commodity exchange is the main social and economic relationship.

It was his preoccupation with the actual material foundations of society that enabled Marx to criticise the social ideas of those who, in thinking about society abstractly, merely reproduced in theoretic form their own alienation. Starting with economic relationships themselves, instead of with the manner in which they might be reflected in this or that individual consciousness, Marx succeeded, even at this early stage of the development of his ideas, in making a substantial contribution to the new science of sociology.

The history of industry and the established objective existence of industry are the open book of man's essential powers, the exposure to the senses of human psychology. Hitherto this was not conceived in its inseparable connection with man's essential being, but only in an external relation of utility, because moving in the realm of estrangement, people could only think man's general mode of being (religion or history in its abstract-general character as politics, art, literature etc.) to be the reality of man's essential powers and man's species activity. We have before us the objectified essential powers of man in the form of sensuous, alien, useful objects, in the form of estrangement, displayed in ordinary material industry... Since all human activity hitherto has been labour - that is industry - a psychology for which this, the part of history most contemporary and accessible to sense, remains a closed book, cannot become a genuine, comprehensive, and real science.[24]

In the relationship between private property and alienated labour Marx already in the 'Economic and Philosophic Manuscripts of 1844' had recognised both the essential character of capitalism and the means by which it might be overthrown.

> From the relationship of estranged labour to private property it...follows that the emancipation of society from private property,etc., from servitude, is expressed in the political form as the emancipation of the workers; not that their emancipation alone was at stake but because the emancipation of the workers contains universal human emancipation - and it contains this, because the whole of human servitude is involved in the relation of the worker to production, and every relation of servitude is but a modification and consequence of this relation.[25]

A similar claim for a materialist explanation of alienation is made by Sartre when he takes as his point of departure the scarcity of nature and the needs of people.[26] But this is, in fact, a different approach from Marx's derivation from productive relations. Why the emphasis on the scarcity of nature rather than on its abundance, on the needs of people rather than on their productive capacity? - except that Sartre betrays the consumption bias which is typical of intellectuals who are cut off from any actual experience of the productive process and for whom the objective world is not something to be actively transformed by labour but something to be passively dependent on for the satisfaction of wants. For such people, as we have noted before, economics is the outlay of limited means on available goods for whose purchase they compete with others. It has little to do with entering into co-operative relations with others in order to produce those goods. Thus Sartre's starting point is Malthusian rather than Marxian and enables him to deduce certain characteristic existentialist conclusions. 'On the basis of scarcity the menace of man for man reveals itself: man is the being by which man is reduced to the state of a haunted object.'

It is true, as Sartre states, that a large proportion of the earth's people are tragically undernourished; but to argue from this that 'scarcity is the fundamental human relationship both in respect to nature and other men' is to regard a situation created by imperialist exploitation, which is only capitalist exploitation in its international form, as the basic human condition and to ignore the example of China where millions upon millions of people under socialism have banished the threat of famine. Sartre's thesis conceals the class differences between exploiters and exploited and offers us instead a fatalistic scheme of social existence in which all people are each other's enemies in an endless competition for too few goods. 'Singular man' thus confronts in the context of society the Other, this Other being the needs of the other members of society which would rob him of his own satisfaction.

From this 'singular man', completely alienated and frustrated at every turn by the malign 'otherness' of the people and objects around him, it is impossible to go forward to any conception of social forces which could revolutionise the system of competition and exploitation. It is not class struggle which is for Sartre the motivation of history but the existentialist, or bourgeois concept of the individual in a life and death battle with the 'other' - that is, the rest of humanity, pictured in zoomorphic terms of 'territorial imperatives', 'survival of the fittest' etc., which are our equivalent of the anthropomorphic account of animals in earlier times. 'Thus the comprehension', Sartre says, 'of the enemy is always more immediate than the comprehension of the ally, since, naturally, the material conditions of scarcity decide what kind of comprehension is possible.' Struggle is the basic human activity but the struggle has no purpose but bare survival in a capitalist nightmare of existence - a tragic conclusion for a man as sympathetic to the plight of the oppressed as Sartre was.

It was because Marx took his stand firmly on the solid base of people's 'objectified essential powers in ordinary material industry', of people's labour which sums up all human activity, that sociology has become ever since, in the work of Weber, Durkheim, Mead, Mannheim and so many others, either openly or implicitly, 'a debate with Marx'.[27] Much of what Marx wrote during the period of the 'Economic and Philosophic Manuscripts' has been found acceptable by sociologists who would certainly reject with alarm any positive prescription for action which would actually transform society. Hence the great popularity of Marx's early writings with revisionists. As long as communism could be described in such general terms as 'the real appropriation of the human essence by and for man, the complete return of man to himself as a social being - a return become conscious, and accomplished within the entire wealth of previous development', as long as communism was, in short, a form of humanism to which people, in spite of any question of class interest, could pay lip-service, sociologists could profess to find Marxism illuminating and perceptive. They could declare with Marx that the 'only alternative to the socialisation of the individual mind and character is its alienation'.[28]

But socialising actual property by forcefully expropriating capitalist owners as one of the conditions for this socialisation of individuals would be another matter. The idea of humanising productive relationships is a perfectly acceptable subject for discussion; but the demonstration that humanism is too vague a concept to be of much use as long as class divisions persist and that such divisions can only be ended by a proletarian revolution tends to stimulate remarkably the critical faculties of ideologists who associate themselves with the interest of the ruling capitalist class.

In his early writings can be found most of Marx's leading ideas in embryonic form; but they have not yet acquired the concentrated, systematic structure of his mature work. They are philosophical jottings about the material conditions of life rather than a science of society rigorously deduced from those conditions as a result of experiencing them directly as a member of the class with whose interests he identified himself completely. In the 1844 Manuscripts Marx has already grasped the basic principle that there is no human essence apart from the 'productive forces and social forms of intercourse' and that 'all history is nothing but the continuous transformation of human nature'; but he still includes statements about human beings in the abstract, about the essential powers of human beings, and he still sometimes speaks of 'alienation' as affecting human beings in general, irrespective of class, as though the original division of labour were like some universal fall from grace through original sin. Four years later, in 'The Communist Manifesto' of 1848, he firmly rejects all such vague references to 'human nature, to man in general, who belongs to no class, has no reality, who exists only in the misty realms of philosophical fantasy'.[29] And in the 'Theses on Feuerbach' he says: 'Human nature is no abstraction inherent in each separate individual. In its reality it is the ensemble of social relationships'.[30]

'Alienation' as something that happens to all people in commodity-exchanging societies in which money mediates all relationships is a term Marx uses less and less in his mature work. He speaks instead of the effects of alienated labour-power which have a clear class reference.

> The exercise of labour-power is the worker's own life activity, the manifestation of his own life. And this life-activity he sells to another person in order to secure the necessary means of subsistence. Thus his life-activity is for him only a means to enable him to exist. He works in order to live. He does not even reckon labour as part of his

> life, it is rather a sacrifice of his life.[31]

The loosely expressed 'universal emancipation of workers' of the 'Manuscripts' becomes the clear statement of revolutionary mission in the 'Manifesto':

> The proletarians cannot become masters of the productive forces of society, except by abolishing their own previous mode of appropriation, and thereby also every other previous mode of appropriation. They have nothing of their own to secure and fortify; their mission is to destroy all previous securities for, and insurance of, individual property...The proletariat, the lowest stratum of our present society, cannot stir, cannot raise itself up, without the whole superincumbent strata of official society being sprung into the air.[32]

In 'Capital' the word 'alienation' hardly appears at all, not that Marx had changed his mind about the range of social phenomena previously comprehended under that term but only that he had found ways of describing them which were more specifically related to the historic task of the working class. Throughout the existence of class-divided society the products of labour have never wholly belonged to those who made them and have thus, to some extent, stood over against their makers as alien objects. It remained for capitalism in the commoditisation of labour-power itself to dispossess workers completely, not only of the product of their labour but of the very tools of their trade so that no work could be done except on the terms of the purchaser of labour-power.

What is doled back to the workers in wages, when they are fortunate enough to be in work, is determined by the subsistence rate based on the value of necessary commodities for a particular time and place and leaves over for the capitalist surplus-value, the substantial difference between the total value produced and that portion of it which keeps the work force alive. The drive for surplus-value sums up the whole motivation of capitalism and engrosses all the vaguer sociological characterisations of capitalist society as 'profit-seeking', 'acquisitive', 'competitive' or 'atomistic'. The concrete fact of surplus-value not only indicates the precise form of exploitation but also, unlike looser qualifications, designates exactly who exploits whom and precisely what the exploited have to change if they are to cease being so.

Surplus-value, as the appropriation through ownership and control of the means of production of this huge difference between goods produced by the working class and goods consumed by it, a difference which increases with every rise in working class skill so that 'human progress' under capitalism can be measured by the greater amount of wealth appropriated by the capitalist, simply is the law of capitalism. Capitalism cannot be changed unless this basic economic law of the appropriation of surplus-value has changed; and any claim that capitalism is gradually turning into something else, as long as this law remains in operation, is mere terminological quibbling.

Monopolisation may have introduced a minor distinction between ownership and managerial control in vast corporations but the personnel of the ruling class overlaps these categories which, in any case, are both equally devoted to the pursuit of surplus-value. The state, which in capitalist society is simply 'the executive committee for managing the affairs of the whole bourgeoisie', may have had to intervene more and more to preserve the system as economic crises grew in severity, taking over and running at the expense of taxpayers, mostly the working class, those essential industries in which surplus-value was small; but, as has been shown before, this represented no real change since once those nationalised industries have been made profitable by infusions of public money they are re-appropriated and those which cannot be made profitable are asset-stripped for immediate profit and disposed of.

Surplus-value is the key to the essential capitalist character of states which may look very different superficially - colonial clients of imperialist countries or imperialist countries themselves, bourgeois democracies or corporate states like Fascist Italy or Nazi Germany.

Nothing that happens to countries from the outside can change this basic nature - only an internal change which puts an end to the private appropriation of surplus-value. Apologists for capitalism like to believe that it is indissolubly associated with liberal bourgeois democracy; but when the Nazi dictatorship required a poison gas capable of annihilating millions of people in the Final Solution, bids were invited from the leading chemical firms in the usual capitalist way and I.G.Farben won the contract fairly and squarely. When the whole fascist state and military administration of Germany was smashed, there among the rubble of the western sector was capitalism, which had invented Hitler to begin with to get rid of trade unions, still seeking surplus-value and only requiring the plasma of money from the capitalist United States to rise out of the ruins as fat and greedy as ever.

As we have seen, the capitalist drive to amass surplus-value means that the quantity and quality of commodities actually produced in a given situation does not depend directly on human needs but on expectations of profit. Those whose labour creates value determine neither by their material demands nor by their conscious will the direction of the productive process. Even those who do control production in their own class interest do not have the same degree of control over the market where this interest and the general effective demand for goods must be resolved in the conversion of commodities into profits. Neither monopolisation nor more intervention by the capitalist state can change the anarchic nature of a system of production based not on supplying people's needs but on exploiting them; and to the ordinary deprivation of the working class in being robbed of surplus-value is added the incidental hardship of economic crises the capitalist class is powerless to prevent. Both classes pay tribute, but by no means in anything like equal proportion, to a state of society in which the process of production has the mastery over human beings instead of being controlled by them. These two classes are quite clearly distinguishable at all times by the fact that only one of them, the working class, in that it must offer for sale on the market its own value-creative ability, assumes itself a commodity form.

The pernicious influences and distortions of vision affecting people in societies based on commodity-exchange Marx describes as 'commodity fetishism'. Commodity fetishism, which involves ascribing value to things simply as they are in themselves rather than as the products of human labour, covers the same social phenomena as were previously referred to by the more generalised term of 'alienation' but now made more specific as particularly relevant to the final stage of commodity production under capitalism. If surplus-value provides the key to the exploitative class relationships of capitalist society, commodity fetishism complements it as a general illusion resulting from the absolute pervasiveness of commodity relations throughout capitalist society. Since value is the common element in all commodities as produced by human labour, and since that labour in all class-divided societies is more or less alienated labour, alienation as an affective state is produced generally as a by-product of the production of commodities. Only under capitalism and the fullest development of commodity production can value, as a social product, presupposing the dissolution of all previous relations of production not completely dominated by exchange, appear in its strict sense as the product of labour completely alienated from the labourers themselves by the outright purchase of their labour-power. And it is this absolute alienation which is reflected in 'commodity fetishism'.

In commodity-exchanging society the social character of people's labour appears to them as an objective value stamped on the product of that labour. 'A definite social relation between men thus assumes, in their eyes, the fantastic form of a relation between things.'[33] The 'relations connecting the labour of one individual with that of the rest appear, not as direct social relations between individuals at work, but as what they really are, material relations between persons and social relations between things.' But these things which embody their relationship with other people in society neither belong to them nor were produced at their instigation, and so the relationship itself tends to become incomprehensible, what Marx calls a 'social hieroglyphic'. Membership in society determines the very nature of individual human beings, but this membership as mediated by things has become a mystery to them. To find an analogy for this strange plight of people in commodity-exchanging society, Marx returns to his earlier comparison of the '1844 Manuscripts', reformulated in the light of his intervening studies in political economy:

> We must have recourse to the mist-enveloped regions of the religious world. In that world the productions of the human brain appear as independent beings endowed with life, and entering into relations both with one another and the human race. So it is in the world of commodities with the products of men's hands. This I call the Fetishism which attaches itself to the products of labour, so soon as they are produced as commodities, and which is therefore inseparable from the production of commodities.[34]

Commodity fetishism, as a particular form of the various aspects of estrangement Marx had noted previously, he describes thus:

The mode of production in which the product takes the form of a commodity, or is produced directly for exchange, is the most general and the most embryonic form of bourgeois production. It therefore makes its appearance at an early date in history, though not in the same predominating and characteristic manner as nowadays. Hence its Fetish character is comparatively easy to be seen through.[35]

But when we come to its highest development under capitalism, this appearance of simplicity vanishes. What was only one area of social existence and could be compared with other areas relatively untouched by exchange relationships comes to pervade the entire framework of life in society, leaving no alternative standard by which its influence might be judged. Just as all the general characteristics of capitalist society disappear only when the law of surplus-value has been abrogated, so commodity fetishism, or people's sense of alienation in capitalist society, will only vanish when production is planned for use, directly determined by the real needs of society, and not for exchange.

Under socialism, the transitional stage to communism, the law of value ceases to be the sole regulator of the proportions of labour distributed among various branches of production because it is limited in its operation by the social ownership of the means of production and by the law of the balanced development of the national economy in the interest of the working masses. As Stalin put it in 'Economic Problems of Socialism in the USSR' written in 1952: How else would it be comprehensible that 'our light industries, which are the most profitable, are not being developed to the utmost and that preference is given to our heavy industries, which are often less profitable?' Without that preferential development of heavy industry the Soviet Union would never have been able to hold off and then defeat the powerful invading force of Nazi Germany. This same waiving of profitability was practised in the cultivation of land in Albania which in capitalist terms would be highly 'uneconomic'. This was necessary as part of the country's need to achieve self-sufficiency in food as part of its condition for genuine independence. Another way of putting the same issue is by distinguishing between private and social profit.

Under full communism the law of value loses its function as a regulator of exchange relations entirely because exchange relations themselves no longer exist.

Value, like the law of value, is a historical category connected with the existence of commodity production. With the disappearance of commodity production, value and its forms and the law of value also disappear. In the second phase of communist society, the amount of labour expended on the production of goods will be measured not in a roundabout way, not through value and its forms, as is the case under commodity production, but directly and immediately -by the amount of time, the number of hours, expended on the production of goods. As to the distribution of labour, its distribution among the branches of production will be regulated not by the law of value, which will have ceased to function at that time, but by the growth of society's demand for goods.[36]

Value will have disappeared because it will no longer be projected as a distinguishable aspect of things by production for exchange and will have been re-absorbed into the integral process of production for use.

In the transitional period of socialism, however, commodity exchange continues as, for example, between agricultural co-operatives and the state purchasing agency. This is because co-operative ownership is not yet full state ownership in the name of the whole people as is the case with factories, mines or, of course, state farms. Even when private property in the means of production which harnesses production to profits rather than to people's needs has been abolished, the law of value, the equivalence between labour expended and the cost of commodities, would still be a guide to distribution even if it no longer dominated distribution absolutely. Until the commodity form of goods disappears entirely, society cannot move from the socialist productive relationship 'from each according to his ability, to each according to his work' to the communist productive relationship 'from each according to his ability, to each according to his need'. In the latter case labour has become so free and products so abundant that needs no longer have to be directly connected with work done.

'Economic Problems of Socialism in the USSR' was Stalin's last theoretical work and it was an attack on revisionism. In an article on the Basic Economic Law in 1962 Stalin is taken to task for suggesting 'that in the course of communist construction commodity and money relations outlive themselves and retard our progress toward communism'. It is argued instead that 'in the expansion and perfection of production the fullest use should be made of commodity and money relations, in keeping with the new content they acquire under the socialist system'[37].

There is more to this argument for making full use, during the transitional period of socialism, of 'commodity and money relations' with the new socialist content they have acquired than Stalin was prepared to concede. However he was right in denying the revisionists' claim that the expansion of production and the higher standard of living attendant on it, without at some stage the liquidation of commodity and money relations, could of itself bring about communism. The question is whether the law of value is being used to go forward toward communism and the communal production of abundance to meet the people's needs or backward toward capitalism and the private ownership of the means of production geared to profits for the few. The revisionist author of the article on the Basic Law and, indeed, all the so-called liberalisers who are really interested in dismantling socialist economies, fly in the face of Marx's conception of the altered relations of production in communist society, which has to be the goal of socialism however many generations it takes to get there.

The labour of the individual is taken from the start as social labour. Therefore whatever the specific material form of the product which he creates or helps to create may be, that which he has bought with his labour is not a special specific product, but a special share of the communal production. For this reason he has no special product that he has to exchange. His product Is not an exchange value. The product does not have to be translated into a specific character form in order to acquire a universal character for the individual. Instead of a division of labour, necessarily ending in the exchange of exchange value, we would have an organisation of labour, which results in the participation of the individual in communal consumption.[38]

Or, in ethical terms, communist morality is not based simply on the availability of plenty, but also on the conditions of human dignity and freedom in which that plenty is produced by conscious, self-expressive labour.

This concern with the commodity, from its inception in the division of labour and the beginning of class differentiation through the development of commodity production which, with the appearance of labour-power in the market place as itself a commodity, leads to capitalism and on from there to the disappearance of the commodity with the end of exploitative relationships in communist society, takes us back to the point from which we started in an attempt to define the word 'good'. Indeed the method of our procedure can be seen, in a sense, as the reverse of Marx's development from the writing of the 'Manuscripts of 1844' to the publication of 'Capital'. He succeeded in giving expression to his philosophical ideas about the ethics of social organisation in the concise, scientific form of an economic analysis of a particular type of society, its network of inner relationships and, as a result, what it was capable of being turned into. We have been trying to release from that systematic construct, under the guidance of Marx and his successors in developing revolutionary working class ideology, its philosophical implications in order to gain a better understanding of morality in general and the ethical problems of our own times in particular - not as an intellectual exercise but in answer to an urgent social need in a period of crisis.

CULTURE AND CLASS STRUGGLE

It remained for capitalism to develop commodity production to the point where it became a cloak for the grossest forms of exploitation and at the same time, for those who penetrated the disguise, suggested the possibility of a society which would have nothing to conceal because no one was being exploited. It is the very impersonality of economic oppression under capitalism which not only permits excessive abuses but seems to put them beyond the reach of moral criticism. If the victimisation of millions of people can be made to appear as the result of the movement of unforeseeable forces, then no one need feel guilty about it.

Are several million workers thrown out of jobs bringing misery to their families? Then they have priced themselves out of the labour market by demanding too much in wages for the current state of economic activity, that is all. Are many many millions of those living in the capitalist world chronically undernourished if not actually starving? Well, the terms of trade must have moved against primary producers. Are under-developed countries constantly thwarted in their efforts to raise their standard of living by the 'assistance' of the original capitalist powers? Ah, that merely proves that the economic conditions for the 'take-off', when industrialisation gains sufficient momentum to be self-sustaining are more complicated than was realised and, perhaps, another book ought to be written about it. And of course many many books must be written to show that this kind of economic system, whereby an impersonal market in commodities automatically robbing workers of their livelihood and impoverishing primary producers is 'freedom', while any attempt by the exploited to assert collective control over their economic destiny and assume responsibility for their actions, both as they affect themselves and as they affect others, is materialistic bondage -'the road to serfdom'.

We have noticed before that this removal from the field of moral consideration of the great issues of how people are to provide for their physical sustenance and what kind of relations they are to establish among themselves in the process has the effect of trivialising ethics, so that people become obsessed with questions of sexual mores and personal life style. Since the utilitarian pleasure-pain principle determines the field of individualistic action much in the same way that supply and demand determine economic action in a free market, people are relieved of any concerns beyond the working out of their own desires in the most satisfactory way. Hence a similar trivialisation of so much of our literature, countless books, ranging from the romantic genre level to the most stylistically exalted elaborations, all dealing with what is not, after all, an inexhaustibly interesting subject, middle class adultery. As Bertolt Brecht has remarked of so many contemporary writers, 'The fact that money-making is seldom the subject of their work makes one suspect that...it may be the object instead.' The great themes that used to be dealt with in the best fiction, all to do with people's understanding of the world they live in so that they can set their personal aspirations in the moral context of their relations with others, have for the most part now to be sought in the novels coming out of the ex- and semi-colonial countries of South Asia, Africa, the Caribbean and Latin America.

Books must also be written for those who do feel some sense of unease at acquiescing in a system that can only function on the basis of the appalling waste and destruction of resources whether natural or human, comfortable people who wish to add to other luxuries and amenities just one more - a good conscience. But what they are mainly offered on the market are further distractions from having a bad one. Of course these people do not wish to purchase a good conscience at the cost of the very privileges which put them in the market for an easy one. They want peace but not at any price. They want peace in a world still tragically divided into rich and poor - a world, therefore, in which war is inevitable, either as the class war which attempts to subjugate those struggling for a decent life or as colonial war waged by capitalist countries like the United States, aided and abetted by junior partners like Britain, which strives to preserve that terrible division in the world.

Nor is it possible for such people simply to close their eyes to it all and seek refuge in a few intimate relationships because in a state of advanced alienation, dominated by objects, those very relationships with others get translated into relations among things. And where are they to look for guidance or relief in this general estrangement? To psychiatrists whose advice is also a commodity? To writers and artists whose very works are not only commodities produced for a market and subject to the same laws as any other articles made to sell but whose talent also, like the labour-power of other workers, is bought and sold at current prices, thus transforming them into commodities too. As was pointed out before, one only has to look at the publishing scene in Britain today - those firms, founded on making available to the public books of merit, now caught up in vast conglomerates whose only concern with books, like any other commodities they handle, is how much profit can be wrung out of them - to see what commoditisation is doing to literature.

> This art...full of the easy gratifications of instincts starved by modern capitalism...is the religion of today, as characteristic of (capitalist) exploitation as Catholicism is of feudal exploitation. It is the opium of the people; it pictures an inverted world because the world of (bourgeois) society is inverted.[39]

How are people to find their way through this commodity-world to the real human relations behind it when the media of information, the newspapers we read together with the news printed in them, the feature programmes we watch or hear, even education itself, are all becoming nothing but commodities offered on the market? Everyone is like Midas, desperately needing natural sustenance and human warmth, yet condemned to turn everything touched into money - itself merely the most general form commodities can take. The awareness of the influence on human relationships of commodity exchange was naturally greater when its effects were first being felt. Shakespeare writes of:

> That smooth-faced gentleman, tickling Commodity,
> Commodity, the bias of the world...
> This sway of motion, this Commodity...
> This bawd, this broker, this all-changing word.[40]

If commercialised life in capitalist countries has become atomised, people set against each other in competition for jobs and the things money can buy, human relationships changed into monetary ones, perhaps these alienating effects can be overcome by a new impulse toward social living; perhaps all that is needed is to recover a sense of belonging to something greater than oneself, a feeling of 'togetherness' with others. But which others? Psychiatric treatment often takes the form of helping one to adapt oneself to living in the commodity world as it is - in spite of the fact that it is just that world which is at the root of the individual psychological problems one started with.

Or one can join some corporate grouping whose principle of unity takes some racist or nationalist or religious form which enables one to participate in irrational feelings of hatred toward those thought to be more alien than oneself. Cultivating such gut reactions may be connected with the upsurge of fundamentalist religion, the 'born again' Christians who preach of a nuclear crusade against the godless communists. The retreat from reason under the inspiration of such superstition has gone so far in some American states that children have to be taught in schools the myth of creationism alongside the science of Darwinian evolution!

Even joining a working class revolutionary movement simply to lose one's personal feelings of estrangement by belonging to something, as a number of intellectuals did in the '30s, is unlikely to have much therapeutic value and certainly does nothing at all for the movements themselves. Revolutionary movements are not substitutes for a religion the individual has precociously lost and fondly regrets. A book published some years ago, 'The God that Failed', is a typical plaint from those who expected to get something out of communism, some personal uplift or sense of social salvation, who hoped thus to recover a lost faith. As one of them, Arthur Koestler, argued: 'A faith is not acquired by reasoning. One does not fall in love with a woman, or enter the womb of a church as a result of logical persuasion'. Therefore the socialist emancipation of the working class from exploitation which is very much a question of dialectical reasoning and logical social practice cannot be an object of faith for alienated intellectuals. Koestler was going to be much happier with a firm belief in the paranormal than he ever could have been with a penchant for communism.

Or perhaps the desiccated individual of capitalist society seeks to undo the alienating effects of the system through love of the people only to find, like the author of 'Nineteen Eighty Four', that he does not like them very much and is quite content to imagine a dystopian hell of endless suffering for his apathetic 'proles'. Genuine revolutionary activity has to be rational through and through to have any hope of success. It has nothing to do with losing oneself in society - only with finding oneself in society, which means becoming fully aware with all its implications of belonging to a class capable of changing that society.

There are two moralities in Britain today existing together - the one bound up with the decaying economic system of capitalism, the other founded on the socialism which grows inside the bourgeois world and in various places has begun to burst forth as a new social order. The situation is not entirely dissimilar to that of an earlier Elizabethan period which, too, was a time of transition, the newer individualistic ethics of bourgeois society co-existing with the tiered order and personal loyalties of feudalism. There was considerable ideological confusion as the result of this moral polarisation under two different standards - a confusion which was to be found in the minds of individuals as well as in society itself. Often a person's sentiments pulled one way and reason another, or that very reason might be divided against itself. The poets and dramatists and thoughtful courtiers were inspired by the bourgeois ideal of a freer and more reasonable society; but they had every hope that these ideals might be realised in an enlightened feudalism as imagined in the glorified court of the Virgin Queen. It is rather like those today who appreciate the virtues of socialism and hope that they can be used not to change but to modify capitalism, thus giving it an 'acceptable face'.

Shakespeare might require at first a noble patron but he was soon living and writing according to the new dispensation of the self-made man, raising himself in the world by the commoditisation of his great dramatic works. But even if his plays are full of the iniquities of feudalism, he saw the bad as well as the good side of bourgeois commercial freedom, expressing a nostalgia for the vanishing order in which people knew their place and what it entailed ethically, 'Take but degree away, untune that string, And, hark, what discord follows'! And he railed passionately against the commercialisation of human relations by the universal commodity gold, the 'common whore of mankind' that 'will make black white, foul fair, wrong right, base noble'.

The major moral contradiction of the time was between the ethos of feudalism and the ethos of burgeoning capitalism; but there were secondary contradictions like that within the bourgeois ethic itself between the promise of freedom under reason for all and the possibility of using the new wealth of London for a new kind of exploitation. The major contradiction was to be resolved in the English revolution, whereupon the secondary contradiction within the bourgeois ethic would begin to be the major contradiction.

At any time when there is fierce contradiction between two whole orders of moral conduct, there are bound to be tragic disruptions of personal life as people who are confused about their class allegiance grapple with the problem of which side they are on. The idea of betrayal which haunted the minds of those poets and dramatists of the first Elizabethan period returns to us in the scenes of the ideological trials at the height of the Cold War when our own Iagos and Bosolas turned courtrooms into theatres and with grand rhetorical flourishes and much breast-beating repudiated briefly-espoused beliefs, informed on old friends thus ruining their lives and cashed in handsomely on the whole staged charade. Sometimes this public delation could not be accounted for solely on the basis of the bribes offered in the name of the established order. There are violent shifts from one set of standards to another. What seems from one point of view to be a kind of incomprehensible malevolence, seems from another to be a return to the true faith after dabbling in heresies. But then intentions are hard to follow across the transvaluation involved in suddenly altering the very standards by which ethical judgment takes place; and the vile actions of such unstable characters seem as unmotivated as Iago's.

Our times are like theirs also in the wild fluctuations from the heights of optimism to the depths of despair, depending on an identification of interest with a world that is being born or one that is visibly cracking up. Like them there is an obsession with sexual relationships - partly from the illusion that physical passion may be the one enduring thing where all else is in flux and partly from the fact that the disjunction between past and future in an age of violent transition precipitates this relationship, like others, from any natural context - so that it becomes isolated, an act in itself, all important and at the same time, meaningless. Despair itself, the sin against the Holy Ghost, can be offered as a nicely packaged marketable commodity by writers who take the alienation of people in bourgeois society, cut off from other individuals, afflicted with a sense of the meaninglessness of life, and turn it into the plight of human beings as such, inhabiting a grey godless limbo and incapable of ever changing it. When these alienated artists write about the 'people' it is never a class-conscious worker with some idea of changing things: it is always a tramp or meths drinker or perverted criminal, in short, someone as alienated materially as they are intellectually.

It is an interesting fact of bourgeois culture that, from the beginning, the best examples of that peculiarly bourgeois literary form, the novel, have all been more or less open attacks on bourgeois morality - that is, the morality actually practised by the bourgeoisie as opposed to the promises of liberty, equality and fraternity which mobilised the working class in support of a revolution that was going to alter the form but not the fact of their exploitation.

Balzac's critical understanding of French bourgeois society, laying bare all its selfish motives and ridiculous aspirations, was so brilliantly reflective of reality that his books were Marx's favourite reading. 'The Eighteenth Brumaire of Louis Bonaparte' itself reads like the witty setting of a nineteenth century novel of manners. But for Balzac there was as yet no vision of a future alternative to the capitalist society that was the legacy of the French Revolution. He had to look backward to find his ideal society in some modified and enlightened form of feudalism. The great English novelists too, like Fielding, Dickens, George Eliot, Thackeray, Meredith all owe their enduring hold on a loyal readership down the years to their exposure of the real nature of bourgeois society underneath the outward show of merited success and well-earned material wealth. Even Henry James who may seem only interested in a stratum of society somewhat removed from working class concern deals in a progressive way with the subtle effects of money on human relationships - a clever woman who cannot see why her young man should not be the heir of an ailing millionairess, a rich father who buys an elegant Italian prince for his daughter, an emissary from wealthy interests in America to an effete Europe who formulates as the only dignified rule of conduct the thoroughly unbourgeois principle 'not to have got anything out of it for himself'.

The birth of capitalism in Britain, its original home, was so brutal and represented such a traumatic experience for those who were uprooted from the countryside and their traditional rural culture and driven into cities where their conditions were appalling that they were for some time inhibited in their own cultural response to the new situation. There was thus a break in British working class culture which facilitated the intervention of the bourgeoisie with a cheap, mass-produced, pseudo-working class culture to be fobbed off on workers in the same double exploitation as that of the company store which takes back at one window the meagre wages handed out at another. Fortunately there are limits to the moral damage that can be done by meretricious mental products manufactured by an exploiting class for the exploited. The heightened class consciousness that accompanies defensive collective industrial action can sweep away at once all the mental rubbish emptied out on workers over a period of years - like froth blown off the top of a mug of beer. One has seen television interviewers covering a strike dashing frantically from worker to worker, some of whom may even have copies of 'The Sun' tucked under their arms, vainly seeking a scab who will put the boss's point of view.

Out of the socialisation of labour during the Industrial Revolution, out of the beginnings of working class organisation in trade unions grew a working class culture. Partly it consisted of songs, petitions, declarations and the protest literature of the labour movement as it matured politically in its struggles with employers. Such social expressions of a collective working class will, like campaigns on behalf of the Tolpuddle Martyrs or the popular upsurge of the Chartist Movement, were reflected culturally. Poets like John Clare who spoke for a peasantry in the course of being proletarianised by enclosures and Robert Burns who belonged to one of the national regions being absorbed by bourgeois imperialism have to be regarded as working class. William Blake, himself a working craftsman, identified himself not only with the working people of Britain but of the world.

> ...on the Land children are sold to trades
> Of dire necessity still laboring day and night till all
> Their life extinct they took the spectre form in dark
> despair
> And slaves in myriads in ship loads burden the hoarse
> sounding deep:
> Rattling with clanking chains the Universal Empire groans.[41]

Blake realised that in spite of their professions of universal freedom and Justice the revolutions in America and France had been merely bourgeois revolutions, 'destroying colonial and monarchic restraints only to establish the irresponsible 'right' to buy and sell.'[42] He also understood dialectics.'Without Contraries is no progression. Attraction and Repulsion, Reason and Energy, Love and Hate, are necessary to human existence.'

And of course Shelley, the great poet of revolt against exploitative tyranny, had grasped the essential fact about class struggle:

Rise like lions after slumber
In unvanquishable number -
Shake your chains to earth like dew
Which in sleep had fallen on you -
Ye are many - they are few.

With the spread of educational opportunities to the people generally, itself a result of concessions won by the working class in struggle, there were considerable accessions to working class culture. For every working class writer who found there was room at the top for him to go over to the class enemy there were many more who found themselves in a position to express to a wider audience the deepest anxieties and aspirations of their class. And there were also many writers and dramatists like Shaw whose political convictions made them side with the working class on many issues and some, like William Morris, who identified themselves with the most fully class conscious workers committed to revolutionary change.

Bertolt Brecht was a Marxist playwright whose commitment to revolutionary change not only determined the content of his great plays but also led him to break with the Aristotelian tradition of drama as a means of catharsis. Brecht did not intend the spectators of his plays by identification with the characters to purge themselves of uncomfortably strong feelings. He used various alienating devices to prevent spectators from losing themselves in the characters and to help them instead to find themselves by thoughtful reflection on the social plight of the characters and whether they could do anything about it. His epic form of theatre instead of implicating the audience in a stage situation to which they merely respond emotionally turns them into critical observers who by penetrating the disguises exploitation wears are aroused to action. Brecht's message to his audience is this:

You have seen the familiar, which always happens.
But we beg you:

What is not strange, find it disquieting!
What is ordinary, find it inexplicable!
What is usual, let it astonish you!
What seems the rule, recognise it as an abuse.
And where you have recognised abuse,
Put things right!

Working class and bourgeois cultures are not watertight compartments. They reflect in a very general way the whole complex of ideas, beliefs, and spontaneous and artistic creativity associated with, on the one hand, those who own their capacity for work and, on the other, those who own the capital for putting others to work. Though there are members of the bourgeoisie who would deny it, this is an exploitative relationship. Both cultures stem from what can be called national culture, the culture of the nation. Nationhood is the essential genius of working people, going back before divisions into classes, who in a particular place over a considerable period of time have developed their peculiar skills and arts and their own culture, including language, for the enrichment of life both materially and spiritually. On the principle of one dividing into two, the principle of dialectics, this national culture can split into different strands, like predominantly working class and predominantly bourgeois culture, but it is by no means negated in the process and continues to make up such a large part of both that no final distinction between them can be made. In socialist society working class culture will begin to have the same prominence that bourgeois culture has now, just as working class ideology will predominate governmentally and institutionally; but all that has been good and progressive in bourgeois culture will continue to be part of the broad stream of national culture. As Mao Tsetung, himself a poet, says:

> The literary and artistic works of the past are not a source but a stream; they were created by our predecessors and the foreigners out of the literary and artistic raw materials they found in the life of the people of their time and place. We must take over all the

> fine things in our literary and artistic heritage, critically assimilate whatever is beneficial, and use them as examples when we create works out of the literary and artistic raw materials
> in the life of the people of our own time and place.
> Therefore, we must on no account reject the legacies of the ancients and the foreigners or refuse to learn from them, even though they are the works of the feudal or bourgeois classes.[43]

Nothing could be more ridiculous than those members of the petty-bourgeois pseudo-left who think it is elitist to enable working class children to claim their heritage of the great art and literature of the national culture which they have enjoyed themselves. But taking over a cultural legacy from the past and making the best possible use of it must never replace the artistic task of creating contemporary working class culture.

> There is suffering from hunger, cold and oppression on the one hand, and exploitation and oppression of man by man on the other. These facts exist everywhere and people look upon them as commonplace. Writers and artists concentrate such everyday phenomena, typify the contradictions and struggles within them and produce works which awaken the masses, fire them with enthusiasm and impel them to unite and struggle to transform their environment, Without such literature and art, this task could not be fulfilled, or at least not so effectively and speedily.[44]

And when it comes to the greatest transformation of all:

> Revolutionary culture is a powerful revolutionary weapon for the broad masses of the people. It prepares the ground ideologically before the revolution comes and is an important, indeed essential, fighting front in the general revolutionary front during the revolution.[45]

As ridiculous as those pseudo-leftists who would deny working class children their cultural heritage are those who decry nationalism as reactionary and would substitute for it some form of wishy-washy cosmopolitanism, thus allowing racists and fascists to drape themselves in the Union Jack. The working class must take pride in their national culture and have as part of their revolutionary perspective becoming custodians of the national honour. As Lenin said of Great Russia:

> Is a sense of national pride alien to us, Great-Russian class-conscious proletarians? Certainly not! We love our language and our country, and we are doing our very utmost to raise her toiling masses (i.e., nine-tenths of her population) to the level of a democratic and socialist consciousness. To us it is most painful to see and feel the outrages, the oppression and the humiliation our fair country suffers at the hands of the tsar's butchers, the nobles and the capitalists...We are full of a sense of national pride, and for that very reason we particularly hate our slavish past when the landed nobility led the peasants into war to stifle the freedom of Hungary, Poland, Persia and China...We are full of national pride because the Great-Russian nation has, too, created a revolutionary class.[46]

During and just after the first Elizabethan period were in circulation all the ideas from which the English people were to find the courage and resolution to rebel against their king and by his execution to destroy the last vestiges of feudalism. Raleigh in rejecting a cyclical view of history enabled people to think of politics as an art or a science related to changing social and economic circumstances. Bacon drew from the practice of artisans a scientific philosophy of nature governed by laws and of people redeeming themselves from error through science. As Christopher Hill writes of the political results of such ideas:

> Unless we can expect effects to follow causes in a rational and predictable way, leaving room for human freedom, there is no stimulus to that moral effort to which Hakewill (and the Puritans) attached such importance.[47]

George Hakewill, much influenced by Raleigh and, in turn,

influencing, among others, Milton, put it thus in his 'Apologie': 'The first step to enable a man to the achieving of great designs is to be persuaded that by endeavour he is able to achieve it.' He also expressed the moral indignation of the age at 'venal courtiers and judges, at gentlemen who strip the backs of the poor, that they may apparel their walls, and snatch meat from their mouths, that they may give it to their hawks and dogs.'[48]

Spenser, Raleigh, Pym all asserted the power of humanity to escape by the use of reason from 'an ineluctable cyclical decline'. Raleigh's and Bacon's conception of history made the idea of controlled change conceivable. Just as, subsequently, 'Bacon's former secretary, Thomas Hobbes, could say that politics was a science because men made the state, so Harrington could conceive of history as a science because men could control it.' All of which was leading up to a social confrontation enabling Gerrard Winstanley to say to the poor people of England:

> Let all men say what they will, so long as there are Rulers as call the Land theirs, upholding this particular propriety of Mine and Thine; the common-people shall never have their liberty, nor the Land ever be freed from troubles, oppressions and complainings; by reason whereof the Creator of all things is continually provoked. Therefore you dust of the earth, that are trod under foot, you poor people, that makes both scholars and rich men your oppressors by your labours, take notice of your privilege, the Law of Righteousnesse is now declared.[49]

And Milton could say of the execution of Charles I:

> And if the parliament and military council do what they do without precedent, if it appear their duty, it argues the more wisdom, virtue and magnanimity, that they know themselves able to be a precedent to others; who perhaps in future ages, if they prove not too degenerate, will look up with honour and aspire towards these exemplary and matchless deeds of their ancestors, as to the highest top of their civil glory and emulation; which heretofore,

in the pursuance of fame and foreign dominion, spent itself vaingloriously abroad, but henceforth may learn a better fortitude - to dare execute highest justice on them that shall by force of arms endeavour the oppressing and bereaving of religion and their liberty at home: that no unbridled potentate or tyrant, but to his sorrow, for the future may presume such high and irresponsible licence over mankind, to havoc and turn upside down whole kingdoms of men, as though they were no more in respect of his perverse will than a nation of pismires.[50]

With capitalism being restored in the Soviet Union after a successful socialist revolution one is reminded of what Milton wrote, almost at the cost of his head, about another post-revolution restoration:

If we return to kingship, we may be forced perhaps to fight over again all that we have fought, and spend over again all that we have spent...by our ingrateful backsliding...making vain and viler than dirt the blood of so many thousand faithful and valiant Englishmen who left us this liberty, bought with their lives; losing by a strange after-game of folly all the battles we have won.

But all was not lost with the shameful return to kingship. The last vestige of feudalism in Britain had been swept away much earlier than anywhere else in Europe and, though the bourgeoisie quickly assumed the seats of power, some measure of liberty left by those 'faithful and valiant Englishmen', renewed by class struggle from generation to generation, has lasted British workers right down to the present when, with capitalism in decline, it is under serious threat.

Just as the ideas of the first Elizabethan period were the ideological preparation for a bourgeois revolution, so in Britain today there already exists the ideology which will enable the working class to find the courage and resolution to make the proletarian revolution. Marxism, with all the creative contributions to it made by those who have been actively involved in revolutionary practice, mainly Lenin and Mao Tsetung, simply is the ideology of the working class. That is not to say that working class revolutions will take the same form and establish the same post-revolutionary institutions everywhere. They will differ from place to place as much as national cultures differ; but they will all have in common the ending of the exploitation of one person by another and the beginning of the historical period when human beings, working together co-operatively, have assumed control of their own destiny.

The further development of this ideology and the propagation of it among working people will not be easy -particularly as class struggle sharpens with the decline of capitalism. 'The class which has the means of material production at its disposal, has control at the same time over the means of mental production.' And, of course, the mass media are so much more vast, influential and monopolised than they were in Marx's time. Little overt censorship is required to police the interdiction on revolutionary works: they can always be rejected on the grounds that they are not commercially viable propositions by film companies, editorial boards and publishers who all have a vested interest in keeping things as they are no matter how bad they get for working people.

Commercialisation which has penetrated every cranny of life in a capitalist country like Britain can not only drown the voice of protest but even distract from hearing it the very people for whom it is intended. Updating that remark of Phocion's, 'any time you succeed in getting any work published or performed which receives highly favourable publicity and wins you considerable material rewards, look carefully to see if you have not in some way served the interests of the capitalist class and betrayed your fellow workers'. There are many forms of hidden censorship. Replacing grants with sponsorship by commercial firms can help eliminate from subsidised theatre any plays which challenge or criticise the capitalist system. Making television and radio programmes dependent on advertising can turn all drama into 'soap opera' which is unlikely to clean up any of the dirtier aspects of big business. Emphasis on 'best-sellers' can pull the critical teeth of literary fiction. But as long as the working class continues to struggle, continues to resist, does not capitulate, working class culture will be fed from a myriad sources and continue to flourish.

THE WORKING CLASS AS THE AGENT OF SOCIAL CHANGE

As Lenin applied Marxism to Russia, as Mao Tsetung applied Marxism to China, as Ho Chi Minh applied Marxism to Vietnam, so by applying Marxism to Britain today can we help our British working class acquire the revolutionary ideology for changing the relations of production here. Thus the working class in Britain itself is changed from a class-in-itself, which the capitalist mode of production creates whether that class realises it or not, into a class-for-itself, which is that same class fully aware of its revolutionary mission.

The British working class is assisted considerably in this process by the fact that Marx developed his ideas about how the capitalist system really works in this country and first applied them in social practice here in his work with the more class conscious victims of British capitalism. What is the proof that the application of Marxism can have such an effect here, that Marxist theory can so grip the British working class that it becomes a material force in changing this society? And the answer has to be the test of socialist practice, the fact that proletarian revolutions have been made in the Soviet Union, China and Vietnam. It may be pointed out that in the Soviet Union we have seen the 'end of socialism' and are told that 'the communist era has come to a close'. We will have to consider that charge in detail and think about what effect, if true, it would have on our attitude toward revolutionary change in Britain. But what can be said here and now is that applying Marxism to the conditions of countries yields very different programmes for change depending on the forces and relations of production in the particular country studied. In no case will a Marxist analysis lead to the discovery of principles which can be imposed on working people to produce a certain type of society: it can only indicate how those working people themselves can organise to bring about, through social change, a certain type of society. Economic exploitation gives the working class its incentive to revolt against existing conditions; a state of crisis in those conditions provides the occasion; and the consciousness of the possibility of some other ordering of society in which the role of workers would no longer be that of wage slaves lends political direction to the revolutionary impulse. This is Lenin's revolutionary situation: when the ruling class can no longer rule in the old way and the working class is no longer prepared to let itself be ruled in the old way.

We shall have to consider just how serious the crisis of British capitalism has become and also the extent to which the British working class is developing its own ideology. Working class interests were for some considerable period looked after paternalistically by the more liberal wing of the bourgeois ruling class. When the Labour Party was formed, it was much influenced by bourgeois liberalism and had a social democratic programme of reform from which, quite recently, any vague references to socialism have been removed. What signs are there that the working class, particularly as organised in trade unions, is developing its own ideology which can be nothing but an understanding of how to end exploitative relations of production in order to establish a socialist society in Britain?

The basic division between workers and capitalists is the main contradiction in capitalist society and conditions the whole outlook of these two forces in their irreconcilable opposition. As we have seen in our analysis of commodity-exchanging society, the division between work done and satisfactions enjoyed results in very different experiences for those who sell their labour-power under pain of deprivation of satisfactions and those who traffic in the labour-power of others. A class which does no physical work and is mainly concerned with manipulating intellectually as well as physically those who do, a class who sees reality constantly refracted through the abstract spectacles of prices, stock quotations and unit costs and only handles the physical world through the kid gloves of money easily acquires the illusion that ideas command the existence of things, that desires, with ready cash as their ponce, create the substance of their own fulfilment.

This idealistic illusion held by a non-productive ruling class can be expressed in economic terms as the distorted view that money, from being simply a measure of the equivalence of values as created by a common human labour, appears actually to have called that labour into being. An abstraction thus seems to be the real source of all value. If more money is to be made in exporting capital abroad where labour is cheap than in making goods at home, then the thing to do is just stop making goods and only make money. And where will goods come from if capitalists generally only make money? Oh you can always buy goods if you've got money! Carried to such extremes this distorted vision incapacitates a ruling class and its apologists for coping with real social issues. Money and the abstract speculation which is its ideological reflection, instead of being recognised as the by-products of a system of commodity exchange, are seen as the whole purpose and justification of what has become no longer industrial but finance capitalism. Difficulties arising from contradictions in the material base of this final capitalist phase can either be 'bought off' or 'thought' out of existence.

Workers can have no such illusions. For them useful articles are always the result of specific labour and desires are only satisfied to the extent that labour-power has been sold. They can never really forget the connection between utility and value, no matter how obscured it may have become behind the movement of commodities. Because they themselves have largely assumed the qualities of a commodity by having to sell their labour-power in the market, they preserve within their own nature, however unconsciously, that essential relatedness of the amount of work done and the worth of things made. For them duty and pleasure, reason and emotions are not driven so far apart as is the case with members of a class whose nature is essentially that of the buyers of the labour and services of others.

In daily working contact with their physical environment industrial workers certainly cannot but be aware through their own muscles and their own brains of the real origin of all our values and the ultimate source of all our knowledge. Tell a worker with calloused hands that the world beyond his finger tips may be an ideal illusion and his response is likely to be that of Doctor Johnson's to Berkleian idealism - only rather more personally directed! Working class ideology is slower to develop among so-called white collar workers who also sell their labour-power but whose conditions of work often involve them in a more isolated capacity dealing largely with abstractions; but once they do begin to grasp the ideology of the class they really belong to, that very familiarity with abstractions may deepen their theoretical understanding of it.

The capitalist class, on the other hand, more and more detached from the workshop, mill or mine where muscle and brain transform nature and quite unlike the early masters who remained in close association with a small number of workers at the point of production, increasingly loses touch with reality. In cutting themselves off completely from the productive process they are cutting themselves off from the source of correct ideas. They are being by-passed by the epistemological transmission belt of the knowledge-producing mass line - from the perceptual experience of the working masses to conceptualisation in theory and then back to the masses again for verification in social practice.

> Where do correct ideas come from? Do they drop from the skies? No. Are they innate in the mind? No. They come from social practice, and from it alone; they come from the three kinds of social practice, the struggle for production, the class struggle and scientific experiment.[51]

With the socialisation of the labour force, the gathering together of workers in ever larger factory complexes, there has inevitably been a socialisation of the thinking and habits of workers. They have realised from their own daily experience of class struggle in these mass conditions that their unity was their strength, that an injury to one had to be regarded as an injury to all, that their shop-floor leaders must be protected from victimisation by the class enemy. Extreme individualism they recognised as the characteristic of those too selfish to join a union and fight the employer but willing to accept any advances others might win by their sacrifices, the utilitarian outlook of the bourgeois spy in their midst, of the scab.

As victims of an exploitative system they learned to hate not just their own exploitation but exploitation as such. Their sense of class unity embraced workers in other lands. During the American Civil War while the British capitalist class supported the Confederate South, the source of the cotton which fed their textile mills, the working class supported the Union North in a war to extend to slaves the civil liberties enshrined in the Constitution. This sympathy with fellow labourers everywhere became the only real internationalism, to be invoked against the international crimes of economic imperialism - 'Workers of the World Unite!'

Thus in the womb of capitalism has been developing another morality, a morality as different from the rugged individualism and selfish acquisitiveness of capitalist ethics as the conditions of the working class differ from those of the bourgeoisie. That is not to say that workers always act in accord with these ideals: a regimen from which no one ever departs is not morality but natural law. But it is a morality that honestly declares its class character as serving the interests of workers, the vast majority of people everywhere. The bourgeois morality of individual selfishness pretends to be universal but it no more applies to those whose exploitation yields the profits for capitalists to be selfish about than bourgeois democracy has ever meant that the working class could vote on the question of whether it was to go on being exploited or not. The bourgeois morality of individual selfishness serves the double purpose of both providing an apology for actions of the capitalist class on the grounds that self-interest is the only form of social motivation that works and also of offering an argument against social change on the grounds that human nature never alters and the most that people can do is to change one lot of exploiters for another.

The collective morality of workers withdrawing their labour to bring about better conditions for their class in the future at the expense of shared sacrifices in the present leads to the individual worker's morality of subordinating the consumption side of his or her nature to the productive co-operative side.

The individual amorality of utilitarianism according to which the owner of means of production self-interestedly satisfies the desires of personal consumption in the belief that he is in that way also contributing to the growth of social production leads to the collective immorality of mass exploitation.

The organisational form of this working class morality of the factory is the trade union. 'The trade union movement' as Engels says, 'is the real class organisation of the proletariat, in which it fights out its daily battle with capital, in which it trains itself.'[52] And Marx in his 'Instructions for Delegates to the Geneva Congress of September 1866' has this to say of the past and future of trade unions:

> The immediate object of trade unions was therefore confined to everyday necessities, to expediencies for the obstruction of the incessant encroachments of capital, in one word, to questions of wages and time of labour. This activity of the trade unions is not only legitimate, it is necessary. It cannot be dispensed with so long as the present system of production lasts. On the contrary, it must be generalised by the formation and the combination of trade unions throughout all countries. On the other hand, unconsciously to themselves, the trade unions were forming centres of organisation of the working class, as the mediaeval municipalities and communes did for the middle class. If the trade unions are required for the guerrilla fights between capital and labour, they are still more important as organised agencies for superseding the

> very system of wage labour and capital rule.
>
> Apart from their original purposes, they must now learn to act deliberately as organising centres of the working class in the broad interest of its complete emancipation. They must aid every social and political movement tending in that direction. Considering themselves and acting as the champions and representatives of the whole working class, they cannot fail to enlist the non-society men into their ranks. They must look carefully after the interests of the worst paid trades, such as the agricultural labourers, rendered powerless by exceptional circumstances. They must convince the world at large that their efforts, far from being narrow and selfish, aim at the emancipation of the down-trodden millions.[53]

It was on the basis of this same working class morality of the factory, as organised in trade unions, that Lenin formulated the principle of democratic centralism.

> Is it really so difficult to understand that, before a decision has been taken by the centre on a strike, it is permissible to agitate for and against it, but that after a decision in favour of a strike (with the additional decision to conceal this from the enemy) to carry on agitation against the strike is strike-breaking? Any worker will understand that.[54]

And this principle of democratic centralism originating in the discipline and democracy of the factory is the organisational form of Lenin's 'party of a new type', the political conscience of the working class.

> We have already more than once enunciated our theoretical views on the Importance of discipline and how this concept Is to be understood in the party of the working class. We define it as unity of action, freedom of discussion and criticism. Only such discipline is worthy of the democratic party of the advanced class. The strength of the working class lies in organisation. Unless the masses are organised, the proletariat is nothing. Organised - it is everything. Organisation means unity of action, unity in practical

> operations...Therefore the proletariat does not recognise unity of action without freedom to discuss and criticise.[55]

This workplace origin of the idea of the communist party led one of the Mensheviks to complain that Lenin seemed to look on the party as though it were a 'huge factory', to which Lenin replied:

> This dreadful word of his at once betrays the mentality of the bourgeois intellectual unfamiliar with either the practice or the theory of proletarian organisation. For the factory, which to some seems a bogey, represents that highest form of capitalist co-operation which has united and disciplined the proletariat, taught it to organise, and placed it at the head of all other sections of the toiling and exploited population. And Marxism, which is the ideology of the proletariat trained by capitalism, has been, and is, training unstable intellectuals to distinguish between the factory as a means of exploitation (discipline based on fear of starvation) and the factory as a means of organisation (discipline based on collective labour united by the conditions of a technically advanced form of production). The discipline and organisation which come so hard to the bourgeois intellectual are easily acquired by the proletariat just because of this factory schooling.[56]

In so far as the working class movement is not completely under the influence of working class ideology as expressed in the political line of a vanguard communist party, 'the most advanced and resolute section of the working class', having 'no interests separate and apart from the proletariat as a whole'[57] that movement will be subject to the pressure of two petty bourgeois tendencies disguised as working class sentiments. When no revolutionary organisation exists, but a movement of resistance to ruling class domination is growing, 'we observe two opposite extremes which, as is to be expected (when we look at the matter dialectically) meet, that is, absolutely unsound Economism or the preaching of moderation and, equally unsound, excitative terror'.[58] These two tendencies may be characterised as opportunism or reformism on the one hand and anarchism or adventurism on the other.

As Lenin says: 'Anarchism is not infrequently a kind of penalty for the opportunist sins of the working class movement. The two monstrosities complement each other.'[59] This can be seen in the rise of various anarchic groupings in western Europe as a result of the revisionism, countenanced by Khrushchev, affecting so many communist parties. As Lenin points out, these two 'monstrosities', opportunism and adventurism, are two sides of the same coin which, flipped, yields the same result: heads the capitalist wins, tails the workers lose. Though they may clothe themselves in revolutionary language they are equally counter-revolutionary in effect, the one by deterring workers from fights they can win, the other by luring workers into fights they cannot win, not yet anyway. In every struggle in which workers are involved, from the factory or office right up to the country as a whole, they will always be presented with these two equally false alternatives, the ultra-leftist one of raising the stakes to an impossible level for that stage of conflict or the rightist one of finding sound excuses for not fighting after all.

Lenin describes opportunist reformism as 'economism', the separation of the economic demands of the working class from any political movement. Such a separation suits the bourgeois interest very well and in relatively good times there is a willingness to make some concessions to buy off the working class from any political commitment to all out class conflict. The working class for its part, when trade union activity on the economic front is capable of winning improvements in wages and conditions, is prepared to accept a separation between politics and economics. Organised British workers created the Labour Party as their political representative in Parliament while they concentrated on their trade union struggles for economic demands within the capitalist system - the essence of social democracy. But, of course, economics and politics cannot be divided, any more than the forces of production can be separated from the relations of production. Politics delegated by the working class to somebody else will, whenever it comes to the crunch, become politics united with somebody else's economic interests. But at the same time any economic struggle which workers push through to a victorious conclusion has political implications.

The Communist Party of Great Britain was founded as a Marxist party. As Lenin had said: 'Marxism is the ideology of the proletariat'. But with 'The British Road to Socialism' the CPGB showed that it too was social democratic. A communist party, Lenin's party of a new type, is the organisational form of the mass line based on democratic centralism. It takes the scattered and unsystematic ideas of workers from all over society; through study it turns them into concentrated and systematic ideas; then it goes to the workers and propagates and explains these ideas until the workers embrace them as their own, hold fast to them and translate them into action. The communist party is the brain and heart of the working class, its ideology and its conscience. It does not struggle on behalf of the working class: it is the working class's morale in struggle. Least of all does it rule on behalf of the working class: it teaches the working class how to rule itself. Outwardly it is the voice of the working class which must be heard in every forum of society. Inwardly it is the working class's constant guide and counsellor.

The communist party does not fight elections. That is to turn itself into one more political party among others which, by abandoning the working class's mission of changing the system and ending exploitation, becomes at best a party of social democratic reformism. In the revisionist period communist parties all over the West turned themselves into reformist parties involved in bourgeois elections and, no longer fulfilling their role as the ideology of a working class-for-itself, shrunk in size and collapsed.

After World War II the Labour Party was swept to power by a working class which included the bulk of those returning from the various fighting fronts, all determined that post-war Britain would not be like the Britain of the depression years. A policy of full employment was adopted and the foundation was laid for a welfare state with progressive reforms in health, education and benefits for the disadvantaged. But at the same time the Labour Party fully supported British imperialism, aware that Malayan rubber and tin exports almost exactly balanced the amount of aid the United States was supplying, and, indeed, the Labour Party has generally acquiesced in Britain's becoming United States imperialism's junior partner in trying to prevent any part of the capitalist world from 'going socialist'.

Right up until the end of the '70s there was enough of a consensus between the two major political parties on trying to maintain an acceptable capitalism, with its effects on the working class cushioned by welfare, for them to be able to take turns in governing the country. But as decline set in, Labour was as obedient as the Tories in imposing International Monetary Fund conditions on the economy; and when it was felt that the power of the trade unions had to be curbed, Labour anticipated the Tory's Industrial Relations Act with its own In Place of Strife. Labour has been as persistent as the Tories in imposing wage freezes, wage cuts and 'solemn and binding agreements' on the organised labour movement to restrict collective bargaining. The so-called 'winter of discontent' when the labour movement re-asserted with massive industrial action the right of collective bargaining was directed against a Labour government.

That industrial action was a perfect example of the political implications that can follow what was undertaken as a purely economic struggle. If British capitalism in decline could no longer survive when there was a trade union movement free enough and strong enough to smash the Tory Industrial Relations Act and defend against Labour the principle of collective bargaining, then that successful industrial action had a revolutionary character, even if the workers waging it were not altogether aware of it. The determined defence of reforms which capitalism simply cannot afford and still remain in business is not reformist but quasi- revolutionary.

If the labour movement was not altogether conscious of this implication, capitalism was. The Thatcher Government was a pre-emptive counter-revolution, committed at whatever cost to weaken and dismantle the trade unions. The Labour Party is still trying to come to terms with a situation in which there is much smaller scope for a reformist, social democratic political body. Some think it may still be possible for Labour to put itself forward as the party which can run an avaricious 'share-owning democracy' more benignly than the Tories and some think it is time the split between politics and economics was finally ended and Labour and the labour movement should combine in finding the only answer there can be to counter-revolution -the revolution which that counter-revolution was launched to stifle.

The tactics of workers, whether in the jungles of Asia, Africa or Latin America or in the cities of the advanced capitalist countries, in order to avoid the two wrong alternatives of opportunism or adventurism at a time when the class forces ranged against them are relatively stronger, have to be guerrilla tactics. Workers have to learn not to become involved in confrontations with superior forces either in the form of the imperialist armies of mercenaries which freedom fighters might inadvertently encounter head on or the power of the capitalist state which workers might challenge in an attempted general strike before they are ready to make such industrial action on a national scale part of a revolutionary strategy. They have to learn to concentrate their forces for the main blow, to be mobile and flexible, able to operate in self-reliant detachments with great initiative and ingenuity without losing sight of the plan of campaign; they have to be able to use the enemy's weapons, whether material or ideological, against him. They must have secure bases, deep in the forest or in a completely organised factory, mill, office or other institution from which they can operate.

In Britain, the oldest working class in the world is, probably, the best organised for this kind of struggle in a highly industrialised country. The essence of it is to counter the employers' tactics of laying off workers where profits are low by withdrawing their labour where profits are high. They have developed in their defensive fight against redundancy and closures where profits are low or non-existent such tactics as occupying factories and holding to ransom the capitalists' assets like goods and machinery. Indeed, their very success in this limited kind of industrial warfare may have been a factor in their having been a bit slow to develop revolutionary class consciousness, believing that it might always be possible to win concessions within the system without having to attack the system itself.

But during the '80s there was a change in the nature of class struggle. Where previously most industrial action was directed against private owner or management over the question of better wages and conditions, since 1979 most strikes have been directed against the government itself, not just over questions of wages and conditions in the public sector but also over questions of mass redundancy and privatisation in the nationalised industries and over the vital question of the very survival of the National Health Service, state education and all the rest of the welfare organisation won by working class struggle in the past. This has meant a change in those who were most heavily involved in working class struggle from predominantly industrial workers, like engineers who for many years waged successful guerrilla actions which set the rate for wage settlements for the class generally, to largely white collar workers like teachers, health workers, council employees and civil servants many of whom were finding themselves in industrial action for the first time.

There was also the difference that in wage battles with the employers it was possible to win limited engagements which the employers would hope to make up in the next round; but the government can never accept defeat without jeopardising its very ruling position. Therefore class conflict, from having the character of guerrilla struggle, took on the character of protracted struggle, with workers in this or that threatened industry or institution having to dig in for a long drawn out defence. Class struggle, instead of being between the working class and the individual capitalist boss with the government in the background making sure that the scales were always tipped in the boss's favour, now became quite overtly between the working class and the government itself; and that means that every member of the working class is affected in some degree by any industrial action at all; and since there is no corner of the industrial and social scene which does not have its own peculiar form of that class conflict between workers and government, it makes perfect sense to call on the entire working class to 'Fight Where You Are!' be it factory, mill, mine, school, office, hospital or even in the home. And that fight, as it is joined on the scale that it must be, has an increasingly revolutionary character.

An example of this class conflict waged against the government was the miners' strike. Dealing with the NUM must have been one of the major commitments of Mrs Thatcher when she took office in 1979. An earlier miners's strike had been instrumental in bringing down Heath's Government and she must have seen the NUM as a bastion of working class industrial strength. For years she made her preparations, switching some power stations from coal-fired to oil-fired, building up huge stocks of coal at others, helping lorry drivers to become self-employed and not subject to TGWU discipline, and most important of all organising the police on a national basis for the first time with operational headquarters in London so that the whole country could be brought under a paramilitary strike-breaking network.

Then when everything was ready she imported an expensive American axe-man, who had already wrecked havoc in the steel industry, with a plan for closing dozens of pits and making thousands of miners redundant, knowing that it was a gauntlet the miners would have to pick up. The year-long strike, not just for their own jobs but for the very right to work of all workers and of workers yet to be born, was one of the magnificent pages in the history of the

British working class. And Mrs. Thatcher did not win. She had set out to destroy the NUM, 'to see them off'. But they outlasted her and though the Tory Party has largely succeeded at great social cost in denying to British industry its own coal, the NUM and its President are still very much with us and the spirit that supported the miners in their year-long strike can still plague the post-Thatcher anti-working class Tory Government.

There could be no better example than the Government campaign against the miners of how the fight to weaken the trade unions has resulted in the weakening of British industry where the trade unions are strongest. The closing of mines in this country to import cheaper coal from abroad to make more money for the privatised energy suppliers while the whole country's huge balance of payments deficit is greatly increased just shows what anti-national lengths a capitalist government will go to in its war against workers in the interest of private profit!

But there are lessons the working class has to learn from the miners' strike, as also from the teachers' strike and from the print workers' strike. Sections of workers courageous enough to take up struggle on behalf of the class must not be left practically on their own with nothing but cheering words and a few coins contributed to the cause. Other sections must answer the call 'Fight Where You Are!' and divert pressure from those already engaged. The TUC must not content itself with votes of support but must become on such occasions what it was originally intended to be, the headquarters of a trade union movement in active conflict with the class enemy.

The Thatcher Government showed its anti-working class character by creating massive unemployment to weaken the unions and passing a lot of anti-trade union laws; it transferred by tax cuts, privatisation and cuts in expenditure on health, education and the public services vast sums from the pockets of wage-earning tax payers into the pockets of the very rich. But it also did great harm to British industry which is barely at the level of 1979 and what with cuts in research, higher education and severe losses in basic industrial skills cannot hope to recover. Some £50bn from North Sea oil which might have been invested in British industry was frittered away instead covering up the huge trade gap that appeared when for the first time since the Industrial Revolution Britain became a net importer of manufactured goods! Some three and a half million people desperately want work; repairs and improvement of the whole infrastructure of the country desperately want doing; but these two vital needs cannot be put together because it would not earn any private entrepreneur enough profit. Meanwhile the number of people living below the poverty line has doubled, millions of children are being brought up in circumstances of dire need and among these new poor the infant mortality rate is climbing and the life expectancy rate is going down - as though Britain having lost its overseas empire was now cultivating an under-developed world enclave of misery and degradation within.

This Robin-Hood-in-Reverse policy of robbing the poor to increase the wealth of the already rich is nothing new for capitalism.

The law that always equilibrates the relative surplus population, or industrial reserve army, to the extent and energy of accumulation, this law rivets the labourer to capital more firmly than the wedges of Vulcan did Prometheus to the rock. It establishes an accumulation of misery, corresponding with accumulation of capital. Accumulation of wealth at one pole is, therefore, at the same time accumulation of misery, agony of toil, slavery, ignorance, brutality, mental degradation, at the opposite pole, i.e. on the side of the class that produces its own product in the form of capital.[60]

What is new is that this polarisation of wealth and misery is no longer associated with an expanding industry whose products are being exported all over the world. What we have now is a profound economic crisis in which Britain's stagnant or declining industry is no longer capable of paying for the imports we still require to keep going at all. There is simply no way that a system of production for profit can save a country's industry when through asset-stripping and lack of investment that industry is ceasing to be profitable.

Although the Labour Party did not succeed in defeating Mrs Thatcher at the polls, the working class with its 'Thatcher Out' line did finally make her unelectable, so that her own party got rid of her. The working class often fails to realise just what strength it has in unity. The proletariat which is much more numerous than the bourgeoisie and grows simultaneously with it but under its rule...gradually gains strength, becomes an independent class playing the leading role in history, and finally seizes political power and becomes the ruling class.[61]

'The proletariat of each country must, of course, first of all settle matters with its own bourgeoisie.'[62]

Since the whole political point of a socialist revolution is the investing of the working people with real state power, so that they do take their destiny in their own hands, there is no question of ever carrying out a revolution on their behalf, of imposing socialism from above. They make the revolution themselves and they make it when they are ideologically and materially strong enough to do so. There are no short cuts by way of coups, putsches or conspiratorial plots - only the protracted struggle of developing 'the self-conscious, independent movement of the immense majority, in the interest of the immense majority'. The revolution itself is not an unfortunate necessity imposed on people by the intractable nature of social change; it has intrinsic value as the assertion through united action by the vast majority of a common human dignity hitherto suppressed; and also it is the only training ground for the subsequent tasks of carrying out the building of a socialist society on the basis of democratic centralism.

> This revolution is necessary, therefore, not only because the ruling class cannot be overthrown in any other way, but also because the class overthrowing it can only in a revolution succeed in ridding itself of all the muck of ages and become fitted to found life anew.[63]

The struggle to end exploitation is not a necessary evil but an eloquent expression of all that is best in the consciously achieved solidarity of exploited peoples everywhere. And just as material values are measured by the labour incorporated in them, so moral values can only be judged in terms of the amount of human thought and effort involved in their realisation.

> A revolution is not a dinner party, or writing an essay, or painting a picture, or doing embroidery; it cannot be so refined, so leisurely and gentle, so temperate, kind, courteous, restrained and magnanimous. A revolution is an insurrection, an act of violence by which one class overthrows another.[64]

Marxists are often criticised for holding the view that the end justifies the means and therefore countenance, if they do not actually encourage, violence. But the violence of revolutionary force is only the other face of the violence of counter-revolutionary repression inherent in the existing situation, and since the latter form of violence goes uncriticised, one must assume that it is not really the means which are being objected to but the end - the abolition of the exploitation of one human being by another. Revolution is the expression in social practice of the working class's detestation of a system that degrades human beings and uses them only for the purpose of profit-grubbing.

> Clearly the weapon of criticism cannot replace criticism of weapons, and material force must be overthrown by material force. But theory also becomes a material force once it has gripped the masses.'[65]

After all, what can justify any means except the end? And yet because the end also conditions the means of attaining it, Marxism categorically rejects, for any short-term organisational advantages in this place or that, any methods which break the unity and fellowship of the international working class. This means it regards as weapons the capitalist class employs in its incessant efforts to divide and rule the working class all forms of chauvinism which try to substitute for class unity some spurious and exclusive order. The morality of means must be considered in terms of a normative judgment about ends; and the evidence is overwhelming that the effort to preserve a system incorporating obvious injustices denies itself the use of no weapons, no matter how vile and destructive, while the effort to re-organise society on a more equitable basis shows, in the midst of struggle, a concern for the quality of human life with every liberated area becoming a promise of the socialism to be. The ends, exploitation of the many by the few or emancipation of the many, colour through and through the respective means used.

Violence does not only take the form of forcible detention or corporal punishment or mass killings, though no system of exploitation has ever been able to dispense with such means either explicitly or implicitly. Millions upon millions of people living at a bare subsistence level are also the victims of violence, even if no guns are being fired at them. If a man is sitting on another man's back, their relationship may appear to be non-violent - until the man on the bottom tries to get up. Pity for the victims of this kind of violence which is not combined with active detestation of its perpetrators is pretty futile. Peace movements which fail to specify the source of aggression in capitalist imperialism or would put a halt to all armed struggle including people's war when so many millions live under conditions of intolerable economic oppression are friends of an exploiting class.

The revolutionary force which Marxism sanctions as the only way to liberate people from economic bondage and establish the basic conditions for genuinely moral relationships is not directed at individuals but at a class and the state institutions which maintain its domination. Getting rid of the capitalist class in Britain does not, of course, mean destroying individual British capitalists, only their property rights in the means of production which enable them to exploit others. The class of criminally negligent motorists, for example, could be liquidated without a single person being subjected to violence - unless, of course, those motorists insisted violently on their right to drive just as they please.

The truly remarkable thing about the revolutionary transformation of even so vast a country as China is the economy of force used. This is because it is directed only against the real enemies of the people who are very few and, as the revolution advances, the confused dupes of those enemies desert in their millions to the working people's cause. The soldiers of a liberation army adhere to the strictest moral discipline in relation to the people in whose interest they fight, not 'taking so much as a piece of thread without paying for it'. Indeed, it is the kindly, helpful conduct of these troops which first convinces the masses that this is an entirely different movement from any of the brutal incursions of soldiers they have been subjected to in the past. Even in the treatment of the enemies of the people the effort is always made to rehabilitate those who have been misled by lies and bribes - 'to kill the disease in order to save the patient'. This tends to be obscured by the media in the capitalist world since the trial and execution by a people's court of one vicious landlord gets more attention than the freeing from serfdom and misery of millions of peasants.

Reducing politics to the question of individual rights is a way of evading real political issues, just as stressing the individual act avoids any consideration of the real problems of ethics. As long as the ruling class can limit political and moral criticism to the rights and duties of the individual they have effectively put their own interested acts as a class beyond the reach of working class criticism in social practice.

We have already seen how the full development of commodity production under capitalism, by substituting money relations for personal ones and by treating the members of a community as units competing with each other in the market for jobs and goods, has the tendency of atomising society and isolating the individual. This alienated individual can be generalised as the subject of political study and this person's abstract rights can be enshrined in the charter of bourgeois society - the right to vote or the right to own property, the right to pursue one's own happiness or the right to think as one pleases. But these abstract rights, important as they are, become almost meaningless to the head of a family who is on the dole. They do not of themselves provide the means for anyone to publish dissident views nor obtain work paying a living wage nor so much as buy a single loaf of bread; nor, on the other hand, do they limit in any way the privileges exercised by those who have amassed the means for turning abstract rights into material benefits.

The capitalist class is not threatened by the isolated individual which capitalism tends, unless checked by the socialisation of labour, to produce - hence the concern for the preservation of this harmless product, as when the right of the individual to scab is legally upheld even when a secret ballot shows a majority in favour of strike action. In class-divided society there is always the question of democracy for whom. The existing social order in Britain which is described by capitalism's apologists as one of the great democracies is, from the point of view of the working class, a dictatorship of the bourgeoisie, while the emancipation of the working class is, as far as the bourgeoisie is concerned, a proletarian dictatorship. One class's 'open society' is another class's 'totalitarian state'.

One of the main contradictions of capitalism is that, for extending its sway or defending what it already holds, it has to depend on those who are not themselves capitalists. It is the essential nature of capitalists as a class to be exploiters. They do not exist apart from that exploitative relationship with others. It is not the essential nature of workers to be exploited but to transform nature co operatively to meet human needs - a task they can perform infinitely better freed from the exploitative relationship. The capitalist class cannot do without workers but the working class can do very well without capitalists. Workers are the source of all capitalist profit: organised, those same workers are the greatest threat to capitalist profit. Capitalism could only ensure its own peaceful future if it no longer raised an army of workers against it by robbing them of surplus-value; but then the profit motive having been abandoned, it would have ceased to be capitalism. All reformism says, in effect, if only capitalism were something other than what it is, it would not be necessary to change it.

History affords us no example of a privileged minority, as a distinct class, voluntarily resigning its special position and sharing its worldly goods with other members of that society, simply because such a class is by definition those who benefit from a particular form of exploitation and whose membership of that class carries with it the ideological conviction of the 'rightness' of that position. And even if it were conceivable that such a class would be moved to some such act of general redistribution, it would not satisfy the Marxist condition for a system of morality based on human relations of production in a society from which exploitation has been excluded. Charity on the widest scale might mitigate some of the more obvious forms of distress but it would not alter the relationship between dominant and subject classes. Being able to give away goods is itself an expression of a special position in society, however rarely indulged by the rich and the powerful. On the other hand, to be grateful for gifts of what they have made themselves would, from the point of view of the working class, merely add humiliation to injustice.

We have seen how a polarisation of class forces in modern capitalist countries results in the splitting of society 'into two great hostile camps, into two great classes directly facing each other: Bourgeoisie and Proletariat.'[66] In the colonial and semi-colonial world a similar polarisation takes place when a popular uprising of the working people threatens the puppet regime through which imperialism rules.

> At such a time, foreign imperialism and domestic reaction stand quite openly at one pole while the masses of the people stand at the other pole, thus forming the principal contradiction which determines or influences the development of the other

contradictions.[67]

In the imperialist phase of capitalism the most naked and brutal exploitation has prevailed in the colonial and semi-colonial countries. Since World War II this polarisation of forces between imperialist rulers and colonial peoples has been the main contradiction as far as the older industrialised countries are concerned. But already at the end of the twentieth century, with the completion of class polarisation in a country like Britain and with British capitalism in serious decline, the main contradiction could well become that between classes in one of the very heartlands of capitalism. It would be fitting if the first capitalist country in the world, the country which produced the first proletariat, were also the first major industrialised country to have a socialist revolution.

In some cases of polarisation where the masses of people confronting an imperialist aggressor have represented an alliance of classes including a large peasantry under the leadership of a relatively small working class, the revolution has been carried out in two stages. This, Mao explains, 'is a special historical feature, a feature peculiar to the revolution in colonial and semi-colonial countries and not to be found in the revolutionary history of any capitalist country'.[68] Where the polarisation of classes is a result of the simplifying of class antagonism to that between capitalist class and workers, as in Britain, the working class goes directly for socialism under a proletarian dictatorship established in a one stage revolution.

In the first case of polarisation, under colonial or semi-colonial conditions, the national question predominates to begin with and the class question then comes to the fore in determining whether the liberated country is to develop self-reliantly on a socialist basis under working class rule or slip back into some form of neo-colonialism. In the second case of polarisation, in developed capitalist conditions, the class question predominates to begin with and the national question is then raised as the ruling bourgeoisie, unable on its own to solve the class question to its permanent advantage, seeks to internationalise its class struggle against the working class. This is what the British ruling class has done in sacrificing its sovereignty by allowing the United States to establish a military presence in Britain in the interests of United States imperialism and by joining the monopoly-capitalist alliance of the European Economic Community, now the European Union.

The bourgeoisie exploited nationalism to build their capitalist imperialist state - just as they used working people to defeat feudalism and then more or less disenfranchised them; but once the bourgeoisie have no further use for nationalism, since profit knows no nationality, it is for the working people who developed nationhood down the centuries as their particular form of co-operative value-creativity to liberate nationalism from the trammels imposed by capitalism, thus freeing their own genius, skill, courage, intelligence and initiative for the service not only of themselves and of their children and of their children's children but of a whole world from which exploitation is being eliminated.

In dealing with these two forms of class polarity what must never be done is to counterpose one against the other. The working class struggles in the colonial territories are complementary to working class struggles in the metropolitan countries: they both have the same enemy - capitalist imperialism. Any tendency to see them as being in opposition only serves the divide-and-rule policy of that common enemy. As Lenin has said:

> The revolutionary movement in the advanced countries would in practice be a sheer fraud if, in their struggle against capital, the workers of Europe and America were not closely and completely united with the hundreds upon hundreds of millions of 'colonial' slaves who are oppressed by capital.[69]

The best service workers in the imperialist countries can perform for their fellow workers in the underdeveloped countries is to make a revolution at home. 'In proportion as the exploitation of one individual by another is put an end to, the exploitation of one nation by another will be put an end to.'[70]

The ruling capitalist class, not just in this country or that, but all over the world is corrupt and deceitful. By its very nature it uses as an unfair advantage in every deal struck its privileged private possession of the only means workers have of turning their labour into the goods they need to live -and then pretends to have dealt with its employees justly. In the final phase of financial capitalism rules about mergers, take-over bids, asset stripping and the like are all governed by a legal system based on the recognition of the almost unrestricted rights of private property. Any questionable operations are covered up by slanted news or lying statistics peddled by all the media sympathetic to capitalist rule. If the poor could eat all the cooked figures they are constantly fed they would get fat! Concerned only with immediate profits capitalism can find no remedy for long term decline. It can guarantee no security to the world at large because it cannot properly control the very economic forces it seeks merely to profit from.

The working class, though individual members and even whole sections may vacillate and try in this way or that to opt out of the role for which history, the sum of human actions, has cast it, is not, simply by the nature of its relationship to the means of production, corrupt. Labour itself cannot be corrupted: it is the human source of all value. And the working class, in so far as it consists of those who, however venal they may be individually, collectively produce value for the whole of society, is a creative force which cannot in its productive character be corrupt. It is not power which corrupts. Power wielded for the general good in a socialist society by the working class which makes up the 'immense majority' of that society does not corrupt but dignifies, as the freedom of people in control of their own destiny. It is power wielded partially, in the service of exploitation which corrupts.

The very word 'exploitation' implies a moral superiority of the exploited over the exploiters which can only be denied by contending that there is no exploitation, that all people in society get their just rewards and that if there are people suffering from poverty and malnutrition they deserve it - even if they are new-born babies. But mere knowledge of the inhumanity of exploitation does not change anything. Not till this knowledge has become the morale of a working class determined to put a stop to the exploitation of human beings by human beings can real social change occur. In our era a belief in humanity and a hope for its bright future can take no other rational form than the social homoeopathy of working class revolution - active involvement with the value creators against the despoilers in class struggle to put an end to classes.

It would certainly seem that the decline of capitalism in Britain has gone too far to think in social democratic terms of merely reformist changes, a bit of 'piecemeal technology' here or a touch of 'social engineering' there. Increasingly the working class is going to be confronted with a situation in which there are only two alternatives: they can be capitalism's mercenaries or they can be freedom fighters in the cause of working class emancipation. British workers who have shown themselves in the past to be so skilful, inventive and well-organised in making things of use to the whole world are going to have to make something for their own survival - revolution. Increasingly, with the massive high technology armaments capitalism uses to keep the world's people in submission, with its criminal waste of the world's resources and its pollution of the world's environment for private profit, the revolution British workers make here for their own survival is also a blow for world survival.

We have been looking at the politics of revolutionary working class struggle from a moral point of view. What Marxism says in ethical terms is that the free development and activity of individuals, the possibility of humanising production and laying the foundation of truly moral personal relationships, requires them 'to bring under their own conscious control the material conditions of life, conditions which have previously been abandoned to chance and which have thus acquired an independent existence over against individuals'.[71]

The ethics of the very struggle to lay the foundations of a truly ethical society can be summarised thus:

> Our morality is entirely subordinated to the interests of the class struggle of the proletariat (because) only the proletarians, fired by a new social task to accomplish for all society, to do away with all classes and class rule, are the men to break the instrument of that class rule - the state, the centralised and organised governmental power usurping to be the master instead of the servant of society.[72]

The 'interests of the class struggle of the proletariat' may seem an inadequate expression of the moral ideal but it contains by implication all that is necessary in the way of ethical principles for establishing the material basis of a higher moral order of society from which the exploitation of one human being by another has been eliminated.

In the concept of 'struggle' is that Marxist thesis that the point is not simply to understand and interpret the world but to change it. In the concept of 'class' is all the comradeship and common purpose which unites workers all over the world. Dialectically combined they represent the 'self-conscious, independent movement of the immense majority in the interest of the immense majority', the liberation of all people from the slavery of exploitation in any form to build co-operatively a universe of the greatest possible material and spiritual value for all of us to share.

MARXIST SOCIALISM IN PRACTICE

At the beginning of this book Marx was quoted as saying:

The question whether objective truth can be attributed to human thinking is not a question of theory but is a practical question. In practice man must prove the truth, that is, the reality and power, the this-sidedness of his thinking. The dispute over the reality or non-reality of thinking which is isolated from practice is a purely scholastic question.[73]

Marx also says that the mechanical materialist doctrine that men are simply the products of circumstances and upbringing forgets that men can change circumstances, can revolutionise them, and change themselves in the process.

The coincidence of the changing of circumstances and of human activity can be conceived and rationally understood only as revolutionary practice.[74]

Capitalism's apologists have taken the socio-economic collapse of the Soviet Union as 'the end of socialism'. Indeed one American commentator has called it the end of history itself in so far as history has been thought of as 'an account of the contradictions in human life which could not be resolved in the context of modern liberalism' - thus consigning humanity to the exploitative system of bourgeois liberal capitalism for all eternity!

We must consider carefully just what implications the collapse of the Soviet Union has for the thesis that the 'truth, the reality and power, the this-sidedness of Marxism can be tested by revolutionary practice.

The first thing that has to be decided is just what socio-economic system did collapse in the Soviet Union in 1990-91. Some Marxists have claimed that there has never been socialism in the Soviet Union, that 'socialism is the unrealised potential of capitalism' and can only come about as the result of revolution in a fully developed capitalist country. What was established after the October Revolution, they argue, was a kind of bureaucratic state capitalism. But the fully developed capitalist world would hardly have been galvanised into such obsessive opposition nor would the undeveloped world have been inspired to such heroic liberation struggles against that capitalist world by the emergence on the stage of history of a state capitalist Soviet Union. However, what expired in 1990-91 was certainly not a dictatorship of the proletariat which was Marx's name for democratic socialism in the period when there were still class enemies within the country and external enemies without. If it had been democratic socialism, it could not have been disposed of without major resistance on the part of the working people of the Soviet Union.

The best description of what has been collapsing into anarchy is state socialism which had been allowed to decline into bureaucratic stagnation. The only feeble resistance there was came from the bureaucrats themselves who obviously felt that they had most to lose. But the question is whether the socialist society free of exploitation which the Russian workers and peasants under Lenin's Marxist leadership staged a revolution for and fought so hard to defend from the capitalist interventionists and the Nazi invaders was bound to turn into the inert, industrially backward bureaucracy which is ending in chaos.

The fact that the first working class socialist revolutions in the case of both Russia and China did occur in economically backward countries with no tradition of bourgeois liberalism is pretty good sociological evidence that they had to start in such countries whatever limitations there might be in developing a genuine working class democracy where there had been no bourgeois democracy before. One Marxist theoretician insists that a country like Russia was entirely unsuited for the first attempt at creating a modern socialist society. 'Marxism was never intended to be a theory and practice of how desperately backward societies could leap, isolated and unaided, into the twentieth century; and the material consequence of such an attempt is generally known as Stalinism.'[75]

Lenin, as has already been noted, was aware of the problem posed by the underdevelopment of the masses of people liberated by the Russian revolution and their consequent inability to assume a more popularly assertive role in the new relations of production established. He did not, however, call off the October Revolution and he would not have agreed that for a 'desperately backward society' to try 'to leap into the twentieth century' should be called 'Stalinism'!

There is no doubt that Lenin intended a socialist democracy in which soviets and trade unions would play a full and active part in achieving 'an immense expansion of democracy, which for the first time becomes democracy for the poor, democracy for the people, and not democracy for the money bags: the dictatorship of the proletariat (that is, the assumption of state power by the working people) imposes a series of restrictions on the freedom of the oppressors, the exploiters, the capitalists. We must suppress them in order to free humanity from wage slavery.[76]

Had the conditions existed for an organic process of internally generated change such democratisation might well have been carried out by the working class and peasantry once the vast majority of them had been won over for the aims of the revolution; but under the external threat of invasion, with no proper economic base and with the working masses quite inexperienced in the struggle for and day-to-day utilisation of democratic institutions, political leadership over the entire post-revolutionary period was assumed by the Communist Party as 'the vanguard of the working class'. This dictatorship of the Party on behalf of the working class was, under the circumstances, the only alternative to abandoning the very attempt to build a socialist society after the victorious revolution.

The bureaucratic state apparatus set up by the Party did manage to carry out socialist policies at enormous speed - the collectivisation of agriculture, the electrification of the country, the construction of huge new industries and the extension of popular education and health services over the whole of the immense Soviet Union. All this demanded great sacrifices and there was severe repression of resistance. However, it represented a great improvement in living standards for the broad masses. Lenin said of the organisation which made all this possible:

For hundreds of years states have been built on the bourgeois model, and now for the first time a non-bourgeois form of state has been discovered...However bad our state apparatus is - still it has been created: a most important historical invention has been made, a proletarian type of state has been created. Therefore let the whole of Europe, let thousands of bourgeois newspapers, carry news about the horrors and poverty and sufferings which the workers endure in our country - still all over the world workers are attracted to the Soviet state.

A dozen countries including all the fully developed capitalist powers invaded the Soviet Union a short time after the Revolution, determined to strangle socialism in its cradle. And all during the desperate years of creating the economic foundation which would enable the first workers' state to survive, hundreds upon hundreds of spies and saboteurs were sent into the country to conspire with dissidents on the inside to penetrate the army and wreck industry. In spite of which in just about fifteen years the creative energy of Soviet workers, from a position of industrial backwardness and economic ruin, constructed a productive base of heavy industry which supplied the modern weapons needed to smash the Nazi war machine - the most powerful aggressive army ever assembled.

Of course, if Lenin's voice had been listened to at Versailles, calling for no reparations, no annexations and no punitive actions against Germany for a war of competing capitalist imperialisms in which there were no blameless participants, there would not have been the basis for the Nazi rise to power to begin with. Once Hitler claimed that Bolshevism was the real foe of a revanchist Germany, the British and French governments connived at German rearmament and refused to negotiate with the Soviet Union to keep peace in Europe by guaranteeing Czechoslovakia's frontier. Nazi Germany could be allowed to finish the job they had begun with their Interventionist War. But, of course, Nazi Germany did not restrict its aggression to the Soviet Union. The people of Britain were to play their part in turning what began as an anti-communist war into an anti-fascist war. It was grimly ironic that the Soviet Union which had done most to prevent the second World War from ever occurring, had to play the greatest part in defeating Nazi Germany and at the greatest cost - some twenty million Soviet citizens killed and a third of the country laid waste.

Even before World War II was over the United States had started the Cold War against its temporary ally, the Soviet Union. The atomic bomb, ostensibly directed against Japan which had already offered to surrender, was really pointed at the Soviet Union. Henry Stimson, the senior man in President Truman's cabinet, proposed in 1946 a treaty with the Soviet Union whereby the United States would impound its atomic bombs and cease their development, provided the Soviet Union and Britain would do the same and the three nations would agree not to use the bombs unless all three decided on that use. The proposal which would have saved the world from the terrible dangers and pollution of the nuclear arms race was rejected by Truman. The United States while still enjoying its monopoly seriously considered using the threat of nuclear attack to force the Soviet Union to open its doors to capitalist exploitation. The Soviet Union's rapid development of its own nuclear weapons kept the United States from using them again against civilian targets as at Hiroshima and Nagasaki. It was thought by many Americans of high office in army and state that in order to avoid humiliating defeat nuclear weapons should have been used in the war against Vietnam. It was possession of nuclear weapons by the Soviet Union and China that kept the United States from doing so.

One of the most important consequences of the October Revolution was the encouragement and help given to colonial countries to liberate themselves from capitalist imperialism. The assistance given to these countries, often at the expense of the Soviet people, was the exact opposite of their exploitation by western capitalism and was in the finest tradition of Marxist morality. All over Asia, Africa and Latin America Marxist leaders sprang up who mobilised people against their continued exploitation by the imperialist powers - Britain, France and, mainly, the United States. So successful have these movements been that Britain and France have ceased altogether to exist as direct colonial powers and the United States has been practically driven out of Asia and much weakened elsewhere, having more and more to resort to exploitation indirectly through the World Bank and the International Monetary Fund - just as more and more it has to carry out its vicious punitive acts of aggression against countries challenging its dominance by arming thugs to fight instead of by sending in the marines. However, this has changed with Iraq!

After Lenin's death, Stalin used the party-managed dictatorship of the proletariat, often in a severely repressive way with the firmest suppression of any criticism, to advance the cause of Leninist socialism. What was required and what may have begun to be brought about had Lenin lived longer was working class political democracy. The 'party of a new type' instead of continuing to rule on the working class's behalf should equip the working class ideologically to rule itself. The party through the democratic centralism of the mass line becomes the working class's political conscience and thus fits the working class to enter fully into economic planning through its trade unions and to choose and change its government democratically. Certainly for Lenin party membership always meant serving the working class. It never meant acquiring special powers and privileges which increasingly differentiated party officials and nomenklatura bureaucrats from the working class. That was not Lenin's 'morality which serves the purpose of helping human society to rise to a higher level and to get rid of the exploitation of labour'. It was the old bourgeois 'morality' of claiming that in serving one's own self-interest one was thereby helping society.

After Stalin's death In 1953, the ferocious way the party dictatorship had been used to carry out Lenin's socialist ideas was roundly criticised by Khrushchev at the Twentieth Party Congress - not for the purpose of switching to a more democratic means of carrying on with the development of socialism but in order to use the same Party dictatorship for an ill-thought-out and unrealistic policy of 'catching up with the West' in the shortest possible time.

The motivation for this policy was not the further advance of socialism but the promise of more consumption goods like those which capitalism boasted of making available in unlimited quantities. The October Revolution had rejected the individualistic commodity fetishism responsible for the growth of western capitalism and had chosen instead the collective work ethic which was to create a socialist society of shared benefits for all. That individualistic commodity fetishism was now to be invoked to get the Soviet people to increase the production of consumer goods and this promised abundance was then to be called 'socialism' - a 'socialism' which could be achieved by appealing to the incentives of capitalism! Productive power was no longer to be stirred into action by the driving force of enthusiasm for a collective system of future peace and plenty for all but by present individualistic demands for more and better consumer goods here and now. The competition between the capitalist and socialist worlds was no longer concerned with the goals of life but only with levels of consumption.

Khrushchev presented as 'a creative development of Marxist-Leninist theory' what was in fact a complete departure from Marxism-Leninism. Collaboration with imperialism which he labelled 'peaceful co-existence' was exalted as the general line of the foreign policy of all socialist states in opposition to Lenin's principle that the foreign policy of a socialist country could only be based on proletarian internationalism - 'an alliance with the revolutionaries of the advanced countries and with all oppressed peoples against the imperialists.' For the sake of peaceful co-existence at all costs Khrushchev made it clear that he was prepared to give up international class struggle, renouncing on behalf of the colonial peoples any right to liberate themselves from oppression and reassuring capitalist governments by emphasising 'peaceful transition to socialism' or the parliamentary road as the only correct line for communist parties everywhere. He wrongly assumed that if only United States imperialism were given to understand that their economic and military positions all over the world were not going to be challenged, then they would give up their aggressive designs against the socialist bloc.

The 'creative development of Marxism-Leninism' was simply the division of the world into Soviet and American spheres of influence in which each was to enjoy unquestioned supremacy - a twentieth century version of the Pope's demarcation line sharing out the new world between Spain and Portugal. 'Then,' Khrushchev was to say 'if any mad man wanted war, we, the two strongest countries in the world, would have but to shake our fingers to warn him off' - and included among the 'mad men', of course, were any popular leaders wishing to take their countries out of imperialist bondage. Instead of challenging the policy of nuclear blackmail which the Unites States had used ever since the war to keep the world safe for the operations of monopoly capitalism, Khrushchev was going to use the Soviet Union's nuclear capacity to get in on the act.

The 'creative development of Marxist-Leninist theory' put forward at the Twentieth Party Congress was no more successful on the domestic front than it was internationally. By replacing socialist goals with planned increases in the production of consumer goods there might be a reduction in the oppressive measures for driving the country on to a socialist future; but since there was no democratic involvement of the working people and their creative capacity to give life to planned increases in production, the result was bureaucratic stagnation. Throughout the Brezhnev period the country, industrially speaking, lived off the fat of the great achievements of the first phase of socialist development and failed to replace outworn equipment or to keep up with technological advances in the capitalist world - except in armaments where to lag behind the West would invite another attempt at military conquest in spite of all the talk about peaceful co-existence.

During this time there was a mental stagnation in Marxist understanding and the inspiring of youth with socialist ideals which was a reflection of the way the whole economy had bogged down in a bureaucratic mire. 'The low level to which the Party's political competence to develop correct policies descended is shown in the superficial babble of the programmatic book Perestroika by Mikhail Gorbachev, which purported to announce the beginning of a new epoch of Communism.'[77] What it actually announced was the beginning of the degeneration into state capitalism with all the accompanying features of black marketeering, currency swindles, protection rackets and the invasion of foreign entrepreneurs to cash in on the chaos. Socialism had not failed the Soviet Union: revisionism had.

In other parts of the socialist world there was great opposition to the revisionism of the Twentieth Party Congress. The Chinese Communist Party under Mao Tsetung's leadership denounced it and in 1960 with the publication of Long Live Leninism declared its loyalty to the ideals of socialism. At the Moscow Conference of 81 Communist and Workers Parties convened toward the end of 1960 the Chinese delegation with the support of other communist countries, mainly Albania, succeeded against Khrushchev in getting changes made in the draft declaration which strengthened its Marxist-Leninist content. The present epoch was described not as one of peaceful co-existence and economic competition, but as one of 'transition from capitalism to socialism...of struggle between the two systems, the epoch of socialist revolutions and of national liberation revolutions.'

Enver Hoxha in support of the anti-revisionist stand of the Chinese pointed out in opposition to Khrushchev's line of peaceful co-existence that 'the Albanian people detest war but they are fully aware of the warlike moves of the imperialist powers. Imperialism, particularly United States imperialism, has changed neither its skin nor its nature. It is aggressive, it will be aggressive while even a single tooth remains in its mouth.'[78]

China having waged a communist-led liberation war against Japan and having defeated in a revolutionary civil war the Kuomintang class oppressors backed by the United States, established in 1949 a people's democratic dictatorship as the first step in creating a socialist China. The problems were tremendous: a huge under-fed population the victims of both natural and man-made disasters and an economy based on primitive agriculture with little developed industry. And yet within some fifteen years China was able to feed, clothe and house one quarter of the world's population, educate them and provide them with adequate health care. Because it is only possible to do anything constructive about birth control when the mass of the people enjoy a standard of living such that they have something to lose, China has been able to make a start on ensuring that the quality of life for all was not going to be overwhelmed by the quantity of new births - a problem which has so far defeated most non-socialist underdeveloped countries. As a result of China's revolutionary achievements never again will the apologists for capitalism be able to say that poverty and famine are the inevitable concomitants of underdevelopment and nothing can be done about them but to beg for aid from the west at the cost of political and economic independence.

'Maoist economic development thus brought about in Sichuan a transformation in aggregate capabilities, a modest increase in power capita consumption, the laying of the foundation for future growth via industrialisation and infrastructure construction, a massive reduction in spatial inequality, and put paid to the landlord and the rich peasant. That this was achieved in the face of a hostile world environment makes it all the more remarkable.'[79]

Mao Tsetung was determined that these achievements should not be put at risk by Khrushchevian revisionism. The Great Proletarian Cultural Revolution was his way of imbuing the youth of China with socialist ideals. Since there were revisionists within the Communist Party leadership, it was necessary to launch the struggle against revisionism outside the Party, first among young people, then among organised workers in the great factories of Shanghai and other manufacturing centres and finally among the people in the communes in the remotest parts of China. This involvement of the people in the fight for socialism was also a very real extension of democracy.

No doubt individual mistakes were made in searching out and holding up to scorn officials and Party members who could be designated 'capitalist-roaders' but it was a practical example of the way the dictatorship of the proletariat or democratic socialism could begin to be meaningful in a country containing well over a billion people. Deng Xiaoping who, after Mao's death, was to introduce reforms of a revisionist nature into China was correctly singled out and labelled a 'capitalist roader' by the Cultural Revolution. Perhaps it is unfortunate that the policy of 'Kill the disease; cure the patient' left an uncured Deng Xiaoping around to gain control of party and state and embark on a policy of economic reforms with the pragmatic observation that he 'did not care what colour a cat was as long as it caught mice'. Perhaps the same moral and political indifference covered his military invasion of his socialist neighbour, Vietnam, and his joining hands with United States imperialism in supplying arms to the murderous Pol Pot to use against the people of Cambodia and the Vietnamese who came to their aid.

There can be no Marxist objection during the socialist period of making limited use of a free market and some measure of private enterprise as adjuncts to planned production for satisfying the needs of all; but it is clear that Deng Xiaoping's 'reforms' go far beyond this. As William Hinton, one of the most sympathetic interpreters for the west of China's great socialist achievements has put it:

> The surprising thing is the speed with which these reforms brought China to the crisis it's in today. The crisis is the direct outcome of reform policies, of the privatisation of agriculture, the attempted privatisation of industry, of the free market and of the decentralisation which threw important economic decisions to the regions who then, making money fast and loose, bid against interior China for scarce goods, particularly raw materials.

> Conditions developed that brought the country close to economic chaos. The government could not guarantee supplies...prices soared out of control, corruption became endemic, and all the moral degradation of the old society started to come back.[80]

Of course, the western media present this as 'the last gasp of communism and the ultimate result of having carried out a communist revolution' instead of what it really is: 'the ultimate result of having betrayed the revolution ten years ago.'

Is it being suggested that the failure of bureaucratic socialism in the Soviet Union was inevitable 'due to the contradictions at the very beginning, so that the October Revolution was a heroic, but misguided, premature birth? Only one who disregards the role of reflection (and that means the purposeful intervention of human beings in history) can accept such a deterministic fatalism. Sound application of Marxist dialectics could have led to an understanding of the contradictions in the first socialist social system arising initially from the immaturity of the conditions and then from the co-existence of two antagonistic social systems. This understanding could have led to strategies other than those that have now brought about the dissolution of socialism.'[81]

Let us say instead that this understanding will lead to strategies which can bring about the further development of socialist society - perhaps in China when it is realised how much of the people's social gains are being frittered away by capitalist privatisation and the utilitarian argument that 'getting rich is a good thing for everybody', perhaps in Russia when the working people see that their country is not gaining by joining with the western capitalist countries but is merely being exploited by them, perhaps in the capitalist countries themselves as the internal contradictions of an exploitative system become increasingly aggravated.

Meanwhile let us not allow the apologists of capitalism to erase from history all the achievements of Marxist socialist practice in various parts of the world.

Under Ho Chi Minh's communist leadership the people of Vietnam liberated themselves from the Japanese; and when Britain at the end of the War helped the French renew their colonial control of Vietnam, the Vietnamese defeated the French and drove them out as well. They were then invaded by the most powerful imperialism of all time, the United States, which dropped more bombs on Vietnam than had been dropped on Germany during the whole of the second World War and rained down on the unprotected people napalm, defoliants and other chemical weapons which had never been used in warfare before. Over a million Vietnamese were murdered, thousands of children were born deformed as a result of the toxic chemicals used and vast tracts of land were so polluted that they will not yield agricultural produce to this day. The United States suffered a complete and humiliating defeat and were driven out.

It might have been hoped that at last the Vietnamese would be left alone to get on with building socialism in peace; but the United States has continued to find mean and furtive ways of venting its hatred against the Vietnamese for the defeat suffered at their hands. Not only have weapons been supplied the genocidal Pol Pot clique to use against the Vietnamese but the United States has persuaded its junior partners in capitalist crime, Britain and other west European countries, to boycott Vietnam completely. It is the only underdeveloped country in the world which has been allowed to receive no aid nor assistance of any kind from the United Nations.

The colonial and semi-colonial world owe a great debt of gratitude to Vietnam. It was going to be a long time before United States imperialism would use its own troops to invade any country larger than Grenada. Instead they developed on a world scale the policy of hiring others to do their fighting for them and to sow with thousands of land mines any place where the people looked like being able to throw off the capitalist imperialist yoke and begin to make a decent life for themselves - in Chile, in the Philippines, in Guatemala, in Nicaragua, in Angola, in Cambodia...Just as the developing world owes a great debt to the Soviet Union for not again, after the mistake over Korea, allowing the United States to wrap itself in the mantle of the United Nations to carry out some act of imperialist aggression - not until the betrayal over Iraq that is.

But in spite of all the difficulties placed in their way by the vengeful United States and in spite of the fact that the main sources of their foreign trade, the Peoples Democracies and the Soviet Union, have dried up, Vietnam has not abandoned socialism. It has been necessary for the Vietnamese to institute certain reforms and to come to terms with the capitalist world - but as an independent country not as a colony. They remain loyal to the vow of Ho Chi Minh:

Our mountains will always be, our rivers will always be,
our people will always be;
The American invaders defeated, we will rebuild our land
ten times more beautiful.

At the other end of the scale from China, little Albania, about the size of Wales with a population a bit over two million, which at the beginning of the second World War was the most backward country in Europe without a single university and with eighty per cent of the population illiterate, also liberated itself by its own efforts, from both fascist Italian and Nazi German occupation. Albania turned its fight for freedom into a revolutionary war barring the return of the old regime of exploiters. Within a few years of the end of the War Britain and the United States were engaged in what amounted to a completely unjustifiable undeclared war on Albania. For this purpose they trained those expatriate Albanians who had collaborated with the fascists and parachuted them back into Albania to carry out acts of sabotage, subversion and espionage.

An ironic twist to this Anglo-American unprovoked aggression was that when the Americans chided the British with not making enough of an effort to knock out what was thought to be the most vulnerable member of the East European Communist Bloc, the British agreed to put in charge of the whole operation one of their top security people who had been chief liaison officer between MI6 and the CIA and enjoyed the Americans' complete confidence - one Kim Philby! No doubt Philby was able from time to time to get word to the Albanians when they could expect their next delivery of spies and saboteurs; but the real reason that this aggressive effort was abortive was because most of the Albanian people were united behind their communist leadership to build a socialist society in the land they had freed from external and internal oppressors.

Because of Albania's size forms of democratic centralism were possible there which would be impractical in a country as large as China. A few years ago when it was agreed that education should be 'revolutionised' to bring it into accord with the socialist economic base under construction and to enable it to serve the needs of the working class better, there was a nation-wide forum lasting a whole year during which all teachers, all students from the ninth year on and the whole working class, as parents concerned with the proper training of their children in socialist ways of life and as workers concerned with the qualifications of recruits to production, were free to make any suggestions they liked. There were 21,000 meetings attended by 600,000 people, or more than half of the adult population, at which contributions were made by 160,000 individual citizens. All proposals made, whether they were contradictory or not, provided they were not at variance with general socialist principles, were collected in a document which was resubmitted to the people for further discussion; and finally the reorganisation of the entire educational system on the widest possible basis of agreement was set in motion. This is the mass line, 'from the masses, to the masses' operating in the most democratic way. 'They corroborated in practice,' the Head of the Central Committee for the Revolutionising of Education said at the end of the public consultation, 'the principle that the socialist revolution forges ahead through class struggle, with the active participation of the masses who are not only the object but also the subject of the ideological and cultural revolution.'

Albania made great efforts to become completely self-sufficient but being cut off by its stand on revisionism from help from the Soviet Union and, later, from China, too, greatly hindered industrial development. There is no doubt that there were serious flaws in the way the politics and the economy of Albania were managed by the party bureaucracy on behalf of the Albanian people. Perhaps they could have been considerably rectified by the Ramiz Alia government which succeeded the government of Enver Hoxha and in a free democratic vote of the whole people, monitored for fairness by supervisors from half a dozen European countries including Britain, received over 60 per cent of the vote. But he was not to get the chance. While the American-sponsored invasion of the country by Albanians who had collaborated with the Nazis failed back in the early 'fifties a new invasion of Albanians who had lived for some time in the United States and had acquired a thoroughly capitalist outlook, collaborating with the townspeople of Tirana and the other major towns who were tempted by the glitzy goods capitalism was supposed to offer everyone, managed to stage a 'democratic' counter-revolution. It brought about great suffering, particularly in the countryside where land was privatised, but this, of course, could all be described as 'the legacy of socialism'!

What has given capitalism's apologists some credibility for their claims about the 'end of socialism' is the misconception many of us had that the October Revolution began a unilinear process which could be finally judged in terms of whether it resulted in a fully-developed socialist society or not. This attitude tended to make the Soviet Union the sole embodiment of socialism with us would-be socialists in other lands watching developments there with the care and anxiety of relatives at the bedside of a family breadwinner whose health was in doubt - often instead of getting on with applying Marxism to conditions in our own countries. The practice of socialism in the first workers' state should be seen instead as the first stage of a transition not unlike the passage through several centuries from feudalism to capitalism. This transition from capitalism to socialism will also involve revolutions and counter-revolutions, victories and defeats, advances and retreats in the eventual transformation of capitalist barbarism into socialist civilisation.[82]

This transition will not take so long, however, because it is a much more conscious development. The change from feudalism to capitalism was fought out under a variety of banners, religious and national as well as liberative, while those involved in the ideological conflict between capitalism and socialism are much clearer about the class interests, private profit or the collective good, which are respectively served.

Our main concern with the ex-Soviet Union ought to be our realisation of how little we British socialists were able to do to mitigate the terrible distorting pressures our government, together with other capitalist governments, mainly the United States, imposed on the first workers' state by interventionist wars, trade blockades, the denial of access to advanced technological development and the crippling effect of being forced to keep up with massive armaments production devised to keep the world safe for capitalist exploitation and, in the process, making it thoroughly unsafe for all human kind. We ought to express our deepest gratitude for the tremendous sacrifices made by the ordinary heroes and heroines of the first proletarian revolution and our sincerest appreciation for the lessons we have learned from their mistakes - such as not realising that any party or bureaucratic organisation which continues to operate on behalf of the working class and not under their political influence, in spite of socialistic pretensions, will sooner or later betray them. Those lessons will be invaluable to us as we move into that phase of the transition from capitalism to socialism which takes the struggle into the very heartland of the capitalist empires.

Because with all the changes that have occurred in the socialist world western capitalism has not changed fundamentally. It continues in Marx's words to 'establish an accumulation of misery' at one pole, 'corresponding with an accumulation of capital' at the other, whether within the metropolitan capitalist country itself or, even more catastrophically, within its economic empire. Indeed a lot of the jubilation over the 'end of socialism' has been for the purpose of drowning out the angry protests and despondent cries of the millions upon millions of those who are exploited and oppressed by the capitalist system. What a marvellous opportunity was being provided by the collapse of bureaucratic socialism in the USSR for capitalism to sweep its crimes against the people under the carpet. By showing over and over again the pollution of the atmosphere by Soviet heavy industry, constructed at a time when the world was not so aware of the problem, the United States could conceal the fact that it continues to be the world's number one pollutant on a massive life-threatening scale.

Capitalism cannot be dissociated from war, whether wars of conquest to engross into its economic empire new sources of raw materials and cheap labour and a larger market for the distribution of its products or great wars between rival capitalist countries to determine how the world is to be split up among them. The armaments industry has a special place in domestic capitalist economies. It is a form of enterprise which transfers huge sums of money from the pockets of tax-payers to the capitalist's pocket without his having first to sell his product on the market. Arms sales abroad are enormously profitable as well as politically useful for exerting influence on whole regions. Flooding semi-colonial territories with weapons can turn the local divisions on which imperialism thrives into destructive civil wars wrecking progressive governments and impeding liberation movements. Millions upon millions of people have died in these capitalist wars - so many that the inflated figures of crimes charged against the Soviet Union in establishing the first workers' state against enemies within and without look utterly trifling by comparison.

Capitalism cannot be dissociated from waste. Production for profit instead of to meet people's needs is bound to result in the overproduction of junk commodities which were expected to sell and did not. There is the waste of built-in obsolescence because it is more profitable to provide commodities which have to be replaced ever so often than those which last. There is the waste of asset-stripping since today's profits always take precedence over tomorrow's needs. Natural resources have been plundered with a wasteful prodigality which now threatens shortages of many essential materials. And most terrible of all there is the waste of human labour because massive unemployment is the only means the capitalist has of weakening the workers' power to bargain over wages and conditions. Large underdeveloped countries could be fed and clothed on the waste products of a single major capitalist power.

Capitalism cannot be dissociated from pollution which has reached such a scale that the very future of life on the planet is threatened. No capitalist country is thinking seriously about the problem of ever-increasing motor traffic in terms both of exhausting resources and spreading pollution. In Britain, once waste-disposal was deregulated, big profits have been made by inviting other countries to dump their polluted rubbish on this small crowded island! The main proposal of the capitalist countries for dealing with this problem is, while doing little or nothing about it themselves, to warn underdeveloped countries of the pollution large scale industrialisation is likely to cause and to suggest that they remain unindustrialised in the interest of world health.

The Gulf War, launched only a short time after the collapse of bureaucratic socialism in the Soviet Union, demonstrated all these characteristics of capitalism: armed conflict using up the weapons capitalists had made millions of dollars and pounds out of supplying illegally, the murder of thousands of innocent people in the victimised country, the destruction of natural resources and pollution on a massive scale, children going hungry and without medical treatment through the prolongation of sanctions - all to maintain an imperialistic grip on the rich Middle East oil reserves for the sole benefit of capitalist profit. It also showed that it was perfectly possible to use the media in such a way as to make the whole dirty business look like a harmless electronic game the public was allowed to sit in on. That is the 'New World Order': murderous, destructive and highly profitable attacks on underdeveloped countries now that the Soviet Union no longer exists to block the use of a compliant United Nations to conceal imperialist aggression in a spurious cloak of internationalism.

Or take the war in Bosnia precipitated by Germany's taking advantage of the disruption of Yugoslav unity to extend its influence over Croatia which had collaborated with the Nazis during the War. Such a move was bound to provoke all-out attack by the Serbs and the unleashing of ethnic and religious conflict embroiling in the most vicious struggles people who had formerly lived together amicably. The intervention of the capitalist countries of Europe now including Russia and the United States under cover of a United Nations mantle without being able to resolve their different interests and come up with an acceptable plan for peace is another example of the 'New World Order'.

There is no lack of intellectual apologists to pave the way ideologically for the military imposition of this New World Order. The ultra-relativism of postmodern thought disarms any criticism which claims to be based on truth going beyond what is currently accepted as 'good in the way of belief'. This 'good in the way of belief' has been primarily established at any particular time by the media, generally influenced by the class interests of profiteering owners of the means of communication and strictly controlled under such circumstances as the Gulf War by the capitalist government. Neo-pragmatists like Richard Rorty contend that the only kind of truth that counts is the power to enter into meaningful conversation with the members of one's own interest-group, or 'interpretive community' who share the same 'good in the way of belief'. Those members fortunate enough to belong to Rorty's interest group, 'North Atlantic postmodern bourgeois liberal democracy', must learn to appreciate its virtues and give up any thought of questioning them, partly because they have no choice in the matter since its 'values' are the very cultural air they breathe and the only means of conversing with a wide enough receptive audience to count and partly because - even though he has denied himself the logical right to say it - they are the best set of values that have so far emerged in the 'cultural conversation of mankind'!

Pragmatism gets the relationship between truth and what works, between theory and practice the wrong way around. What is true, in so far as we can discover it, always works but what works at any particular time may only establish the most fleeting and ephemeral of truths. Neo-pragmatists like Rorty are only interested in the ephemeral truths of public opinion at a given time within a particular 'interpretive community' and deny the very possibility of any truth that might challenge them. Nor is this the only reversal serving the interests of American imperialist capitalism. Postmodernist literary theory denies the commonsense view that narrative is accountable in any way to truth-telling probity and contends that the literary text should serve as the paradigm instance of a language that disowns all truth-claims or realist illusions. But as Christopher Norris points out: 'there is a path that leads directly from the textualist or neo-pragmatist suspension of determinate historical truth-claims to the supine moral and political acquiescence that equates truth with some existing state of received consensus belief'[83] - like the pronouncements of Francis Fukuyama written under the auspices of a US State Department think tank.

Marxist critical realism which subjects theoretical truth to the social practice of collective action is not really affected by these attacks of postmodernist intellectualism, whether they take the form of the deconstruction of the Cartesian ego or the undermining of the 'truths' of an idealistic text. The idea that because there are no meta-narratives like Marxism in a textualised existence which has no truth of contact with basic reality, that because there is only the contingent, the ephemeral and the discontinuous, everything has to be taken less seriously and we can only delight in the chaos of life as if it were some kind of game is not an idea that is going to appeal to any but bored, uncaring, comfortably-off intellectuals completely cut off from any kind of useful work.

In spite of such postmodernist terms as 'post Fordism', capitalism has not changed in essence, nor will it. What has changed is the growing realisation that a system motivated primarily by private profit is incapable of achieving the social justice either internally or in its relations with those under its economic domination necessary for all around equitable and peaceful development. Nor, as a system sacrificing everything to today's profits, is it capable of genuine concern for world ecology or a proper care for and a fairer sharing of limited world resources. Our planet is too small and crowded a place for individuals or classes or countries mainly motivated by an uncaring selfish greed. The so-called 'collapse of socialism' has not altered in the slightest capitalism's growing disparity of the rich getting richer and the poor getting poorer: it has merely brought additional countries under that vicious dispensation.

The collapse of the Soviet Union and the communist regimes of eastern Europe, the post-Maoist economic 'reforms' in China whereby the country of 'Long Live Leninism' has become the place where 'It is good to get rich' have enabled the apologists for capitalism to argue that their system is inevitably associated with democracy and a free market while socialism is just as inevitably associated with totalitarianism and centralised economic planning. Hence its demise. But it is easy to refute historically any claim to a watertight division between democracy and a free market on the one hand and dictatorship and a planned economy on the other.

There is nothing more democratic than a revolution. Democratic freedom cannot be bestowed nor imposed from above: it has to be won by the people and then preserved collectively. The popular results of the revolutions of the Enlightenment in Britain, France and America were taken over by the bourgeoisie to establish a form of bourgeois 'democracy' confirming their property rights against feudalism and turning freed serfs into waged labourers. Capitalism or private profit based on their ownership and control of the means of production was their way of beginning to turn the 'individual rights of all' into their rights to all.

The October Revolution, led by the Communist Party, established the basic rights of working people against their capitalist exploiters; but the Party was unable for historical reasons to do much to help the people create their own socialist democratic institutions to preserve that freedom from exploitation. Instead, a bureaucratic government more or less detached from the people was set up to run the economy on their behalf.

Global capitalism has no use for those bourgeois democratic institutions so useful at the time of early industrialism and has completely exhausted any moral legacy borrowed from the Enlightenment. Marxist Communism, grounding those ideal rights of the Enlightenment in the material reality of the essentially human, value-creative process of production which provides the goods for equitable distribution to meet the needs of all, must enable the working people of the world to establish collectively their own correct socialist institutional guarantees against immoral political dictatorship or economic exploitation.

Democracy means a lot more than periodic elections when people are allowed to vote for one of several capitalist parties but not on whether they are to go on being exploited or not. Ironically, at the very time when so many east Europeans were opting enthusiastically for western-type democracy, here in Thatcherite Britain democracy, in the form of the democratically-elected metropolitan government of London or the regional democracy of freely-elected local governments or the trade unions which are the democracy of our places of work, was either being abolished altogether or severely restricted.

The so-called free market is only free in the sense that it enables huge international monopoly capitalist enterprises to operate freely all over the world and frees speculators who contribute nothing whatever to the creation of value to make enormous profits on the world exchanges. The 'free' market only responds, of course, to effective demand, which rules out of consideration the needs of the growing number of poor and unemployed at home and the starving millions upon millions of poverty-stricken people in capitalism's economic empire. Adam Smith would laugh his head off at anyone's calling 'free' a domestic market dominated by price fixing monopolies to whose number in Britain have recently been added the huge price-fixing monopolies of water, gas and electricity. Internationally the so-called free market is merely the form of exploitation exercised by highly industrialised capitalist countries against under-developed countries depending mainly on primary production whereby manufactured goods are grossly over-priced and natural produce ridiculously under-priced. The current name for denying the right of under-developed countries to do anything about this kind of exploitation is the General Agreement on Tariffs and Trade.

This is not, of course, to suggest that there is no democracy and no market freedom in the capitalist west: only that such democracy and market freedom as exist all too obviously favour a growing gap between rich and poor people in capitalist countries and between rich and poor countries in the capitalist world and that this development cannot be in the long-term interest of real democracy anywhere.

It certainly cannot be argued that there is any direct two-way logical or practical relationship between democracy and free markets. During World War II the Nazi dictatorship of Germany operated a free market, as when the contract for the poison gas to effect the 'final solution' was put out to free tender and eagerly bid for by the leading chemical companies. And the democratically-elected government of Britain operated a tight socialist economy of centralised industrial planning and equitable distribution of rationed consumer goods. People with any say at all in their destiny would hardly allow a war for national survival to be settled by the vagaries of profit-seeking in a 'free' market!

It has been argued that socialism is impossible because centralised planning cannot take the place of a free market when it comes to dealing with all the complicated interactions of things and all the difficult interrelationships of people that go to make up the proper economic functioning of a large modern country. We have to choose between a planned economy that does not work and a free economy that for some strange reason goes on enriching the well-to-do and punishing the poor and starving. Various intermediate forms between the two extremes have been proposed. It has been suggested that some way might be found of 'socialising' the capitalist free market and thus softening some of its harsher effects or of introducing a competitive entrepreneurial character into socialism to give it a bit of a shot in the arm.

In fact, of course, neither system exists nor could exist in absolute purity. What these compromisers are leaving out of account is the question of class. What matters is whether a capitalist country in which political power is enjoyed by the owners of the means of production is temporarily introducing certain social reforms to persuade the working class to go on being exploited for profit or whether a socialist country in which the working class is in power, while maintaining a socialist system of production to meet the needs of the people, allows a considerable amount of competitive free enterprise and consumers' choice in non-basic goods. This does not mean, of course, that there would be private ownership of the means of production, only that the law of value would be allowed to operate in a relatively free-market way in this sector of the economy.

In both Britain and the United States we have seen recently what happens to social reforms like welfare for the disadvantaged in capitalist countries which are challenged by foreign competition or recession. The Keynesian remedy of deficit financing is hardly applicable to countries which through incompetent government are monstrously in debt.

The ironic thing about using the arguments in favour of a free market to win approval for free private enterprise is that private monopolistic ownership of the means of production is, as we have seen, one of the main limits on market freedom. Some considerable degree of market freedom is necessary during the socialist phase of development but it does not follow that there must be private instead of public ownership. The argument that private ownership produces more successfully than public ownership is demonstrably false. In Britain the private management of many heavy industries to secure high profits while keeping investment low so ran them down that it was necessary to nationalise them, in order that tax-payers could finance their reinvigoration to the point where they were worth reprivatising - often only to be asset stripped! For decades and decades, public ownership and operation of the water supply provided good water so cheaply that we took it for granted, like air. Now under privatisation we are supplied with polluted water at many times the former cost so that managers can pay themselves huge salaries and share holders can collect big dividends. It is proposed to privatise the railways but every expert with any knowledge at all of transport knows that this will result in a much poorer service at a much higher cost. The only thing private ownership of public services or the means of production supplies in abundance is profit for the few - at great social cost for the many.

The change in the relations of production brought about by a working class revolution means that production to make profits for the few is replaced with production to meet the needs of everyone. In any civilised society production must be planned to meet the basic needs of all; but in the distribution and consumption of non-basic goods there is every reason why relative differences in tastes and talents, reflected in relative differences in responsibilities undertaken and income received, should be part of the motivating force driving the whole system forward. On the foundation of a planned economy to meet general needs there would be a free market in non-basic goods, with continuous growth in the number of non-basic goods which come to be considered basic. This is the situation that might obtain during the long period of socialist development when the principle is 'from each according to ability, to each according to work' and 'right' is the claim on goods one is entitled to make as measured by the value of one's labour.

Marx was thinking of basic production to meet the needs of all when he speaks of 'socialised man, the associated producers, rationally regulating their interchange with nature under conditions most worthy of their human nature' as still remaining in a realm of necessity. The additional effort expended to earn certain non-basic goods of choice might be the beginning of 'that development of human energy which is an end in itself, the true realm of freedom, which, however, can blossom forth only with the realm of necessity as its base'. This moral balance between collective work to meet the needs of all and the satisfaction of certain individual wants which call for extra effort starts us on the way toward the ending of commoditisation and its necessary link between the value of labour expended and the value of goods acquired. Communism or fully developed socialism, which however long it takes us to reach remains a goal for directing our co-operative human effort, achieves such an abundance of co-operative wealth that it can afford to take from each according to his or her ability and give to each according to his or her needs without any niggling over amounts of work done and needs met, because work itself, productive and creative labour, will have become one of those needs, 'not only a means of life but itself life's prime want'. We will have arrived at last in that realm where 'the free development of each is the condition for the free development of all'.

But in spite of all that can be said to prove, events in eastern

Europe and the Soviet Union notwithstanding, that capitalism has not changed its exploitative character and socialism is still the only answer the working class has to exploitation, there are liberal-minded people who now falter at calling themselves socialists. They criticise Marxism on the grounds that 'respect for the person along with freedom of speech and other liberal rights ought not to be dismissed as mere bourgeois hypocricies, whatever injustices may have been perpetrated in their name.'[84]

As has been frequently pointed out, Marxism does not reject 'liberal' rights; but it knows that individual liberal rights like freedom of speech are turned by the bourgeoisie through private ownership of the media into the freedom of speech of capitalist exploitation against the expression of socialist liberation. It knows that such individual liberal rights do not include the right to work, let alone the right to withhold one's labour to secure fair pay and working conditions and they certainly do not include the right to organise with other workers to make demands backed by concerted action. It knows that such individual liberal rights as workers do enjoy are constantly under threat in capitalist society and will never add up to collective working class emancipation, while revolutionary liberation of the working class can spread individual liberal rights among the vast majority of the population.

Our liberal critic goes on to admit: 'that in an age of impending nuclear catastrophe, of massive economic exploitation and ecological destruction there seems something increasingly immoral about any refusal to extend the domain of the 'moral' beyond inter-personal relations.'

That is precisely Marxism's point. The liberal principles of individual human freedom and justice have been turned into the rights of those privately controlling the means of production, upheld by the courts, to extort huge profits from the working people of their own and other countries - at whatever cost to world peace and ecology. Marxism does not so much reject individualistic morality as raise it to a higher collective level where it can condemn an exploitative ruling class for its crimes against the people and not simply indict for personal reasons the individuals who make up that class. Marxist morality establishes the right of those who are exploited, the vast majority of human beings, to emancipate themselves collectively in order to find in socialist society a co-operative individual freedom at no one else's expense. In an exploitative society individual morality cannot defend individual rights against the exploiters but collective morality can liberate the exploited and endow them with individual rights which can be collectively maintained.

Our liberal minded critics of Marxism may feel that the term 'socialism' has become so discredited that it might be better to talk instead in other terms - the policy goals of socialism like 'demilitarisation, ecological sustainability, social justice, democracy, gender and racial equality'.

In other words they are intimidated by the biased contention that capitalism is 'the ultimate condition for democracy' and therefore should not be challenged. Instead these liberal-minded people intend to join with those who share their views in working for the policy goals of socialism in a society that remains capitalist - in spite of the fact that, as contemporary history keeps proving, no system of production based on private profit is going to pay more than lip service to demilitarisation, to ecological issues or to any social justice which would involve the ending of exploitation. In other words our liberal-minded people are opting for social democracy as a form of pursuing the goals of socialism without challenging capitalism directly. But while the Labour Party in Britain has ceased to call itself socialist, its fate in recent elections proves that it has to abandon all socialist goals also if it is to win a bourgeois election, as it did again in 1997.

All genuinely caring people uniting in order to fight with all their might for the goals of socialism and joining with all those they must have on their side in order for there to be any chance of success, will find that if they do achieve those goals it is because, whether or not they realised the necessity of it or even the possibility of it to begin with, they have got rid of capitalism. Socialist goals are quite incompatible with capitalism and capitalists are much too canny to allow socialist goals to sneak past them - even when they hypocritically declare that they are 'caring capitalists'! If people do not wish to call this getting rid of capitalism by forcing through the political changes necessary to realise socialist goals 'working class revolution' but 'emancipatory transformation', let them feel free. A red red rose by any other name...!

So that brings us back to the point where this examination of Marxist socialism in practice started. Socialist goals are not something we realise under capitalism: they are the fruits of the socialism we replace capitalism with, not without struggle. That struggle is class struggle leading to socialist revolution, 'the self-conscious, independent movement of the immense majority in the interest of the immense majority' which is working class democracy. This revolution represents the transfer of political power from a small capitalist ruling class, the traffickers for profit in the labour-power of others, to a huge socialist working class, all of us who live by the sale of our labour-power whatever form it may take. The strategy of the revolution is the occupation and control of all workplaces. By this means ownership and control of the means of production are transferred from private capitalists, not to the state, but to those who use them for the public good, whether they are land, factories, shops or all the buildings and facilities of public service. This ownership of the means of production by those who use them for the benefit of society is the basis of the socialist democratic institutions which will be the guarantee of freedom from exploitation.

It is a profoundly moral movement because it liberates the British working class from capitalist exploitation at home and contributes to the liberation of working people abroad from imperialism in which Britain plays any part. It represents our determination to create a world where we do not eat because others starve, where our individual liberties are not at anyone else's expense, where our personal morality is not discredited by the terrible crimes committed in our country's name by capitalist profiteers. Having expropriated them we take hold collectively of the means of production and use them to create equitably shared value for all.

CHAPTER IV ALIENATION AND POLITICAL CHANGE.

1 *Marx, 'Capital' vol I p490*
2 *Lenin, 'The Tasks of the Youth Leagues', Selected Workers, vol II pp669-70*
3 *Marx, 'The German Ideology' p74*
4 *Lenin, 'The State and Revolution', Selected Works, vol II p 145*
5 *Marx, 'Capital' vol I p604*
6 *Marx, 'Capital' vol III p799*
7 *Lenin, 'What Is To Be Done?', Selected Works, vol II p145*
8 *Ibid., p168*
9 *Marx, 'Economic and Philosophic Manuscripts of 1844' p156*
10 *Ibid., p124*
11 *Ibid., p69*
12 *Ibid., p70*
13 *Marx, 'The German Ideology' p22*
14 *Marx, 'Economic and Philosphic Mnuscripts of 1844' p156*
15 *Ibis., p70*
16 *Ibid., p164*
17 *Ibid., p114*
18 *Ibid., p140*
19 *Ibid., p137*
20 *Ibid., p116*
21 *Ibid., p119*
22 *Marx, 'The German Ideology'*
23 *Roger Garaudy, 'Humanism Marxiste', p68 (my translation)*
24 *Marx' 'Economic and Philosophic Manuscripts of 1844' pp109-10*
25 *Ibid., p82*
26 *Jean-Paul Sarte, 'Critique de la Raison Dialectique'*
27 *T.B. Bottomore and Maximilien Rubel, 'Karl Marx, Selected Writings in Sociology and social Philosophy' p45*
28 *Werner Stark, 'The Sociology of Knwoledge' p142*
29 *Marx and Engels, 'The Communist Manifesto', Selected Works, vol I p55*

30 *Marx, 'Theses on Feuerbach' Selected Works, vol II p 366*
31 *Marx, 'Wage Labour and Capital', Selected Works, vol I p77*
32 *Marx and Engels, 'The Communist Manifesto' Selected Works, vol I pp42-3*
33 *Marx, 'Capital' vol I p72*
34 *Ibid.*
35 *Ibid., p82*
36 *Stalin, 'Economic Problems of Socialism in the USSR' p22*
37 *'Vosprosi Ekonomiki', no. 1, 1962*
38 *Marx 'Grundrisse', as quoted in 'The Ethical Foundations of Marxism' by Eugene Kamenka p56*
39 *Christopher Caudwell, 'Illusion and Reality' p 107*
40 *Shakespeare, 'Knig John', II, i*
41 *William Blake,"The Four Zoas'*
42 *David V. Erdman, 'Blake, Prophet against Empire' p226*
43 *MaoTsetung, 'Talks at the Yenan Forum on Literature and the Arts', Selected Works, vol III p86*
44 *Ibid*
45 *Christopher Hill, 'Intellectual Origins of the English Revolution' p200*
46 *Lenin, 'On National Pride of the Great Russians' 1914*
47 *Christopher Hill, 'Intellectual Origins of the English Revolution.*
48 *George Hakewell, 'Apologie', as quoted byb Christopher Hill*
49 *Gerrard Winstanley, 'The New Law of Righteousnesse'*
50 *Milton, 'The Tenure of Kings and Magistrates'*
51 *Mao Tsetung, 'Where Do Correct Ideas Come From?', 'Four Essays on Philosophy' p134*
52 *Engels, 'Critique of the Gotha Programme'*
53 *Marx, 'Documents of the First International, 1864-1870'*
54 *Lenin, 'Letter to the Central Committee of the Russian Social Democratic Labour Party' Selected Works vol VI pp 329-30*
55 *Lenin, 'Party Discipline and the Fight aginst the Pro-Cadet Social Democrats' Collected Works, vol II pp320-1*
56 *Lenin, 'One Step Forward, Two Steps Back', Selected Works vol I p324*

57 *Marx and Engels, 'The Communist Manifesto' Selected Works, vol I p324*
58 *Lenin, What Is To Be Dne?' Selected Works, vol I p240*
59 *Lenin, 'Left Wing Communism, an Infantile Disorder', Selected Works, vol II p580*
60 *Marx, 'Capital' vol I p604*
61 *Mao Tsetung, 'On Contradiction', Selected Works, vol I p334*
62 *Marx and Engels, 'The Communist Manifesto' Selected Works, vol I p43*
63 *Marx, 'The German Ideology' p69*
64 *Mao Tsetungvestigation of the Peasant Movement in Hunan', Selected Works, vol I p28*
65 *Marx, 'Critique of Hegel's Philosophy of Right', 'Early Writings' (Pelican Marx Library) p251*
66 *Marx and Engels, 'The Communist Manifesto' Selected Works, vol I pp33-4*
67 *Mao Tsetung, 'On Contradiction' Selected Works, vol I p332*
68 *Mao Tsetung, 'Introduction to the Communist', Selected Works, vol II p287*
69 *Lenin, 'The Second Congress of the Communist International', Selected Words, vol II p660*
70 *Marx and Engels, 'The Communist Manifesto' Selected Works, vol I p49*
71 *Marx, 'The German Ideology' p75*
72 *Marx, 'The Civil War in France' (first draft)*
73 *Marx, 'Thesis on Feuerbach' Selected Works vol II p201*
74 *Ibid.*
75 *Terry Eagleton, 'Ideology' p115*
76 *Lenin, 'State and Revolution' Selected Works vol II p201*
77 *Hans Heinz Holz 'The Downfall and Future of Socialism' p112*
78 *Enver Hoxha, 'Speech at the Moscow Conference of 81 Communist and Workers Parties 1960*
79 *Chris Bramall, 'In Praise of Maoist economic Planning: Living*

Standards and Economic Development in Sichuan since 1931 p113

80 *William Hinton, 'The Privatisation of China: the Great Reversal' p188*

81 *Hans Heinz Holz, 'The Downfall and Future of Socialsm'*

82 *Randhir Singh, Preface for Bertell Ollman's 'Marxism, an Uncommon Introduction'*

83 *Christopher Norris, 'Uncritical Theory:Postmodernism, Intellectuals and the Gulf War'*

84 *Kate Soper, 'Marxism and Morality' article in New Left Review 163*

BIBLIOGRAPHY

ABERCROMBIE, NICHOLAS, 'Class,Structure and Knowledge' Basil Blackwell, Oxford, 1980

ALTHUSSER, L., 'For Marx', translated by B. Brewster, Allen Lane, the Penguin Press, London, 1969

ARISTOTLE, 'Politics', translated by William Ellis, J.M. Dent, London, 1912

ARISTOTLE, 'The Nicomachean Ethics', translated by D.P.Chase, J.M.Dent, London1911

AYER, A.J., 'Language, Truth and Logic', Gollancz, London, 1947

AYER, A.J., 'The Problem of Knowledge', Penguin Books, Harmondsworth, 1956

BENTHAM, J. 'Introduction to the Principles of Morals and Legislation', 1789

BERLIN, I., 'Historical Inevitability', Oxford University Press, London, 1954

BLAKE, W.J., 'Elements of Marxist Economic Theory and Its Criticism', Cordon co.,New York, 1939

BOEHM-BAWERK, E. von, 'Capital and Interest', translated by W.Smart, Macmillan, London, 1890

BOTTOMORE, T.B. and RUBEL, M., 'Karl Marx, Selected Writings in Sociology and Social Philosophy' Watts, London 1956

BRADLEY, F.H., 'Appearance and Reality' Allen and Unwin, London, 1908

BROGNARD, A., 'Lutte de Classe et Morale Marxiste' A. Brognard, Paris 1969

CAMERON, K. N., 'Humanity and Society: A World History', Monthly Review Press, New York, 1973

CAMERON, K. N., 'Marxism: the Science of Society', Bergin & Garvey, Massachusetts, 1985

CAMERON, K. N., 'Stalin' NC Press , Toronto, 1987

CAUDWELL, C. 'Illusion and Reality', Lawrence and Wishart, London, 1946

CROOK,D. and CROOK, I., 'Revolution in a Chinese Village', Routledge and

Kegan Paul, London, 1959
CROSSMAN, R. 'The God that Failed', Bantam Books, New York, 1952
DOBB,M., 'Political Ecconomy and Capitalism', Routledge and Kegan Paul, London,,1950
EAGLETON, T. 'Ideology', Verso, London, 1991
ENGELS, F. 'Marx and Engels, Selected Works', 2 vols, Foreign Languages Publishing House, Moscow, 1951
ENGELS, F., 'Herr Eugen Duhring's Revolution in Science', Cooperative Publishing Society of Foreign Workers in the USSR, Moscow, 1934
ERDMAN, D.V., 'Blake, Prophet against Empire', Princeton University Press, Princeton, 1954
EWING, A.C. 'Second Thoughts in Moral Philosophy', Routledge and Kegan Paul, London, 1959
FISK, MILTON, 'Ethics and Society' The Harvester Press, London 1980
GARAUDY, R., 'Humanisme Marxiste', Editions Sociales, Paris, 1957
GIDDENS, A., 'The Class Structure of the Advanced Societies', Hutchinson University Library, London, 1973
GOLLOBIN, IRA, 'Dialectical Materialism' Petras Press, New York 1986
GRICE-HUTCHINSON, M., 'The School of Salamanca',Clarendon Press, Oxford, 1952
HALL, E.W., 'What Is Value?', Routledge and Kegan Paul, London, 1952
HARE, R.M., 'The Language of Morals', Clarendon Press, Oxford,1952
HEGEL, G.W.F., 'The Phenomenology of Mind', translated by J.B. Baillie, Allen and Unwin, London, 1931
HILL, C., 'Intellectual Origins of the English Revolution', Panther, London, 1972
HINTON, W., 'Fanshen', Monthly Review Press, N.Y. 1966
HINTON, W., 'The Privatisation of China: The Great Reversal' Earthscan Publications, London, 1991
HOLZ, Hans Heinz, 'The Downfall and Future of Socialism' MEP Publications, University of Minnesota, 1992
HOXHA, E., 'Selected Works', The 8 Nentori Publishing House, Tirana, 1974

HOXHA, E., 'Report to Vth Party Congress', Naim Frasheri Publishing House, Tirana, 1966

HUME, D., 'A Treatise of Human Nature', Clarendon Press, Oxford, 1896

KAIN, PHILIP J., 'Marx and Ethics', Clarendon Press, Oxford 1988

KAMENKA, E.,'The Ethical Foundations of Marxism',Routledge and Kegan Paul, London, 1962

KANT, I., 'Fundamental Principles of the Metaphysic of Ethics', translated by T.K. Abbott, Longmans Green, London, 1946

KAUTSKY, K., 'Ethics and the Materialist Conception of History', translated by J.B. Askew, The Twentieth Century Press, London, 1906

LAMONT, W.D., 'The Value Judgement', University of Edinburgh Press,1955

LENIN, V.I., 'Selected Works' 2 vols, Lawrence and Wishart, London, 1947

LENIN, V.I., 'Selected Works' vol VI, Lawrence and Wishart, London, 1936

LENIN,V.I., 'Collected Works', vol 11, Lawrence and Wishart, London, 1962

LENIN,V.I., 'Philosophical Notebooks', 'Collected Works', vol 38, Foreign Languages Publishing House, Moscow, 1961

LENIN, V.I., 'Materialism and Empirio-Criticism', Foreign Language Press, Peking,1972

LOCKE, J., 'Second Treatise of Civil Government', Basil Blackwell, Oxford, 1946

LUKACS, G., 'Studies in European Realism', Hillway Publishing co, London, 1950

MAO TSETUNG, 'Selected Works', 4 vols, Foreign Languages Press, Peking, 1967

MAO TSETUNG, 'Four Essays in Philosophy', Foreign Languages Press, Peking, 1968

MARX, K., 'Selected Works' 2 vols Foreign Languages Publishing House, Moscow, 1951

MARX, K., 'Capital', 3 vols, Foreign Languages Publishing house, Moscow, 1954

MARX, K., 'Economic and Philosophic Manuscripts of 1844', Foreign Languages Publishing House, Moscow, 1959

MARX, K., 'The German Ideology', International Publishers, New York, 1963
MARX K., 'The Holy Family', Foreign Languages Publishing House, Moscow, 1956
MARX,K., 'The Poverty of Philosophy', Foreign Languages Publishing House, Moscow,
MARX, K., 'Theories of Surplus Value', translated by G.A. Bonner and Emile Burns, Lawrence and Wishart, London, 1951
MARX, K., 'The Pelican Marx Library, Early Writings', Penguin Books, London, 1975
MILL, J.S., 'Utilitarianism', Basil Blackwell, Oxford, 1949
MOORE, G.E., 'Principia Ethica', Cambridge University Press, 1903
NORRIS, C., 'Postmodernism, Intellectuals and the Gulf War', Lawrence and Wishart, London, 1992
OLLMAN, B. ,'Alienation: Marx's Conception of Man in Capitalist Society', Cambridge University Press, 1971
OLLMAN, B., 'Marxism: An Uncommon Introduction' Sterling Publishers, New Delhi, 1990
OLLMAN, B., 'Dialectical Investigations', Routledge, New York 1993
PLATO, 'Laws', translated by A.E. Taylor, J.M.Dent, London,1935
PLATO, 'The Republic', translated by A.D. Lindsay, J.M. Dent, London, 1935
POPPER, K., 'The Poverty of Historicism', Routledge and Kegan Paul, London, 1961
PRICHARD, H.A., 'Duty and Ignorance of Fact', British Academy Annual Philosophical Lecture, 1932
ROBINSON, J., 'Economic Philosophy', Watts, London, 1962
ROLL, E., 'A History of Economic Thought', Faber, London, 1945
ROSS, W.D., 'Foundations of Ethics', Clarendon Press, Oxford, 1939
SARTRE, J.P., 'Critique de la Raison Dialectique', Librairie Gallimard, Paris, 1960
SEMMEL, B., 'Imperialism and Social Reform', Allen and Unwin, London, 1960

SHEHU, M., 'On the Experience of the National Liberation War', Naim Frasheri Publishing House, Tirana, 1947
SINGH, RANDHIR, 'Of Marxism and Indian Politics', Ajamta Publications, India, 1990
SMITH, A. ,'Wealth of Nations', J.M. Dent, London, 1910
SOHN-RETHEL, A., 'Intellectual and Manual Labour', Macmillan Press, London, 1978
STALIN, J.V., 'Works', Foreign Languages Publishing House, Moscow, 1952
STALIN, J.V.,'The Foundations of Leninism', Foreign Languages Press, Peking, 1965
STALIN, J.V., 'Ecnomic Problems of Socialism in the USSR', Foreign Languages Press, Peking, 1972
STALIN, J.V., 'Marxism and Problems of Linguistics', Foreign Languages Press, Peking, 1972
STARK, W., 'The Sociology of Knowledge', Routledge and Kegan Paul, London,1958
TAWNEY, R.H., 'Religion and the Rise of Capitalism', Penguin, London, 1938
THOMSON, G., 'Studies in Ancient Greek Society' 2 vols, Lawrence and Wishart, London, 1949
THOMSON, G., 'Aeschylus and Athens', Lawrence and Wishart, London 1941
TOULMIN, S., 'The Place of Reason in Ethics', Cambridge University Press, 1950
VENABLE, V., 'Human Nature: the Marxian View', Dobson, London, 1946
WEBER, M., 'The Protestant Ethic and the Spirit of Capitalism', translated by T. Parsons, Allen and Unwin, London, 1930
WITTFOGEL, K.A., 'Oriental Despotism', Yale University Press, New Haven, 1956

INDEX